Teaching Diversity:
Challenges and Complexities, Identities and Integrity

Edited by William M. Timpson
Silvia Sara Canetto
Evelinn A. Borrayo
and Raymond Yang

Atwood Publishing
Madison, WI

Teaching Diversity: Challenges and Complexities, Identities and Integrity

Edited by William M. Timpson, Silvia Sara Canetto, Evelinn A. Borrayo, and Raymond Yang

© Atwood Publishing, 2003
2710 Atwood Ave.
Madison, WI 53704
USA
www.atwoodpublishing.com

Printed in the United States of America.

Cover design and illustration by Tom Lowes, Inc.

The editors of this volume wish to thank their academic departments, colleagues, and families for their support and encouragement. In addition, we particularly want to thank Alicia Cook, James Boyd, Sue Ellen Charlton, Kevin Oltjenbruns, David MacPhee, and Karen Wedge for their initiative and leadership.

And, we especially want to thank Jeanne Clarke and student assistants—Laura Zimmerer and Katie Willitt—from the Center for Teaching and Learning, for their organization and keeping the project moving to completion.

Library of Congress Cataloging-in-Publication Data

Teaching diversity : challenges and complexities, identities, and
integrity / by William M. Timpson ... [et al.].
    p. cm.
Includes bibliographical references and index.
  ISBN 1-891859-45-5 (pbk.)
  1. Multicultural education—United States—Case studies. 2.
Education, Higher—United States—Case studies. 3. College
teaching—United States—Case studies. I. Timpson, William M.
  LC1099.3 .T4215 2003
  370.117—dc21

          2003006498

Table of Contents

Table of Contents

Walking Our Talk:
The Special Challenges of Teaching Diversity

William M. Timpson

Introduction

When Silvia Canetto and I first discussed this book in early Spring of 2000, the issues seemed compelling enough. How do we as instructors best handle sensitivities around ethnicity and social class, gender and sexual orientation when class discussions turn those ways? What do we do with faith-based opinions? How safe are our classrooms? When does self-disclosure go too far? How do we teach our own disciplinary canons while incorporating new and long excluded voices?

Silvia had been teaching several courses with diversity content and wanted an outside opinion of the interactions among her, the students, and the content. As director of our university's Center for Teaching and Learning, I had consulted with other faculty about issues in their own courses. I eagerly took up this challenge. Over the course of the semester, I observed each of her three classes on five separate occasions, chatted with students about their learning, and conducted formal midsemester and end of semester student feedback sessions. Regularly I shared with Silvia what I was seeing and hearing, and we talked about the implications, what choices she had about the ways her classes could be organized and conducted.

After Linda Babler at Atwood Publishing expressed interest in the book and we launched our efforts, we began to look around for others on campus who taught courses with diversity content. We wanted instructors from different disciplines to describe their experiences through a series of case studies. We found them in teacher education, counseling, community college leadership and educational psychology, human development and family studies, philosophy, English, social work, ethnic studies, speech communication, natural resource management, and qualitative data analysis. In time, we also recruited two more to help us as co-editors. Ray Yang is a senior scholar in human development and family studies. Evelinn Borrayo is a more junior colleague who also teaches psychology courses with diversity content.

Over a two-year period, the group met regularly, shared readings, discussed concerns and successes, and began to share drafts of our individual stories. By basing this effort on one campus, we wanted to capitalize on the synergy possible when instructors in various disciplines joined together in order to better understand their common struggles. We also wanted contributors who were active in their own sub-disciplines and could bring some fresh thinking to our discussions about diversity. Unlike other edited volumes that feature expert opinions from different campuses, by people who work largely in isolation from each other, we believed we could create something special by working together over time.

In hindsight, we now can see what a struggle it has been to make sense of our own individual experiences. We worried about the generalizability of our own cases. We drew on our own disciplinary literatures to frame these stories—why we did what we did and how we understand the underlying issues. As such, the stories are rich and varied, thick with descriptions about teaching and learning, content and process, rapport, classroom climate, and communication.

Into this diverse mix of contributing scholars came events —globally, locally, and personally—that impacted our thinking and, at times, exploded on the world scene. In the aftermath of the attacks on September 11, we reminded ourselves of the importance of our efforts to help instructors bridge differences, to calm fears, and to promote respectful dialogue even when disagreements run deep. Helping young people overcome the hatreds and prejudices taught by their elders—and too often reinforced by society—is no simple task. Helping them clarify their own thinking while they listen, debate, and learn from others is an enormous undertaking, impossible to address through lecture and multiple choice assessment. The completion of the entire manuscript came together as another round of horrific violence escalated in the Middle East.

Along the way, I myself had other experiences that affirmed the value of this work on diversity that we were doing together. In the summer of 2000, I attended a conference in Germany, visiting the Jewish museum in Frankfurt and seeing the history of their persecution through the ages, periods of calm and prosperity mixed with segregation and brutal oppression. A few days later I was on the beaches of Normandy, where American, British, and Canadian troops, my own dad among them, put their lives on the line to combat the Third Reich and end Hitler's demonic pursuit of power and racial superiority. I was taken off guard when my own tears welled up so quickly as I stepped into the American cemetery, with endless rows of white crosses gleaming in that bright July sun. The soldiers were twenty, twenty-one, twenty-two years old. Their lives and possibilities snuffed out so young. The Germans had their own cemetery, smaller and further back from the beaches. It was affirming to see that kind of respectful provision for everyone's losses, including the "enemy's." We can keep some measure of a civilized attitude even in the wake of a horrific war.

A week earlier I had been in Estonia, my father's nation of birth. As a small country, it was historically easy prey for more powerful neighbors—the Danes and Swedes, Russians and Germans. Yet through it all, its people always seemed to keep their hopes alive for independence. Soviet occupation in the post-WWII era included the deportation of Estonians and the in-migration of Russians who used their superior power to create a two-tiered system of privilege. When the rumblings for independence began to grow louder in neighboring Poland and Lithuania in the late 1980s, a groundswell of Estonians joined with them despite the presence of large numbers of Soviet troops and tanks in their midst and no army of their own. Following age-old tradition, they called for citizens everywhere to come to their capital city of Talinn and sing their national songs, long suppressed and discouraged by their Soviet lords. As one forty ish woman store clerk told me, "We came and sang and held our breaths. We call it the singing revolution. And the Russians left."

The following summer I had the good fortune to attend another conference overseas, this time in Johannesburg, South Africa. A highlight was hearing from one of my own heroes on this issue of acceptance, Nelson Mandela. In his 1994 autobiography, *Long Walk to Freedom*, he articulates his vision for a multi-racial and harmonious future where Black South Africans would have to resist the urge to repay the brutal oppression they had suffered through the apartheid years and forge a multiracial, peaceful future.

> It was during those long and lonely years [in prison] that my hunger for the freedom of my own people became a hunger for the freedom of all people, white and black. I knew as well as I knew anything that the oppressor must be liberated just as surely as the oppressed. A man who takes another man's freedom is a prisoner of hatred; he is locked behind the bars of prejudice and narrow-mindedness. I am not truly free if I am taking away someone else's freedom, just as surely as I am not free when my freedom

is taken away from me. The oppressed and the oppressor alike are robbed of their humanity. (624-625)

On the urging of colleagues who had spent considerable time abroad, I extended this trip to visit India and Nepal. With longstanding pressures from historic inequities, prejudices, and hierarchies overlaid with large and growing populations, this part of the world also offered examples of tolerance and peaceful progress. I could see first-hand the legacy of Mahatma Gandhi, whose life stood for nonviolent cooperation in the face of our most conflicted differences.

As our group members each discovered in our own experiences with teaching diversity content, there are no simple and easy answers. At the same time, we were also able to affirm the importance of what we did as individuals and what our students would be able to do. To quote Gandhi:

> I do not believe in short-violent-cuts to success...However much I may sympathize with and admire worthy motives, I am an uncompromising opponent of violent methods even to serve the noblest of causes...Experience convinces me that permanent good can never be the outcome of untruth and violence...Possession of arms implies an element of fear, if not cowardice. But true nonviolence is an impossibility without the possession of unadulterated fearlessness...It does not mean meek submission to the will of the evil-doer, but it means pitting one's whole soul against the will of the tyrant. Working under this law of our being, it is possible for a single individual to defy the whole might of an unjust empire to save his honor, his soul, and lay the foundation for that empire's fall or its regeneration. (Easwaran 1972, 43, 84, 156)

Noted historian and ethnic studies scholar Ron Takaki (1993) goes further to connect fundamental democratic principles with this desire for inclusiveness, a set of principles and values that can energize students and communities to push for progress. Here he describes the insights that immigrant sugarcane workers gained as they watched their children moving through the schools:

> Many schools...were not preparing these children to be plantation laborers. They were learning about freedom and equality and reciting the Gettysburg Address and the Declaration of Independence. "Here the children learn about democracy or at least the theory of it," said a University of Hawaii student. They were taught that honest labor, fair play, and industriousness were virtues. But they "saw

that it wasn't so on the plantation." They saw whites on the top and Asians on the bottom. Returning from school to their camps, students noticed the wide "disparity between theory and practice." This contradiction was glaring. "The public school system, perhaps without realizing it," the university student observed, "created unrest and disorganization." (265)

Throughout our group's work together, we also came to better appreciate the complexities inherent in the issues that surround diversity. Any progress seems fraught with difficult choices and competing interests. Assimilation into the good life, for example, has its own shadow side, as reflected in the writing of Native American scholar Vine Deloria (1997). Schools, colleges, and universities can be simultaneously part of the problem as well as the solution:

> Nothing is calm beneath the veneer of Indian country, and it may be that we are seeing the final absorption of the original inhabitants in the modern consumer society. The push for education in the last generation has done more to erode the sense of Indian identity than any integration program the government previously attempted. The irony of the situation is that Indians truly believed that by seeking a better life for their children through education, much could be accomplished. College and graduate education, however, have now created a generation of technicians and professionals who also happen to have Indian blood. People want the good life and they are prepared to throw away their past in order to get it. (2)

Be that as it may, we now see the importance of this work on diversity so much more clearly. Participating in the Special Interest Group (SIG) on peace education through the American Educational Research Association, for example, I have heard extensively about the struggles of educators in Northern Ireland to find a nonviolent, inclusive way forward for groups that have been at each other's throats for hundreds of years. Teachers and professors from the Middle East regularly attend and bring reports of work with allies in communities, organizations, and businesses. Stories from South Africa remind us of the clarity, commitment, and effort needed to make a vision into a reality.

Our Challenge

As faculty, staff, and students at Colorado State University, we have come together in this volume to explore the challenges associated with courses that have diversity content. By this we mean courses that incorporate a critical analysis of various dimensions of diversity, including age, culture, gender, social class, religion, sexual orientation, national origin, language practices, and physical disabilities. With respect to classroom dynamics—including instructor-student and student-student interactions—differences in learning (and teaching) styles, personality, development, and region crop up as well, providing a complex, fascinating, and, at times, problematic overlay of factors. At the heart of this book, we want to explore one central question: How can instructors and students contribute to a positive classroom climate that permits an honest and respectful consideration of a range of ideas and issues, no matter how difficult, emotional, or sensitive?

Without some skills and a certain knowledge base, discussions of these topics can too often devolve into a superficial exchange of personal opinions and experiences that lack analytical rigor or reference to any published literature. Discussions can also suffer from emotional shutdown or fear by some students, domination and blaming by others, or submission to what is perceived to be "politically correct." We believe that diversity content is an essential foundation for discussion and, by extension, to a complete education for our students and to their personal and professional competence.

First and foremost, we have come together to share our own experiences, concerns, resources, and learning so that we can enrich our own teaching, better assess the problems we face, share ideas, and support each other in exploring new possibilities. Second, we are hoping to contribute to the scholarship of teaching, to offer something that can help guide others who face these same issues. However, we also recognize that instructors can only go so far on their own; additional resources may be needed to engender systemic campus-wide changes (e.g., research assistance, release time).

Teaching and learning about the diversity of human experiences can be uniquely challenging. First, the teaching materials (e.g., texts) we desire may not exist. Second, learning about diversity may also mean that we have to address broader, complex issues of power and powerlessness, social stratification, dominance, and oppression. Third, these issues may also spark a need for self-reflection about personal histories of privilege, prejudice, or oppression and how instructors and students can perpetuate problems, knowingly or not. We ourselves and our students may be forced to question our beliefs and behavior in both public and private arenas.

Accordingly, diversity content classes are difficult yet exciting classes to teach. Because they deal with emotionally charged material, they tend to arouse strong feelings. Rationality may become confounded with strong emotional reactions, with anger, intimidation, or guilt. Class unity can suffer, at least initially, making us more aware than ever of our differences, our location in the *social map*. They also make visible systems of social stratification, how we benefit and how we contribute. Davis (1992, 232) puts it this way:

> What makes courses in social stratification most exciting to teach also makes them most difficult. The issues of power and powerlessness, advantage and disadvantage, addressed in these courses are charged concepts. They encourage viewing the world as inhabited by winners and losers, locating oneself on this social map, and, consequently, taking sides. Personal identities are shaped and loyalties formed around race, class, and gender. Not only does this characterize students but also instructors, who bring with them racial, class, gender, and other identities. Courses focusing on class, gender, race, sexual orientation, and global stratification also tend to draw more political students and those who feel strongly about ranking systems.

Davis goes on to describe the emotional reactions, including resistance, paralysis, and rage, that often arise for students in these classes. It's not that these feelings arise in every class. However, the climate of each class will be affected by whatever emotions surface. Indeed, multiple classroom mini-climates might exist at a given moment i.e., what some students might experience may be very different from what others experience. What works for some students may not be helpful to others (Marks 1995).

Importantly, reactions of resistance, paralysis, and rage are not simply obstacles to learning. Rather, they often are normal and expected reactions to this kind of sensitive, complex, and challenging material. In fact, they frequently represent stages of thinking and ways of learning, potential catalysts for finding deeper insights and making real shifts. As instructors of diversity content, we ourselves have had our fair share of critical evaluations from students. Yet, we wonder: Do these comments, in fact, represent more impactful course material and process? Be assured, we do not want to excuse ourselves from questions about poor teaching or veiled proselytizing, but rather to suggest that reviews of our student evaluations must take into consideration the distinct possibility that negative reactions may reflect some measure of resistance, paralysis, and rage on the part of students.

Another important issue with diversity content concerns the role of *identity-based expertise*. We question whether personal experience is essential for having expertise about a particular diversity domain and, if so, what kind of personal experiences or "affiliations" count? In other words, beyond our training and expertise, how does our own identity limit (or enhance) us as instructors and experts? This issue becomes especially complicated when a course covers a range of diversity issues such as gender, sexual orientation, social class, religion, ethnicity, nationality, language, culture, and physical abilities. If identity expertise is important, which instructors will be allowed to teach which content? (For a full review of this issue, see Mayberry 1996).

Insights and Recommendations

It is our hope that our expertise, experiences, analyses, and discussions reflected here might spark new conversations, creative thinking, and interest in change for others. The works we cite are, we believe, quite accessible. We ourselves have certainly benefited from sharing a common set of readings as well as from developing a common language as we explored the challenges we have faced and the possibilities for change we have before us. Here are some of the major insights we have achieved.

Diversity

There is now a rich literature on the importance of diversity education as well as various models for understanding student resistance, growth, and development in which their learning is impacted by issues of ethnicity, gender, background, social class, etc. Banks (1989), for example, has long argued for making *more* equal education opportunity, for using the schools to address societal inequalities grounded in ethnicity, social class, and history. Campbell (1999) built on earlier ideas of Dewey (e.g., 1996) in particular to argue for the fundamental importance of multicultural education and its emphasis on particular ideas and skills (acceptance, tolerance, critical thinking, and cooperation) for what is necessary for citizenship in a healthy democracy. Takaki (1993) makes a compelling case for understanding more about the histories of various groups which have immigrated to the U.S.

Nabhan (1997) then makes an equally compelling case for broadening our definitions and including all life forms as well as the processes that underlie the health of our biological diversity. He connects planetary health with our appreciation for human diversity: "[Wherever] empires have spread to suppress other cultures' language and land-tenure traditions, the loss of biodiversity has been dramatic" (37). Nabhan goes on to quote Latin American ethnobiologist Bob Bye, who warns that "[biological] diversity depends on human diversity" (38).

Integration of Diversity Content across the Curriculum

Whether or not instructors recognize the importance of diversity content in their own disciplines is one challenge. On our own campus, courses have been created to address various aspects of diversity directly in a range of disciplines. In Education we have had "Diversity and Communication" and "Multicultural and Special Populations"; in Psychology, "Psychological Perspectives on Female Experience" and "Diversity Issues in Counseling"; in Social Work, "Human Diversity Practice Issues"; in Vocational Education, "Special Needs Foundations and Practices"; in Occupational Therapy, "Handicapped Individual in Society"; in Human Development and Family Studies, "Gender, Work, and Family Relations"; in Sociology, "Contemporary Race-Ethnic Relations," "Comparative Majority Minority Relations," and "Gender Roles in Society." While such courses are now well established on many campuses, offering clear benefits of focus and visibility, there is a danger that some faculty will feel absolved from incorporating references to diversity in their own courses since "it is already covered elsewhere." There is a clear risk of curricular marginalization here with content that itself addresses *marginalized* populations in society.

In truth, diversity content is inherently interdisciplinary. Ethnicity intersects with gender and social class in powerful and important ways. Unfortunately, the various disciplines typically provide particular paradigmatic ways of analyzing events, problems, and conditions. Famed Brazilian educator Paulo Freire inspired spectacularly successful literacy campaigns in Nicaragua, Cuba, and Africa, as well as his own country, by creating small cooperative learning groups that drew on meaningful material to improve their lives. In his book, *The Pedagogy of Hope* (1997), he looked back on these efforts and the importance of recognizing the interactivity of ethnicity, gender, and social class:

> There is…the process of learning that a critical comprehension of the so-called minorities of one's culture is not exhausted in questions of race and sex, but requires a comprehension of the class division in that culture, as well. In other words, sex does not explain everything. Nor

does race. Nor does class. Racial discrimination is by no manner of means reducible to a problem of class. Neither is sexism. (156)

At Colorado State University, a *Multicultural Curriculum Infusion* Project at one time assisted faculty in efforts to incorporate diversity content into mainstream courses. It is our conviction that efforts at overcoming the legacies of oppression and prejudice will require a broad curriculum focus involving faculty both within and across the disciplines. In addition, time and resources must be given over to ongoing professional development efforts if we are to look honestly at these issues, explore our own resistances, integrate our expertise, and explore new possibilities.

Sociolinguistic Style

A number of sociolinguists have written about the intersection of language and culture. Deborah Tannen (1996), for example, makes a solid argument for understanding the different linguistic styles men and women often use. Instead of seeing differences as intractable or innate, Tannen insists that anyone can learn how to communicate better in groups that utilize different styles. This is not to suggest, however, that real differences in power or historic barriers to gender equality can be easily overcome with attention to language alone. However, we do want to challenge ourselves, other instructors, and students to reach across those linguistic barriers, to look deeply at classroom dynamics generally, and take the time needed to nurture new understanding and skills, the kinds of learning that should reap rewards long after formal schooling ends.

Democratic Classrooms

As mentioned, Campbell (1999) makes a good case for the use of democratic principles in classrooms as a viable organizing concept for setting ground rules, empowering students, raising issues, and resolving conflicts. While these ideas can be utilized in any class, they become especially important with diversity content when complex and sensitive issues require substantial understanding and skill to navigate. For example, soliciting feedback from students at various times is one viable way to democratize a classroom, affirming what works, identifying concerns, and considering a range of possible improvements *while there is still time in the semester to make changes* (e.g., Timpson and Bendel-Simso 1996).

Evaluation of Teaching

Despite generally favorable reviews of the validity and reliability of student course evaluations across more than twelve hundred studies (e.g., Marsh and Roche 1997) and widespread use nationally, critiques continue to surface. For example, Trout (2000) raises anew the common complaint about pressures on instructors to "dumb down" their courses in an effort to cull student ("customer") favor. Following this line of reasoning, if low course workload is thought to influence higher student ratings, then diversity content that touches on sensitive issues and demands intense analysis may engender lower student ratings.

Marsh (2001), however, reports that there is a "widespread, mistaken belief that one way to receive good [student evaluations of teaching] is to teach easy, slow-paced courses that require little work and do not challenge students. Although there is clear evidence that this is not the case...the belief persists" (206). Marsh goes on to report that higher student ratings can be achieved through instructor attention to "good" student workload, i.e., appropriate pace with due consideration of capacities and prior learning.

There are also some reports of gender bias where women instructors in predominantly male disciplines like engineering receive lower student course evaluations. Reviewing the existing published literature as well reporting on some of her own field studies, Basow (1998) comes to the following conclusion:

> The pattern that emerges is a complex one. Women faculty may get the same, lower, or higher ratings than their male counterparts depending on many different factors aside from teaching competence. The specific questions asked of students are important. Consistent gender differences do not typically occur on an overall rating question, but women faculty tend to be rated higher on interpersonal qualities and interactions with students than do men faculty. In contrast, men faculty tend to be rated more highly than women faculty on questions relating to knowledge and dynamism/enthusiasm. These differences may relate to gender-typed personality traits or gender-related teaching styles or gender-related student expectations. (149)

Extending her analysis of student course evaluations to factors related to ethnicity and sexual orientation, Basow goes on to note how little useful research is currently available, but how differences and interactions are likely to occur given parallel histories of prejudice.

Marsh and Roche (1997) do note that the accuracy of student ratings will improve with some orientation to the questions being asked. For our discussions here, it is important that students understand the purpose of the diversity content and how best to understand their own reactions, especially in light of possible resistance or other emotional responses. Accordingly, one benefit of mid-semester student course evaluations is to promote the kind of metacognitive awareness—i.e., thinking about thinking (e.g., Meichenbaum et al. 1985)—that can permit students to reflect more deeply about their experiences as learners and better understand their own reactions to complex and challenging material.

First-Year and Capstone Seminars

One new avenue for change could be the efforts occurring nationally to create or revitalize a core curriculum and, especially, first-year and capstone seminars—opportunities to provide some orientation to college-level work as well as some integration and synthesis of what was learned. Orientation courses can help students develop both the knowledge base and the skills necessary to learn from diversity content and from others who are themselves different (see Timpson 2001). Similarly, what is planned as an integrative, concluding experience for students can return to these same issues, since diversity issues have been at the heart of the American experience, for better and worse. These issues have become increasingly important as global interaction and interdependence increase. Colleges and universities can assert a stronger leadership role here.

Prosocial Skills

The literature on cooperative learning, one of the most powerful paradigms for breaking down interpersonal prejudice and promoting appreciation of differences, describes various *prosocial* skills that students need to work successfully in groups (Johnson and Johnson 1994). We now know that the communication skills and group dynamics so important in today's world, from listening to empathy and consensus, can be taught and learned.

Values Clarification

One useful framework for guiding student growth about sensitive issues is values clarification. Here, instructors can help students clarify what they believe, see the choices they have, resist peer pressure to conform, prize their values publicly, and act on them repeatedly and consistently (e.g., Simon et al. 1972; Wolfgang 1999). This model of teaching has been studied in a variety of settings and provides a useful framework as instructors guide students toward making sense of what happens in and out of class. For example, when students hear someone making a cruel ethnic joke, they can begin to see their choices more clearly and understand the opportunity they have to align their core values with a public condemnation of such insensitivity.

Cognitive Development

Perry's (1981, 1999) work stands out as a framework for understanding the various stages students must navigate as they move from dichotomous thinking (right-wrong, yes-no), where *agency* (or authority) is external (in the text or teacher), toward acceptance of different opinions, a search for coherent evidence, and an increasing ability to handle complexity and ambiguity, where agency is internal.

Gilligan's (1982) work explores gender differences in relation to cognitive development. Significantly, she states that often, the criterion used to measure development is based on a male norm, and thus women appear to develop less quickly. For instance, women tend to prize personal relationships above concepts of "success," and so may perceive diversity issues through a different lens.

Belenky and her colleagues (1986) have made an equally persuasive claim that substantive gender differences emerge around classroom discussions about knowing. According to Belenky et al., it becomes important for instructors to encourage participation in classroom discussions because it is in this way that students, and females in particular, "find their voices" and mature intellectually. Early on in this process, acceptance of contributions without harsh judgment can be important for learning and development. There are useful frameworks for debriefing class discussions and helping students better understand their reactions.

However, what makes all of this so complex is the following: What is the instructor's role when a student makes a sexist or racist comment? Should we lessen our critical judgment when students are exploring various ideas? Should we hope that classmates will offer challenges? Or is it useful instead to refer to Perry's, Gilligan's, or Belenky's work and look for the intellectual cohesiveness that ought to underlie any particular statement and that separates personal opinion form something more reasoned?

Emotional Intelligence

Gardner (1983, 1999) and Goleman (1994) both make compelling cases for including more attention to the emotional component of learning, especially where fear and resistance can play havoc with understanding more about diversity and about others who think differently. While college and university instructors ought to be able to assume that students arrive with certain skills in hand, we must acknowledge two truths. First, students have always come to us with a range of prior preparation and ability—no matter their having completed the same prerequisite courses—and consequently, they may well need our assistance in navigating the emotional demands of learning. Second, diversity content presents unique challenges that require much greater emotional sophistication to navigate. Helping students develop greater emotional maturity, listen empathetically, and manage their own feelings, especially when aroused, can enhance their learning.

Other Dreams and Better

Noted historian Patricia Limerick (1996) has criticized traditional American mythologies about Western heroes, noting their legacy of conquest, exploitation, and reliance on governmental subsidies. She describes a way forward, infusing the public discourse with new cultural icons. She envisions a direction ideal for consideration by any college or university, especially when the traditional heroes are being challenged:

> And yet, when the critics of academic historians say that we have discredited the old heroes and failed to replace them with any new ones, they are right. But this is not because we lack the resources. We have all the material we need to put forward a better team, people whose examples affirm a faith of considerably greater promise. It is time for a different kind of Western hero: The sustainable hero who can replace the old, exhausted, and depleted Western heroes. As Wallace Stegner said of the old Western myths, "dream other dreams, and better. (212)

As college and university instructors, we can push for a deeper collegial understanding of the issues surrounding diversity content, such as the heightened emotionality that often complicates more traditional rational discourse, the legacy of prejudice that still lingers and infects us all, and the political winds that swirl and threaten violence. For example, we can affirm the importance of an institutional commitment to professional development for faculty and teaching assistants. Individually, we can address our own issues, biases, fears, and needs. We can insist that we "dream other dreams, and better."

In the summer of 2002, I got to travel through Eastern Europe and follow the trail of Nazi terror and Soviet occupation. In Lithuania, Poland, the Czech Republic, and Hungary, I got to see the worst expressions of human intolerance—the Ponar Forest just outside Vilnius, where 100,000 Jews were systematically slaughtered; the gas chamber and torture cells at Auschwitz-Birkenau, where Jews, gypsies, Communists, union leaders, Catholic priests, prisoners of war, and anyone else who dared to dissent were starved, beaten, shot, gassed, or worked to death. I also visited the Genocide Museum in Vilnius, a former KGB prison replete with its own cells for torture. How quickly the Soviet liberators became repressive as they sought to avenge their losses during the war and impose their own ideology.

Yet, various forms of resistance emerged despite the brutality of the persecution and overwhelming military force. Jews in Vilnius, an historic center for Judaic studies and culture, performed plays, read original poetry, and organized concerts in a courageous attempt to keep their dignity and hopes alive, to continue to learn and nurture the expression of their creative talents. A bit farther south, the Jews in the Warsaw ghetto rose up against their Nazi oppressors as early as 1943—well before the Germans suffered any real military setbacks. Some twelve years later, long after the end of the war and in response to Stalinist oppression and heavy-handed Soviet control, Budapest arose in revolt. The 1968 revolt in Prague presaged the moves for independence throughout all of eastern Europe and the Baltic states as well as the splintering of the USSR itself. Throughout it all, schools, colleges, and universities played critical roles as a part of the problem and as sources for independent, critical dissent and active resistance. We can only hope that our own work here on teaching diversity can contribute something as useful.

References

Banks, James A. 1989. Multicultural education: Characteristics and goals. In *Multicultural education: Issues and perspectives,* edited by James A. Banks and Cherry McGee Banks. Newton, MA: Allyn and Bacon.

Basow, Susan. 1998. Student evaluations: The role of gender bias and teaching styles. In *Career strategies for women in academe: Arming Athena,* edited by Lynn H. Collins, Joan C. Chrisler, and Kathryn Quina. Thousand Oaks, CA: Sage.

Belenky, Mary F., Blythe M. Clinchy, Nancy R. Goldberger, and Jill R. Tarule, eds. 1986. *Women's ways of knowing.* New York: Basic Books.

Campbell, Duane, and Delores Delgado Campbell. 1999. *Choosing democracy: A practical guide to multicultural education.* Upper Saddle River, NJ: Prentice Hall.

Davis, Nancy. 1992. Teaching about inequality: Student resistance, paralysis, and rage. *Teaching Sociology* 20: 232-238.

Deloria, Vine, Jr. 1997. *Red earth, white lies.* Golden, CO: Fulcrum.

Dewey, John. 1996. *Democracy and education: An introduction to the philosophy of education.* New York: The Free Press and Macmillan.

Easwaran, Eknath. 1972. *Gandhi the man.* Petaluma, CA: Nilgiri Press.

Freire, Paulo. 1997. *The pedagogy of hope.* New York: Continuum.

Gardner, Howard. 1983. *Frames of mind.* New York: Basic Books.

Gardner, Howard. 1999. *Intelligence reframed: Multiple intelligences for the 21st century.* New York: Basic Books.

Gilligan, Carol. 1982. *In a different voice: Psychological theory and women's development.* Cambridge, MA: Harvard University Press.

Goleman, Daniel. 1994. *Emotional intelligence.* New York: Bantam.

Johnson, David, and Roger Johnson. 1994. *Learning together and alone.* Needham Heights, MA: Allyn and Bacon.

Limerick, Patricia. 1996. Believing in the American West. In *The West*, edited by S. Ives and K. Burns. Boston: Little, Brown.

Mandela, Nelson. 1994. *Long walk to freedom.* Boston: Back Bay Books.

Marks, Stephan. 1995. The art of professing and holding back in a course on gender. *Family Relations* April:142-148.

Marsh, Herbert. 2001. Distinguishing between good (useful) and bad workloads on students' evaluations of teaching. *American Educational Research Journal* 38:183-212.

Marsh, Herbert, and Lawrence Roche. 1997. Making students' evaluations of teaching effectiveness effective: The critical issues of validity, bias, and utility. *American Psychologist* 52 (11): 1187-1197.

Mayberry, Katherine, ed. 1996. *Teaching what you're not: Identity politics in higher education.* New York: New York University Press.

Meichenbaum, Donald, Susan Burland, L. Gruson, and R. Cameron. 1985. Metacognitive assessment. In *The growth of reflection in children*, edited by Steven Yussen. Orlando, FL: Academic Press.

Nabhan, Gary. 1997. *Cultures of habitat: On nature, culture and story.* Washington, DC: Counterpoint.

Perry, William. 1981. Cognitive and ethical growth: The making of meaning. In *The Modern American College*, edited by Arthur W. Chickering. San Francisco: Jossey-Bass, Publishers.

Perry, William. 1999. *Forms of intellectual and ethical development in the college years*. San Francisco: Jossey-Bass, Publishers.

Simon, Sidney, Leland Howe, and Howard Kirshenbaum. 1972. *Values clarification: A handbook of practical strategies for teachers and students*. New York: Hart.

Takaki, Ronald. 1993. *A different mirror*. Boston: Little, Brown.

Tannen, Deborah. 1996. *Gender and discourse,* New York: Oxford University Press.

Timpson, William M. 2001. *Stepping up: College learning and community for a sustainable future*. Madison, WI: Atwood Publishing and Cincinnati, OH: Thomson Learning.

Timpson, William M., and Paul Bendel-Simso. 1996. *Concepts and choices for teaching*. Madison, WI: Atwood Publishing.

Trout, Paul. 2000. Flunking the test: The dismal record of student evaluation. *Academe* July:58-61.

Wolfgang, Charles. 1999. *Solving discipline problems*. Boston: Allyn and Bacon.

Teaching about Human Diversity: Theoretical and Epistemological Issues

Silvia Sara Canetto, Raymond Yang,
Evelinn A. Borrayo, and William M. Timpson

Introduction

This book is a confluence of journeys. For the editors and authors, the chapters in this volume are an effort still in progress. As instructors in various disciplines, we have tried to understand more about human diversity in all its inherent complexities so that we can best address its meaning for our students, our institutions, and our fields. We have come together to share our findings in the hope that what we have learned can be of use to others.

At various times, all of us have had our own share of struggles when teaching topics that touch on ethnicity, gender, social class, sexual orientation, or religious background. All of us have had to reflect on our own roles and identities and how they have affected our understanding of course material and our students. There is also an exciting, complex, and challenging interweaving of intellectual content and emotional reactions that occurs when these issues surface in class discussions, course readings, student papers, presentations, postings on the web, and interactions through email. In light of this, we all have been challenged to examine our own teaching. Thus, we believe we can offer something both creative and practical to others.

This collaborative journey began with Bill Timpson's and Silvia Sara Canetto's focused exploration of these dynamics in their own courses on diversity. At some point they contacted Linda Babler at Atwood Publishing about the possibility of a book on the subject of teaching diversity. Her enthusiastic responses led them to invite others to explore their own experiences from a variety of disciplinary perspectives. Soon after that, Evelinn Borrayo and Raymond Yang joined the editorial team as well.

In this chapter, we want to provide an overview of those factors that we have come to believe are most important for teaching diversity content. First, we want to deal with meanings and definitions of diversity and then explain what we adopted for this book. Second, we consider how issues pertaining to our "location," experiences, training, and identities affect our choices. A well-established principle in the literature on human diversity is that our cultural location (historically and nationally) and personal experiences (as a result of our individual characteristics and personal history) affect the kinds of issues we explore and the ways in which we frame our questions. It also is generally believed that experiences as an outsider to a dominant system can help with developing a sensitivity to human diversity and a capacity to break out of established frameworks (McHugh, Koeske, and Frieze 1986). Accordingly, we want to offer you some insights into who we are as individuals, our own origins and journeys, what we have come to agree on, what we have learned from each other, where differences still exist, and how we have navigated that terrain.

Meanings of "Human Diversity"

The first dilemma one encounters in this field is that the phrase "human diversity" is used to refer to different domains. To some, human diversity is synonymous with multiculturalism, meaning addressing the experiences of ethnic and some linguistic minority groups as defined by categories used in U.S. bureaucracies and the social sciences (e.g., African American, Asian American/ Pacific Islander, Native American, Hispanic). Other versions of human diversity as multiculturalism focus on categories of stratification (e.g., sexual orientation) or treat all groups as "cultures" (e.g., the culture of physical disability). Consequently, the social hierarchy typically associated with human diversity may be downplayed. For example, framing gay experiences solely as a matter "culture" or "lifestyle" can obscure issues of discrimination and inequity. One perhaps unintended consequence of a "cultural" reference is, as Bell and colleagues (1999, 33) put it, "a superficial acknowledgment or tolerance of difference with no consideration of how differences are socially produced."

To others, human diversity means the *whole* range of human experience. Within this broader definition, teaching about human diversity usually means three things, in particular. First, it means addressing the experiences of any group (e.g., women, lesbians and gays, people of color) that has been absent, underrepresented or misrepresented in the curriculum canon. Second, it means examining the behavior of dominant groups as an important but special case rather than as a universal and standard of human behavior. For example, it means to study men as men, as opposed to men as generic human beings. Finally, it means bringing issues of group status *and* power to the forefront. Group size is no longer the only reference point. This is a critical distinction, because one group can be a minority and still dominate, as is demonstrated by men worldwide or the wealthy or Whites in apartheid South Africa.

This power-based definition of human diversity can also account for variations in the social status and experiences of individuals and groups sharing certain characteristics (e.g., homosexuality) and traditions (e.g., Jews). In other words, a power-based definition of diversity does not assume that certain characteristics are always associated with dominance and others with subordination. Rather, within this definition, what become important are the idiosyncratic meanings, visibility, and consequences of various characteristics or traditions in specific historical and cultural contexts (Rosenfelt 1998).

For example, in some communities, being gay may be associated with pathology (as is the case in the official codes of some southern states in the United States). In other communities, being gay may be viewed as a sign of special blessing, talents, and sensibilities (as is the case among some Native American tribes). In some places one's characteristics may be highly visible and negatively coded (being a Buraku in Japan), while in other places the same characteristics may remain unnoticed and unremarkable (being a Buraku in the United States).

In this book, we argue for a broad and contextually grounded definition of human diversity. Yet, our primary national point of reference is the United States. As a result, our chapters cover the range of human diversity topics that are socially meaningful at this time in the United States. These are gender and sexual orientation; color and ethnicity; social class and privilege; religion; nationality and language; and physical disability. A different selection of topics might have made sense if we were writing from a different national standpoint (Hase 2002; Rosenfelt 1998). For example, if we were writing about India, we would have addressed issues of caste or sexual orientation very differently, perhaps starting with the experiences of the Hjiras (Sharma 2000). Be that as it may, the themes and conclusions that emerge from our analyses of case studies across the various disciplines and our extended discussions over two-plus years should prove generalizable to others teaching diversity content in the U.S. or elsewhere.

Epistemology and Place: Our Location

All the contributors to this volume live and work in the United States, even though our individual journeys to being here have been very different and many of us have had significant experience internationally, living, studying, and working. In general, our experiences have been influenced by a uniquely U.S. mix of populations and history. While our references and arguments all must be considered within this particular context, we want to be up front with this discussion so as not to overstate our conclusions. Every scholar in the social sciences everywhere in the world must struggle with this limitation. Analyses of diversity can never be inclusive of every possible categorization worldwide. Researchers are also constrained by the paradigms (i.e., conceptual models) that dominate their disciplines.

For example, other English-speaking countries with a history of immigration (e.g., Canada, Australia) construct ethnicity in different ways. In Canada, French and English define significant boundaries and loyalties. There are francophones, anglophones, and allophones. Australia also organizes ethnic minorities based on language. However, in Australia, what matters is the language of the country of origin in relation to English. Thus, the Australian classification system for immigrant-origin populations is essentially binary. There are persons of English-speaking origin (which would include England, Canada, New Zealand, and the United States) and persons of non-English-speaking origin, which includes everybody else, from Italians to Turks to Chinese and Filipinos. A third Australian ethnic category is used for Aboriginal people.

To best appreciate how social factors affect the construction of ethnicity—and how culturally specific ethnic classifications are—consider also what happens when people immigrate from one country to another. As an example, think of people moving from Guatemala to the United States (as one of our contributors has). In Guatemala they may have been considered Indigena if they were of Mayan descent and followed traditional ways or Ladinas if they followed modern ways. Or they may have been considered mestizas if they had Mayan *and* Spanish descent. Once they move to the United States, however, these references are invariably subsumed under all-encompassing categorizations like Hispanics or Latinos. Histories and subtleties vanish and re-form in various ways in the new country.

In India, there are uncrossable social boundaries for people of different castes. An upper-caste Indian, a priestly Brahmin would not go to school, live, or eat in the same place as a so called Dalit or a Backward Caste person (or outcastes, as they used to be called). Brahmins and Dalits could not marry. Even casual contact between the two is suspect: For example, a Dalit walking in the shadow of a Brahmin might require a Brahmin to perform ritual purification. Yet, in the United States, all immigrants from India would typically be considered the same, and grouped officially in one Asian American category, together with Chinese, Pakistanis, Laotians, and Tajikistanis. Any study of diversity must address these shifting realities.

Scholars in the social sciences everywhere must examine the ways their work is bounded by the historical and cultural mix of populations under study in their particular countries. So must our own contributors reflect on certain quintessential U.S. beliefs that imbue the culture, underlie certain values, and help to maintain certain traditions. For example, there is the cherished belief that "everyone is an individual," a longstanding notion that tends to discount the effect of social forces in individual lives (see Maher and Tetreault 2001 and Rothenberg 1998 for similar observations in United States classrooms). A corollary of this theme is the common belief in the existence of a meritocracy in the U.S.—that ability and effort are all that matters for social and economic advancement (Bell, Morrow, and Tastsoglou 1999; Rothenberg 1998). There is also the assumption that access to education is all it takes to achieve equality, despite overwhelming evidence to the contrary (Maher and Tetreault 2001).

Consider the confluence of gender and education in the U.S. country. The literacy rate for women is 99 percent. Women represent about half of all college students. Yet, U.S. women lag behind women in many countries, including industrialized (e.g., Italy) and developing (e.g., Kenya) countries, with regard to gender parity in income (Burn 2000). There has never been a female United States president. In fact, the representation of women in the U.S. House and Senate, although rising, never has reflected their numbers in the general population. Alternatively, there has been a female prime minister in Pakistan, a country where women's literacy rate is 22 percent and women represent 15 percent or less of college students (Burn 2000). Considering that the list of countries with a history of female leadership (either prime minister or president) includes Canada, India, Iceland, Ireland, Israel, Nicaragua, Norway, the Philippines, Turkey, and the United Kingdom, it is clear that women's access to education is not the sole factor in their advancement to political stewardship, as many U.S. students wish to believe.

Finally, there is a common assumption that the United States is the standard by which all other countries are to be measured, particularly with regard to "liberty and justice for all." When we teach about diversity and question some of these assumptions, values, and beliefs, tensions inevitably surface. The dissonance with reality can be unnerving for some students. Resistance and denial are common responses. Curiosity and dialogue about human diversity can suffer. Even U.S. scholarship suffers here. For example, while social scientists in Australia commonly cite sources from throughout the English-speaking world, U.S. scholars seem less global in their references.

The editors and authors of this volume are located in different departments but are all at the same institution—Colorado State University. Our university is a public, land-grant, comprehensive research university. As such, it resembles many other big campuses: In 2002, it had a large enrollment (more than 24,000 students), a total budget of over $547 million, as well as inherent tensions between what is required for teaching the nearly 20,000 undergraduates and the demands of its graduate research agenda, which brought in more than $180 million in external grant monies. Courses range from small seminars to large lectures. The University employs 7, 000 people, 1,500 of whom are faculty. Ten percent of the faculty are ethnic minorities. Twenty-five percent of the faculty are women, a proportion that has not changed since 1986. Also, women are clustered more at lower ranks, in untenured positions and in certain disciplines. The overall student/faculty ratio is seventeen to one. Graduate programs are offered in 55 academic departments. The University maintains a large educational outreach program.

The units represented in this collection are Education, Psychology, Human Development and Family Studies, Natural Resource Recreation and Tourism, Philosophy, Social Work, Speech Communication, Resources for Disabled Students, Occupational Therapy, English, and the Center for the Applied Study of American Ethnicities. In addition to our shared experiences in the U.S., our common location on campus means that we also share some things from our broad institutional history and climate. For example, we all are accountable to the same official mission. We all are subject to certain university policies and practices. Like instructors everywhere, we all work in relative isolation, even within our disciplines. Importantly, it has been our shared commitment to explore the teaching of diversity and to contribute something new to the scholarship of teaching that has pulled us together in new, productive, and creative ways.

What we also found out through these interactions were the differences among our own departments with regard to the interpretation and implementation of university policies, including those that affect teaching. We discovered important differences in attitudes about teaching human diversity. We also found differences in the support and authority instructors are given. In any case, our common physical location facilitated direct and often spontaneous interaction as we worked on our chapters. Our conversations evoked additional ideas, which resulted in both revised drafts of chapters as well as invitations for others to join. These discussions have proven invaluable, a major benefit of locating this project on one campus and fostering some of the synergy that is possible.

Epistemology and Time: Our Times

In this last section on epistemology, we want to reflect some on the dominant Zeitgeist about human diversity in academia. We shall start with university demographics and then consider what this profile may mean for teaching and learning about human diversity.

How diverse is the typical university population? This question is important because one way to learn about human diversity is to have it on campus. To the extent that instructional approaches can be student-centered, interactive, and constructivist (i.e., where students are led through inductive processes to define meaning), then the diversity of the student population becomes a rich resource and the campus community becomes a laboratory for learning.

In the U.S. today, the number of females represents the majority of undergraduates (Burn 2000). However, significant differences continue to exist in the mix of females and males depending on the college and the discipline. Presently, the graduation rate of women exceeds that of men and that gap is widening. With respect to ethnicity, minorities now represent twelve percent of all students (Wilder 2000). In fact, over the last decade, the rate of increase in enrollments has been larger for ethnic minorities than for European Americans. Nonetheless, the college participation rates of ethnic minorities still trail by several percentage points when compared with the participation rate of Whites. These data, however, need to be treated with caution given that definitions of ethnicity are political and bureaucratic rather than scientific.

With respect to socioeconomic status, college participation rates have proven to be a direct function of income: Young adults (18-24 years of age) from lower-quartile-income families are less likely to attend college than those from the upper-quartile (55 percent vs. 90 percent), notwithstanding the support provided by special federal and state programs (Swail 2000). Furthermore, the difference in completion rates between students from these quartiles is large (18 percent vs. 65 percent), indicating a higher attrition rate for students from lower-income families. Mortenson (2000) is aware that this difference has always existed but notes that it reached its lowest point in 1980 and that it has increased steadily since then. In a dramatic and telling critique of the rhetoric in higher education about equal access in our purported meritocracy, he concludes: "Today, students born into families in the top income quartile have never had it so good, but students from families in the bottom quartile have never had it so bad…[H]igher education…is making the rich richer and the poor poorer" (42-43).

Furthermore, Mortenson's (2000) analysis of national census data showed that the relationship between formal education and annual income has increased steadily over the last thirty years: more than ever, more formal education equals more income. Yet during the same 30 years, the country's investment in higher education has decreased substantially. Measured as a proportion of the gross domestic product, state and local expenditures fell 23 percent from a 1982 peak; measured as a share of statewide per-capita personal income (the tax base for state appropriations), fiscal 2000 expenditures were $23 billion below the 1979 peak. This steady erosion in funding has had three damaging effects on the financial accessibility of a college education: State support of higher education has decreased, forcing institutions to raise their tuitions (at rates exceeding inflation) and decreasing substantially the ability of educational loans (e.g., Pell Grants) to defray educational costs.[1] In any discussion of diversity, it is essential to recognize the intertwining of social class and ethnicity; changes that impact lower-income families also impact a disproportionately large percentage of ethnic minorities.

There are no comparable national data on sexual orientation among students in higher education. These data are simply not collected. Moreover, given the presence of high levels of prejudice, hostility, and ignorance about lesbian, gay, bisexual, and transgendered people, we doubt that many students would feel safe enough to self-identify and thereby provide reliable reports about themselves. The fact that agencies and universities are not attempting any systematic collection of information on this aspect of student diversity is in itself telling.

An analysis of diversity content in higher education yields mixed findings as well. A majority of colleges and universities around the country have Women's or Gender Studies programs.

Many institutions also have Ethnic Studies and International Studies Programs. In addition, campuses commonly offer a range of courses that address diversity issues. For example, at Colorado State University, we have courses on the "Psychology of Gender," "Contemporary Race-Ethnic Relations," and "The Handicapped Individual in Society." However, these programs, political pressures, and/or courses can be vulnerable due to the vagaries of resource allocation and more traditional disciplinary thinking. As happens with students who themselves are underrepresented, difficult financial times may put courses with diversity content at greater risk.

Epistemology and the Individual: Our Stories as Editors

Our personal histories are themselves diverse. Bill Timpson is of Northern and Eastern European descent. He traces his ancestry to Estonia on his father's side and the Ukraine on his mother's. After teaching in inner-city schools, he completed his Ph.D. in educational psychology with a minor in cross-cultural aspects of learning. Long fascinated with the impact of teachers, personality, content, process, context, and place on learning, he now writes on instructional improvements and innovation in higher education. Silvia Sara Canetto was raised and educated in Italy. Before coming to the United States on her own as an adult, she lived in Israel, where she learned English, Hebrew, Spanish, and French. Her degrees are in physiological and clinical psychology. Her scholarship deals with meanings of gender across cultures, sexual orientations, classes, ages, and abilities. Evelinn Borrayo is Guatemalan. She came to the U.S. as a child with her family. She also is trained as a clinical psychologist. Her research focuses on issues of culture in women's health-related behaviors. Ray Yang's background is Hawaiian. His grandparents emigrated from Korea to work on the sugarcane plantations in Hawaii. His degree is in developmental psychology. His interest is in how at-risk status can be a seedbed for resilient development.

We believe that our own diversity of backgrounds, experiences, training, and interests expands our collective sensitivities as well as the collective expertise upon which we can draw. Our experiences in the United States give us some common references. Our experiences living and working abroad add more. While our histories and locations give us a wide range of reference points on diversity, they could never cover the whole gamut of issues. We hope what we do address, the conclusions we reach, and the recommendations we offer will prove useful to others working with diversity content.

This Book

The book features twenty-one chapters, including an introduction and a conclusion by the editors. The original chapters are all grounded in experiences with teaching. All of the authors were asked to speak in their own voices. We felt that this expectation would best fit the focus of the book, and that it also would be most likely to elicit new pedagogical ideas, fresh frames of reference, and a diversity of interpretations.

The chapters vary in terms of focus. Some address specific issues that emerged in the diversity-content classroom, from how to cover the "canon" as well as address the content the canon omits or misrepresents, to the different ways students respond to human diversity content. Others address institutional issues that affect what students learn and what they may be willing to learn in the classroom. Still others do both. Some address positive experiences in the diversity-content classroom. Others address difficulties and dangers in teaching about diversity; they point out that diversity content classes are exciting but difficult classes to teach because they deal with personally charged material. Some chapters are accounts of pedagogical explorations by new faculty. Others trace the insights and journeys of teachers who have focused on diversity content for decades. For all authors and teachers, these explorations and journeys continue.

The chapters in this book also are varied in terms of style. Some are narrative statements about personal journeys in the classroom. Others more explicitly and systematically reach for the empirical, theoretical, and political literature to get a frame of reference and achieve broader insights. The earlier chapters deal somewhat more exclusively with classroom dynamics, experiences, experiments and stories. The voices of these authors are polyphonic—personal and eloquent, passionate and strong, plaintive and vulnerable. And among these authors is a willingness to expose their vulnerabilities that reflects their deeper courage.

The later chapters delineate the connections between the classroom and the broader context of the university community. This broader context—for example, how teaching about human diversity is understood and evaluated in a department, or the messages about human diversity that are coded in campus artifacts—is an important indirect influence on all community members. These chapters provide a glimpse of the larger context from the perspective of faculty in the classroom. We think you will find them thought-provoking.

Additionally, we must acknowledge that what we are doing on our own campus is a work in progress. While this book represents the culmination of two years of work to better understand the teaching of diversity content in our own classes, any impact of our collective efforts across campus will have to await the test of time, leadership, and resource allocation. We have offered a few workshops along the way and we are just now starting a study group. Stay tuned.

We hope you find this volume informative. As important, we hope that it will be effective at conveying the scientific importance of bringing human diversity content into the classrooms of the modern university. Finally, we hope our experiences, our errors, and our insights will inspire you to go further in the effort to understand the pedagogy of teaching about human diversity.

Note

1. In 2000, the purchasing power of a Pell Grant was about half of what it was during the 1970s. This is one of the reasons why so many college students hold jobs while they attend school.

References

American Council on Education and American Association of University Professors. 2000. Does diversity make a difference? Three research studies on diversity in college classrooms (Executive Summary). Washington, DC: American Council on Education and American Association of University Professors.

Bell, Sandra, M. Morrow, and Evangelis Tastsoglou. 1999. Teaching in environments of resistance: Toward a critical, feminist, and antiracist pedagogy. In *Meeting the challenge: Innovative feminist pedagogies in action*, edited by Maralee Mayberry and Ellen Cronan Rose. New York: Routledge.

Burn, S.M. 2000. *Women across cultures: A global perspective.* Mountain View, CA: Mayfield

Hase, M. 2002. Student resistance and nationalism in the classroom: Reflections on globalizing the curriculum. In *Twenty-first-century feminist classrooms: Pedagogies of identity and difference*, edited by Amie A. MacDonald and Susan Sanchéz-Casal. New York: Palgrave Macmillan.

Kite, Mary E., Nancy F. Russo, Sharon S. Brehm, N.A. Fouad, Christine C.I. Hall, Janet S. Hyde, and Gwendolyn P. Keita. 2001. Women psychologists in academe: Mixed progress, unwarranted complacency. *American Psychologist* 56 (12):1080-1098.

Maher. F.A., and M.K.T. Tetreault. 2001.*The feminist classroom: Dynamics of gender, race, and privilege*. Lanham, MD: Rowman & Littlefield.

McHugh, Maureen C., Randi D. Koeske, and Irene H. Frieze. 1986. Issues to consider in conducting nonsexist psychological research. *American Psychologist*, 41:879-890.

Mortenson, Thomas G. 2000. The crisis of access in higher education. *Academe* 34:38-43.

Rosenfelt, Deborah S. 1998. Crossing boundaries: Thinking globally and teaching locally about women's lives. *Women's Studies Quarterly* 3/4:4-16.

Rothenberg, P. 1998. Integrating the study of race, gender and class: Some preliminary observations. In *The feminist teacher anthology* edited by Gail E. Cohee, Elisabeth Däumer, Theresa D. Kemp, Paula M. Krebs, Sue Lafky, and Sandra Runzo. New York: Teachers College Press.

Sharma, Satish K. 2000. *Hijras: The labelled deviant*. New Delhi: Gian Publishing House.

Swail, W.S. 2000. Preparing America's disadvantaged for college: Programs that increase college opportunity. In *Understanding the college choice of disadvantaged students* edited by A.F. Cabrera and S.M. La Nasa. *New Directions for Institutional Research* 107:85-101.

Wilder, D.J. 2000. *Minorities in higher education, 1999-2000, 17th annual status report*. Washington, DC: American Council on Education.

From a Minority
to a Majority Teaching Environment:
Lessons Learned and Transferable

Chance W. Lewis

"You are the first black person I have ever seen in a teaching capacity at the university level in my life." As I began to teach my first under-graduate-level class in teacher education at this predominantly European American, Carnegie I research institution in the Midwest, I was totally surprised at the mindset of some of the students who were enrolled in my class. I began my university teaching career as an adjunct faculty member in the School of Education (currently I am a new assistant professor). I had high hopes of building upon a successful high school teaching career that had started in the deep southern section of the United States in an inner-city school setting. I was just coming off "Teacher of the Year" honors in Baton Rouge, Louisiana, and I thought I was ready to take the university level by storm. However, on that first day when I stepped into the classroom, I found out that some of my students had never seen an African American in a position of authority at the university level. I must say that this was a very shocking experience for me, and I had to wonder how I would be received as an instructor and how this would impact student learning.

Before I explore these issues, I want you, the reader, to know a little more about my background. I was born in Louisiana in a pre-dominantly African American neighborhood, attended an all African American high school, and graduated from an historically black col-lege where I earned baccalaureate and master's degrees in the field of education. My teaching career began in an African American, in-ner-city high school. It is safe to say here that most of my previous experiences, whether growing up or in my early teaching career, were mainly with other African Americans. After moving to the mid-west to pursue a Ph.D. and then being hired as an assistant profes-sor at the same institution, I was now faced with a question that I have continually asked myself: "How do I transition from teaching a predominantly African American population to teaching a majority European American population in which persons of color have very few positions of authority?"

With the training/professional development workshops that colleges and universities typically provide every year, I have found that diversity training, specifically, and many other workshops as well are geared towards showing European American faculty members how to be successful in teaching European American students along with only a very small percentage of minority students. In my two years here, I have rarely seen the university directly address the needs of the few minority faculty members who teach mostly European American students—students who are very unlikely to have had a minority teacher throughout their entire academic careers.

Where does this leave the minority faculty member, who not only has to adjust to teaching a majority population of European American students but also has to deal with related issues around the campus—especially when diversity is proclaimed as an important part of the curriculum in departments and a focus across campus? What mechanisms are in place to help me fit in comfortably with my classes, other faculty members in the department, and the university community? How can I best help students adjust to me? To provide some perspective, I want to begin with a review of relevant literature. I also want to offer some lessons I learned from my own experiences in the following four areas: (1) majority-student perceptions about having a person of color as a professor, (2) students' feelings about the impact of ethnicity on their learning, (3) student reactions when diversity is addressed directly, and (4) student reactions to my inner-city teaching experience.

Review of Literature

The literature on minority faculty members' experiences in the university community suggests that institutional climate can be "inhospitable." For example, Spann's (1990) study involved seventy-eight University of Wisconsin faculty members. He reported that, at every level of that system, minority faculty were treated, at best, as "a guest in someone else's house" (51). Spann went on to say that European American faculty members and administrators tended to greet minority faculty with an apparent cordiality, projecting an attitude that they are making these "others" feel welcome in "their" space.

Ron Wakabayshi, national director of the Japanese American Citizens League, described this sense of exclusion: "We feel that we're a guest in someone else's house, that we can never relax and put our feet up on the table" (quoted by Daniels 1991, 5). Daniels points out that guests are not family, whose foibles and mistakes are tolerated. On the contrary, guests honor the hosts' customs without question, keep out of certain rooms, and must always be on their best behavior.

Other faculty of color fare worse than "guests" and—according to some of my colleagues around the country—this image is too kind because it describes a situation in which minority faculty members are welcome but with certain limitations. Some faculty members have experienced open or thinly veiled hostility in their academic environments, and even the guest metaphor does not apply. The guest metaphor, however, does serve to explain the discomfort minority faculty members often feel even when a predominantly European American institution is "welcoming" rather than openly hostile. I find it to be an apt analogy for explaining more forms of what could be termed a "chilly climate."

hooks (1997, 97) addresses the issue of the "chilly climate" in her own experiences in academe, saying that "black folks must be overly aware of small details as we go about our lives to be sure we don't enter forbidden territory." She goes on to note that "you learn to turn away from your own pain and memory, and even though you have turned away the memory of past, injustice lingers, comes into the present and you cannot live the way other people live."

Pierce (1989, 297) describes this "chilly climate" stating that "each colored minority faculty member experiences daily stresses as he or she negotiates existence." Jacqueline Mitchell (1982), a black social scientist, describes her academic achievement as full of "contradictions and ambivalent feelings" that were not a result of personal problems but of "being a minority in a European American-dominated society." Overall, this literature highlights the isolation and the "chilly climate" that faculty of color often face on a daily basis.

Student Reactions
to an African American Faculty Member

The first day of my first semester teaching on campus rolled around and I was in my classroom preparing for class. When students, the majority of whom were European American, walked into my classroom, they seemed literally shocked that I was an African American and that I was their professor for the semester. I immediately felt a sudden "chill" in the air. Students were very quiet. At this point, I was thinking to myself, "Are these people from another planet?" As I continued to observe the class, this silence began to look like fear. They did not know how to react to me. It didn't take me long to realize that these feelings impacted the classroom climate before I even had started the course.

Although this was an undergraduate education technology course, I knew we would be touching on some issues of diversity and access. Then I began to wonder: How would these students react when issues of diversity came up during class? How would my race affect discussions about diversity and access to technology? Would students be fearful of speaking honestly on the issues of diversity because I am a person of color? I contemplated all of these questions before saying a word to the class. Then I thought on the words of Cornel West (1994, 4): "Race is the visible catalyst, not the underlying cause." I now had a way to understand this in my classroom.

I quickly decided to begin welcoming these students. I wanted to ease the tension since I thought everyone seemed to be "skating on thin ice." After I went through all of the required particulars of the course (i.e., syllabus and course expectations), I started with individual introductions. When it was my turn, I began by telling students about my previous experiences in higher education and the K-12 setting. Then I addressed the issue of race. This approach has worked well for me in the past. I usually acknowledge the fact that I am African American (even though students can clearly see this) and I explain my purpose for being in the classroom. I inform the students that I am there to help them become "great" teachers and to learn different strategies/techniques so that they can help all learners in their own classrooms. Once I explained all this, I felt the tension start to subside. My African American colleagues who are in faculty positions at other predominantly European American universities (six total) inform me that they also feel the same type of "chilly climate" in their classrooms and, like I do, they address the issue of race/diversity on the first day of class (e.g., Derek Morgan, personal communication, August 15, 2001).

I do find it ironic, however, that I have to defend why I am in the classroom. I know that European American professors I had in my own doctoral program never had to defend why they were in the classroom. I am assuming it was just understood. They had the necessary expertise and experience to compete for and earn their positions, as did I. However, students enrolled in my course were not accustomed to seeing an African American faculty member. Thus, I felt I needed to address the issue right away.

After the first day of class, I noted how these European American students were starting to "warm up" to me. I feel my ethnicity, as an African American faculty member, was an important lesson for my students, as future teachers, in learning how to address the issue of diversity. For example, many students came to my office and privately said, "I'm glad you are here" and "You bring in a different perspective from all of my other professors." One European American student informed me that he wished he could have taken more classes from African American professors because of the "fire" they possess in their teaching. He indicated that he noticed a type of "fire" in me that he also saw in Dr. Martin Luther King, Jr. Comments like these suggest to me that many students at predominantly European American institutions may be missing out on a diversity of viewpoints from their instructors.

The Impact of Student Feelings on Diversity Topics

The students entering my classes came with very different experiences with diversity. The majority of students came from cities or towns that are entirely European American. Those from bigger cities, however, had very different experiences.

Students from smaller towns, who literally had not seen "other" people before, seemed to have very strong viewpoints. For example, I raised this question: "How can we as educators help to bridge the 'Digital Divide' for young students who are currently entering classrooms across the country?" Students from predominantly European American backgrounds made comments such as "I didn't know that a 'digital divide' existed" or "The only reason people of other cultures don't have access to technology is because they are too lazy to go to work and pay for it."

These comments immediately caught my attention and caused much tension in class. I had all types of thoughts going through my mind. However, several students who were from larger cities immediately jumped into the discussion and argued that people of other cultures often are fighting through an "economic" divide that is very prevalent in our society. These students took a very strong stand, further stating that as future teachers, "We cannot afford to look down on students just because of their origins or what they do or do not have." I personally felt a sense of joy as I saw how experiences with diversity could have such a positive impact.

I immediately jumped back into this classroom discussion to give students a "challenge" as future teachers: I asked them to write a paper on how they would approach teaching if the roles were reversed and they were now in the minority instead of the majority: This assignment really made students look at teaching in a very different light. No longer were they in their comfort zones. They now had to face the issue of diversity directly. I saw their "thinking caps" start to turn as they asked themselves how they were going to reach students from different backgrounds.

From this experience, I learned that by addressing the issue of diversity directly, I could give students the opportunity to voice their concerns in a safe environment where they could be heard and accepted. Given my responsibility to prepare future teachers, I was thrilled that these students could actually voice their concerns and hear alternative perspectives. I did not want them to carry their biases out into the schools. I now truly believe that all faculty members, whether minority or majority, should address issues of diversity in every aspect of what they teach. If not, we may never know our students' biases or even our own.

Implementing My Previous Teaching Experiences

I think one of the best ways to teach students in college classrooms is to share our experiences as faculty members. As I stated previously, I want to prepare students to be *great* teachers. In turn, I have found that my students want to know about my previous experiences, especially in dealing with minority students. I find it rewarding that students in my classes continue to ask me how they should handle different situations.

I have explained to students that some of the most memorable moments in my own teaching career have been in the inner-city schools of Louisiana. I have told them how I reacted when one of my students was shot and killed right on the school campus. Initially, these education students were terrified; they had never directly experienced anything of this magnitude. After their initial shock, they wanted to know what I did, how I kept students in my high school class focused after such a terrible incident. I was then able to share the different strategies I had used.

However, I also told these students about some of the positive experiences I'd had in the inner-city school environment that were life changing for me and my students. I told them how I'd reached out to students who had a slim chance of being successful, when the odds were stacked against them. I also explained the joy that I'd received from lighting a candle in the lives of students whom others had abandoned. These university students were amazed at the impact one teacher could have. No longer were these students looking at me as an African American professor. Now, they saw me as a person who was there to help them get prepared for the challenges ahead. Over time, I went from oddity to respected resource, especially when the issue of diversity arose.

I found that bringing my experiences into the classroom made a definite difference in the lives of these students. Stories about my experiences seemed to boost their courage about going out and helping others. Based on these encounters, I now truly believe that I can help all students—no matter their background—to be successful as teachers, especially as they work with those who are different from them. Unfortunately, I believe that many students leave this university without a realistic view of what is happening in the world outside, and that their training is limited by the lack of sufficient diversity locally.

Conclusion

Being an African American faculty member in a predominantly European American environment is not easy. Every teacher/professor wants to be accepted by his or her students regardless of skin color. However, when the legacy of a racist society, with all its stereotypes, comes into the university classroom, minority faculty members may find themselves backed into a corner before a word is spoken. Knowing that you are not welcomed by some on the basis of skin color is hard to take. I had to step back and ask again: Why are minorities not welcomed? Why is it that minority faculty have to be accommodated but not welcomed initially? Why do minority faculty members have to address issues of diversity directly just to prove their worth in the culture of the university environment?

The lessons I have learned as an African American faculty member will continue to be with me throughout my entire career. They will serve as a foundation to handle other "unwelcoming" experiences. As the literature suggests, there is a definite "chilly climate" that I faced as I began my career at this predominantly European American, Carnegie I institution. However, I think the lessons I have learned can serve to help others in similar situations until the day when all people can accept those from different cultural backgrounds as individuals.

References

Daniels, Lee A. 1991. *Only the appearance of diversity: Higher education and the pluralist ideal in the 1980s and the 1990s.* Policy perspectives. Philadelphia, PA: Pew Higher Education Research Program.

hooks, bell. 1997. *Wounds of passion: A writing life.* New York: Henry Holt.

Mitchell, J. 1982. Reflections of a black social scientist: Some struggles, some doubts, some hopes. *Harvard Educational Review* 52(1):27-44.

Pierce, C.M. 1989. Unity in diversity: Thirty-three years of stress. In *Black students: Psychosocial issues and academic achievement,* edited by Gordon L. Berry and Joy Keiko Asamen. Newbury Park, CA: Sage.

Spann, Jeffery. 1990. *Retaining and promoting minority faculty members: Problems and possibilities.* Madison, WI: University of Wisconsin System.

West, Cornel. 1994. *Race matters.* New York: Vintage Press.

Experiencing Diversity in Distance Learning

Timothy Gray Davies

Background to the Case Experience

I began my teaching career in higher education in 1963. I participated in and lived through the tumultuous activities that led to the
development of gender- and ethnic-specific courses and programs
during the next decade. With other campus "radicals," I began working to displace the traditional European American, white-male
"canon" with these separate programs and courses. However, it was
our firm belief that this was only an intermediate step and that these
separate and not-so-equal initiatives would soon become integrated
into the mainstream general education and liberal arts curricula at
the institutions we represented. Personal professional experience
has shown me that this integration of "border knowledge" (Rhoads
and Valadez 1996) into the canon or standard curriculum has not
occurred to the extent many of us had hoped. Now, forty years later,
my personal quest for diversity content integration continues, albeit
in a very different venue.

Several years ago, I developed a new doctoral program in Community College Leadership. Having spent over thirty years in community colleges and almost a decade as a community college
president, I felt it was time to give back to a profession that had been
so generous to me. This program was developed for full-time faculty
and administrators in community colleges. While others outside the
community colleges have joined the program ranks, the vast majority of students have been community college professionals. I developed the courses in the program around the content competencies I
knew community college leaders would need: finance, law, student
development theory, adult learning theory, leadership, and, of
course, research skills.

As important as the content was to the future success of these
students, I wanted to infuse some other strains throughout the cur-

riculum. Research, writing, and team- or cohort-building skills were paramount, but I also wanted to integrate the concepts of diversity in every course and experience throughout the program. Community colleges are well respected for their egalitarian philosophy, evidenced in their open-door admissions; thus, preparing leaders who could develop and protect a diverse and inclusive environment was especially important. While I think I have been able to build such an environment, it was not to take place in any conventional classroom setting.

Once I had accepted the challenge of developing a doctoral program for these full-time working professionals, I realized that the physical distance to the university campus became a primary student and learning issue. With the round-trip driving time between the regional community colleges and the university campus ranging from two to thirty hours, it became clear that the traditional on-campus course schedules would not work. What has seemed to work—after several years of synergistic development and the proverbial trial-and-error experimentation—has been a blending of various learning modalities. Acknowledging that the distance to campus would be a problem, we began to use two-way interactive compressed video for classes one night each week. This distance modality is enhanced by the use of an Internet course software package called WebCT®, which contains asynchronous bulletin boards and private mail capability along with synchronous chat rooms. As course facilitator, I use all these options in various ways to enhance and increase the connectivity of students to one another and to me. I receive and evaluate all papers, exams, and assignments and then return them via this electronic medium. However, I do not believe that the teaching and practicing of leadership skills can be accomplished solely via distance learning modalities; therefore, once each month the cohort meets together for a full day of face-to-face discussion and debate via other modes of experiential learning. I attempt to blend different learning modalities to address the time and distance problem from campus while providing for a rigorous, quality doctoral experience. The case experience that follows took place with the second group of students admitted into this doctoral program.

The Case Experience

The ethnic background of the student cohort in this case experience: four were Hispanic, one was African American, and nine were European American. Eight of the students were female and six were male. They were located at four different distance sites with three sub-cohorts meeting away from the university campus and one sub-cohort meeting on the university campus with me. The course was a seminar in community college leadership, and we were in the first four weeks of the course. Along with some more traditional leadership readings, we read *Gender and Power in the Community College* (Townsend 1995), *Grass Roots and Glass Ceilings: African American Administrators in Predominantly White Colleges and Universities* (Harvey 1999), *Sailing Against the Wind: African Americans and Women in U.S. Education* (Lomotey 1997), and *Democracy, Multiculturalism, and the Community College* (Rhoads and Valadez 1996). These volumes dealt specifically with inclusionary issues from both gender and ethnic perspectives and provided the students with contemporary issues within the community colleges.

This experience began during a class session formatted as a graduate seminar discussion using the two-way compressed video. The content was based on the gender and ethnic inclusion readings from the books mentioned earlier. Using Bloom's cognitive taxonomy (1956) as a framework for the course, students prepared to discuss the assigned readings. This preparation meant that the discussion would not simply center on retelling what everyone had read, which Bloom identifies as the *knowledge, comprehension,* and *application* levels of cognition. Rather, the discussants would need to analyze the works under discussion, take them apart idea by idea, and then rebuild those ideas into a new form or structure that Bloom refers to as *synthesis*. The final activity was to evaluate that which had been recreated from the original ideas in the readings and to integrate those ideas into the students' own professional experiences and campus responsibilities. It was a common seminar discussion format we had used many times before but apparently not with such sensitive material. As might be imagined, these doctoral students had little trouble analyzing the essays and identifying the key issues and challenges presented by the various authors. They were able to clearly and succinctly evaluate the various diversity strategies offered by the authors, whether in curriculum revision, ethnic student recruitment, or hiring a diversified faculty. However, when it came time to connect these diversity strategies to their own campus experiences and their own professional responsibilities on those campuses, they became quiet, sullen, and refused to question and engage one another. This defensiveness engulfed the entire cohort. This was a posture I had not witnessed previously. More than ever the real distances between us added another layer of complexity.

Gently, I attempted to engage them in describing what they had accomplished on their own campuses in terms of applying diversity principles to their hiring practices, their curricular/instructional activities, and their governing/decision-making processes. I attempted not to embarrass them or judge them but rather to draw them back into conversation so that we could regain our communication. I was met with a stony silence! I attempted eye contact across the television studio's conference table, but the three students in the on-campus cohort kept their eyes fixed on their readings. The off-campus television sites revealed the same evasive tactics. If they weren't averting their eyes from the camera, they were staring back across the airwaves in what seemed to me to be a sullen disdain for the questions I was asking. I knew full well that many of them were in positions of responsibility and authority and could have been instrumental in seeing many of these strategies implemented on their campuses. I did not ask them why they had not been able to implement any of the suggestions we had been discussing. I did not admonish them in their silence. But clearly this class behavior was something I had not witnessed before when our discussions were anchored in safer, less-sensitive material. This was a complete anomaly.

I asked what was happening with our process. What was going on within them that created this deafening silence? Still there was no response. I continued to probe to find out where our discussion process had broken down. "I know you have read the readings," I said. "You have demonstrated that in the content portion of our discussion. Now, why can't we talk about this discussion and what is blocking us from talking about racial/ethnic and gender glass ceilings on campus?" Nothing! Not even a twitch was betrayed across the television monitors or across the studio conference table.

I went silent. I could feel my stomach churning. What had I done that was so egregious as to bring us to this deadly silence? What had happened to all of the rapport we had built during the first semester together? We had fifteen minutes left in our class session, but I was completely out of ideas. I didn't know where to go from here. I told them we were closing early; that obviously we all had some thinking to do; that I would see them on Friday for our monthly face-to-face day together.

I felt angry, hurt, rejected, a total failure for the evening—at a minimum for the evening. To paraphrase Parker Palmer (1998), some days the classroom experiences go so well, everything connects, and students explode with ideas and integrate the material so well into their own respective lives that you know you were born to teach. And on other days, things have gone so disastrously that you wonder why you were born at all. This evening was a clear example of the latter for me. I began packing up the computer and closing down the studio amidst hurried goodbyes from my three on campus cohort members. I was amazed at how quickly they had exited, leaving me with my own thoughts as I started my three-mile walk back home.

What went wrong? How could a topic about which they claimed to feel so strongly elicit such a negative reaction? Where had the camaraderie and the closeness demonstrated so often in the past, under so many different circumstances, disappeared on this one evening. As facilitator of this cohort, where had I gone astray? I kept bringing it all back to *me*: What did I do wrong? And that is where I was. I was stuck. It had to be about me and it had to be about right and wrong. I wondered what had happened to me and my own self confidence in my teaching and facilitating abilities. My walk home took an hour longer than usual, and all I had really resolved was that I needed to communicate with the students first thing in the morning via the class bulletin board. What I would say or how I would say it was a mystery as I climbed into bed, but as in any relationship we value, I reminded myself that open communication and keeping in touch are essential.

After a rather restless night, I arrived at the office early. I must admit, I was hoping to find some electronic or phone messages waiting for me—something to show that others were as concerned as I, or even a *mea culpa* from someone. Nothing! I opened the class bulletin board and began to share my own thoughts and concerns from the previous evening. I wrote that I was disappointed in the way the discussion had gone and that I did not feel it represented the quality discussions we had had in the past. Clearly, I wrote, something was amiss, and I wanted to add last night's discussion to Friday's work list when we were all together. While I did receive some responses back to my electronic message, they were simply affirming that it should be on Friday's agenda. There was nothing beyond that, not a trace of what they were thinking or feeling individually or collectively.

Friday came all too quickly. We met at a regional community college and spent the first half of the day listening to faculty and administrative leaders describe their working relationship and their community college's open-door philosophy. Then, after lunch, we had our own time together. I was expecting tension throughout the room once we had reassembled, but strangely that was not the case. I opened our meeting with my own *mea culpa*. Briefly, I told them I felt I had not done a very good job as the facilitator of our group and that we had taken several steps backward and regressed in terms of our relationships with one another. I admitted I was puzzled as to why we were unable to discuss the racial, ethnic, and gender issues on our campuses and what we were doing to become more inclusive campuses and organizations within our communities. I closed by saying I hoped that the afternoon could be spent discussing what had occurred and where we would go from there.

I expected a long silence, the silence that drags on with no one willing to make the first verbal foray into what could be the ensuing abyss. But I was wrong once again. Almost immediately, three people started speaking, giving way to one another, and then establishing an order.

The Hispanic/Latino students asked to begin. They said that initially they were excited about the possibilities our discussion topics held that evening, but that those feelings of excitement had changed to embarrassment for their European American colleagues. Those feelings had then turned to disappointment and anger, and then led to their complete withdrawal from the class discussion. They continued to explain their emotions and were uninterrupted except by requests for clarification. Obviously, the individual cohorts that met together at the different distance sites had been busy communicating with one another over the past few days.

Jose (all names have been changed) began by explaining the feelings of excitement his distance cohort had because they knew the professional positions many of the other students held on their respective campuses. They hoped to hear of the positive movements being made on their campuses as they played a role in making the campus more diverse and inclusive. They wanted to hear that this program was making a real difference on community college campuses. The silence that had ensued that evening despite my specific questions helped change their emotions to embarrassment for their European American colleagues. They sensed that the European American's felt put on the spot and had a certain degree of empathy. But empathy changed to disappointment when their colleagues would not volunteer any information. According to Jose, it would have been better received if their European American colleagues would just have admitted that there really wasn't any change on their respective campuses. Jose said their disappointment then turned to anger because, once again, there had been "much talk but little walk" on the part of their European American members. Not wanting to call their European American colleagues on their silence or check out their perceptions and their disappointment, they became angry and withdrew from the discussion altogether. No matter what I asked, they told the group, they were not going to respond. They felt that many of their European American colleagues held responsible administrative positions from which they could have begun to effect change but apparently had not. Not only would they not share the reasons why they had not moved forward, but they also had refused to speak up and discuss it. Jose said they didn't expect anything earth-shattering but were angered by the apparent lack of trust that their European American colleagues had in them. That, he explained, was why they didn't come forward in the discussion. Jose then asked Millie to respond to what was happening at her distance cohort site, located in the southern part of the state.

Millie was an academic dean and had been offering many creative ways for community colleges to become more diverse and inclusive. She was in a cohort at one of the distance sites where all the students were European American. In speaking about their behavior that night, she said they had spent some time afterwards on the phone and in the chat room talking about what had happened with them. She said their cohort felt very keenly that I had put them on the spot because their cohort had the most leadership responsibility on their respective campuses. They felt some immediate resentment toward me because they felt singled out, even though I hadn't called upon them specifically. Their resentment turned into anger toward the rest of the group, whom they felt had unfair expectations of them because they were in administrative roles. But, Millie said, that feeling turned just as quickly into their own feelings of guilt and inadequacy over the fact that they really hadn't tried to do anything different on their campuses and hadn't even come up with a plan to do so. They really hadn't thought of the discussions around diversity as leading immediately into action at their particular community colleges. Their feelings of embarrassment stemmed from not wanting to tell the group that, in fact, they had a good handle on the readings and on the goal but had not done anything about it.

For two hours, we talked about the feelings that had been generated based on our race, ethnicity, gender, age, professional position, program position (facilitator and student), and even site location. There was discussion over the expectations we held of one another and whether those expectations were really fair. The conversation was animated and appeared sincere and authentic. I asked them where we would go; they replied that they wanted to make amends to one another. We gave ourselves the time that afternoon to each in turn make our statement of amends to the rest of the group, for both what we had said as well as what we hadn't said but had thought. It was one of those rare moments when an entire group of people touches one another at a deeper level of our humanity. We set new rules of conduct for ourselves for the remainder of the term, but the group wanted to pursue this experience further. They agreed that at our face-to-face meeting the next month, we would come prepared to discuss our lessons learned so that they could be passed on to the next doctoral cohort coming the following fall.

This doctoral class did not forget their experience easily, and indeed they returned a month later to their face-to-face Friday meeting and sorted out the lessons they felt they had learned. Furthermore, they were adamant that their lessons needed to be shared with the other doctoral classes that would be following them in the future. What follows is a brief description of these lessons learned.

Lessons Learned

The most important lesson the students felt they learned was actually directed to me as the teacher. They recommended that diversity be developed and presented as a curricular infusion thread that would run throughout all courses in the doctoral program. In fact, the entire class was adamant that the community college's open-door philosophy required that diversity concepts be a well-developed infusion thread throughout the program curriculum. They felt the readings were important for content background, but they also strongly suggested that more time be given to the process of implementing these ideas on a community college campus. They also recommended that diversity be introduced at the beginning of the program and that it be made clear that it was to be a program goal.

The second lesson they felt important to pass on was that the team-building skills needed to be addressed at the outset of each new class and strengthened within and among the cohorts. They pointed out that a cohort is different from a group of students only if planned team-building exercises have been implemented that will help them work with one another with candor and compassion. The development of ground rules for all to follow must be an early undertaking in their cohort life and must include the setting of boundaries for acceptable and unacceptable behavior. Establishing social monitoring of those boundaries, building trust and openness within discussions and interactions, and providing them with the skills to give and receive feedback during sensitive discussions cannot occur just at the beginning of the program, but must be part of an ongoing, planned effort to help them develop and grow.

An important concept that this doctoral class identified was the concept of a "safe place" to which they could return during a sensitive or volatile discussion. Their meaning of a safe place was one built on common ground from past discussions; one to which they could return, regroup, and then proceed with the discussion that was causing both pain and difficulty. This "safe place" could be a specific topic they had addressed, struggled over, come to grips with, and then moved on from, having resolved all the issues and with everyone feeling comfortable and safe. During future difficult discussions, they could return to that previous moment and reconnect with the way they had moved beyond the difficult feelings and emotions. However, they felt completely vulnerable during the evening of the case illustration because there had been no "safe place" for them to go. This had resulted in silence, frustration, and anger.

The third lesson identified by this doctoral class was the need to prepare for sensitive issues. The doctoral cohort felt that diversity issues are initially sensitive. For example, students may have a difficult time talking about their personal feelings relative to being a Latina or a lesbian. In addition, many of the European Americans did not understand their "white privilege"; some were in denial. They felt that personal and professional issues that dealt with race, ethnicity, sexual orientation, and sometimes gender seemed more difficult to discuss. However, once the discussion did get under way, they became more comfortable for a while—until the discussion became more personal or more in depth and rose to a new level of sensitivity. Their suggestion was to prepare for these discussions by leading into them with the readings and reacting to the readings through WebCt®'s electronic private mail journal, which is between the student and instructor. They felt that, in this way, they could explore some of their thoughts and feelings in private before bringing them out to the cohort as a whole.

After they had a chance to explore their ideas and feelings in this way, they felt the next step would be a full discussion in their face-to-face Friday sessions. They believed that being together in person, rather than as television icons or Internet monikers, allowed them the opportunity to explore what people meant by what they said and, as importantly, to follow up on what they didn't say, i.e., with their body language. They said that once this occurred, they would feel quite comfortable having the open graduate seminar discussions on television.

The fourth lesson they felt they learned was the importance of surveying the virtual classroom climate. They believed that a learning environment had to be accepting enough so that a participant could feel comfortable saying, "I'm thinking. Come back to me later," without being judged as having dodged a sensitive issue. They could feel safe in saying, "Your last comment hurt me and I want to discuss it some more to see if we can resolve it" and have that received in a compassionate and understanding way rather than as a threat or a challenge. They wanted a climate where they could ask for, receive, and provide peer and cohort support for and reassurance from each other and from me as facilitator. Accordingly, they suggested that various strategies be used so that the climate of the discussion groups could be checked periodically to ensure the students could confidentially discuss the tough professional issues and challenges that came with promoting diversity on their respective campuses. They wanted a place where they could be supported and feel comfortable offering new ideas and suggestions, but also one where they could choose to just listen or empathize as well. Trust and confidentiality were important. One student even offered a saying from a twelve-step program—"What you see here, what you hear here, what you say here, let it stay here"—as a motto for the trust and openness they wanted in their climate.

The climate survey they recommended was a fairly simple approach of stopping the class discussion, whether on camera or face-to-face, and taking the pulse of the comfort level—i.e., did everyone feel safe enough to risk personal feelings, ideas, and experiences? While not always perfect, when we tried this in subsequent meetings, it did provide the opportunity for people to say they weren't comfortable, that there needed to be some discussion, or that we needed to revert to the "safe place" that had been identified.

I enjoy playing golf, and at one time I subscribed to the old cliché about what a humbling sport it is. On any given day, my drives might be straight down the fairway, my iron shots on the green, and my putts on line. The next weekend, I may not be able to see the fairway for the trees, my iron shots might have ground squirrels running for their lives, and my putts might take me back and forth across the greens. I believed I was learning true humility. In class, when I changed my behavior from the "safety" of lecturing to a more vulnerable role as facilitator, helping students to construct their own knowledge, I began to realize what true humility is for me. The responsibility of helping create a learning environment that not only feels safe but *is* safe is a far more complex task than preparing a lecture ever was for me. Facilitation of learning is more demanding and risky for me than preparing a lecture. When I add the medium of distance learning to this mix, I increase my vulnerability that much more.

I look back on that Friday meeting with this particular doctoral class and wonder about the forward leap we took as a group. Having bid them goodbye at the end of their first year, I returned the next fall to watch new doctoral groups struggle as they attempted to implement the lessons learned by their predecessors. I find I am smiling to myself as I try to help them understand why certain steps are necessary in building an honest and safe learning environment. I share this story just as storytellers of old shared their culture around campfires. As these new doctoral students follow the advice of the doctoral class that went before, they acknowledge their predecessors' wisdom and see the results. Then, understanding the value of this culture and climate, this new group can add its own wisdom as their legacy to those who will follow in their footsteps. In this process of helping students learn, there is no conclusion—only a commencement.

References

Note: This reference list is different from most in that references are included that were not specifically cited in the chapter. This is done because the students had read and discussed these works as part of their program and the background that led up to the case experience. Therefore, I felt it would help you better understand the background the students had coming into this experience.

Belenky, Mary F., Blythe M. Clinchy, Nancy R. Goldberger, and Jill R. Tarule, eds. 1986. *Women's ways of knowing.* New York: Basic Books.

Bloom, Benjamin S., ed. 1956. *Taxonomy of educational objectives: The classification of educational goals: Handbook I: Cognitive domain.* New York: David McKay.

Davis, Josephine D., ed. 1994. *Coloring the halls of ivy: Leadership and diversity in the academy.* Boston: Anker.

Delgado, Richard, and Jean Stefancic, eds. 1997. *Critical white studies: Looking behind the mirror.* Philadelphia: Temple University Press.

Gilligan, Carol. 1982. *In a different voice: Psychological theory and women's development.* Cambridge, MA: Harvard University Press.

Harvey, William B., ed. 1999. *Grass roots and glass ceilings: African American administrators in predominantly white colleges and universities.* Albany, NY: State University of New York Press.

Hill, Mike, ed. 1997. *Whiteness: A critical reader.* New York: New York University Press.

hooks, bell. 1989. *Talking back: Thinking feminist, thinking black.* Cambridge, MA: South End Press.

hooks, bell. 1984. *Feminist theory: From margin to center*. Cambridge: South End Press

Lomotey, Kofi, ed. 1997. *Sailing against the wind: African Americans and women in U.S. education*. Albany, NY: State University of New York Press.

Palmer, Parker J. 1998. *The courage to teach*. San Francisco: Jossey-Bass Publishers.

Rhoads, Robert A., and James R. Valadez. 1996. *Democracy, multiculturalism, and the community college: A critical perspective*. New York: Garland Publishing.

Townsend, Barbara K. ed. 1995. Gender and power in the community college. *New Directions for Community Colleges*, no. 89. San Francisco: Jossey Bass, Publishers.

Turner, Caroline S.V., and Samuel L. Myers, Jr. 2000. *Faculty of color in academe: Bittersweet success*. Boston: Allyn and Bacon.

Creating Safe Learning Environments

Nathalie Kees

Introduction

I have been training counselors for the last fifteen years, and over that time I have consistently received written evaluations from students that could be summarized by the following statement: "Dr. Kees creates an environment in which I feel safe to risk, try new things, and learn." This has been important feedback, because the courses I teach are skills-based courses in which students learn individual- and group-counseling skills, new acquisitions for most of the students entering the graduate program in counseling and career development. I want my students, in turn, to create safe environments for their clients, and it is part of my responsibility to model for them how this can be done.

Creating safe environments for learning is also important to me personally, as one whose first three years of school were spent in fear, watching helplessly as some of my classmates were verbally, emotionally, and physically abused for being slow learners. I learned empathy at a very young age. Creating safety is also important for me as a female working in the traditionally self-reliant, isolating, and hierarchical world of academia. I annually see students, faculty, and staff of all genders and ethnicities leave the university—voluntarily and non-voluntarily—because the one-size-fits-all environment of an institution fails to retain them. Second only to physiological needs on Maslow's hierarchy of needs, a sense of safety and security is an important, if not vital, step toward human beings fulfilling their higher-level needs of self-esteem, love and belonging, and self-actualization (Maslow 1962).

Regardless of my students' feedback, however, I must admit that I know I have never created a truly safe environment. Given the multiple factors at play, creating a completely safe environment is impossible. A recent experience at the Denver International Airport brought this reality into vivid focus. My first air travel experience since September 11, 2001, I waited patiently in lines at the curb, walked past hundreds of people in line at the check-in counters, spent forty-five minutes going through security, and watched people randomly searched at the gate before boarding. And yet, as I boarded the plane, I was fully cognizant of the fact that despite the Herculean efforts of airport staff, thoughts of hijackers' bombs, mechanical failures, human errors, and acts of God were quite easily destroying my feeling of safety.

Given that safety can never be guaranteed, there are still recommendations from the education and multicultural counseling literature that can help create what Ramsey (1999) and others have described as a "safe enough" climate for learning and change to occur. This chapter will offer some of these recommendations, as well as some of my own thoughts and experiences about what seems to create or destroy that sense of safety in the classroom.

What Is a Safe Learning Environment?

The best description I have found of a "safe" learning environment comes from Parker Palmer, a noted consultant to educational organizations and a teacher for thirty years. He says that "to teach is to create a space in which the community of truth is practiced" (Palmer 1998, 90). Speaking in paradoxes, Palmer (1998, 74) says this educational space should:

> ...be bounded and open...be hospitable and charged...invite the voice of the individual and the voice of the group...honor the "little" stories of the students and the "big" stories of the disciplines and tradition...support solitude and surround it with the resources of the community...welcome both silence and speech.

A safe learning environment offers challenges, both intellectual and emotional, within an atmosphere of support, curiosity, cooperation, encouragement, and caring. Above all, a safe environment provides clear and realistic opportunities for success to all students.

How Can Safe Learning Environments Be Created?

In the field of multicultural counseling, the importance of creating safe classroom environments and various recommendations have been offered by several scholars (Kiselica 1999a, 1999b; McAuliffe 2002; Ramsey 1996, 1999; Reynolds 1995; Tomlinson-

Clarke and Wang 1999). This literature generally describes a safe environment as one of respect and trust in which each person's voice is allowed to be heard and people are encouraged to speak honestly (Kiselica 1999a). Rarely happening by chance, this type of environment is generally created over time through deliberate, ongoing processes and interventions on the part of the teacher or facilitator.

In a classroom environment focused on training multicultural counselors, Ramsey (1999) described a highly structured process she engages in with students during the first four weeks of the semester. This process includes norming, mutual goal setting, personal and cultural awareness building, and experiential activities and discussions. Activities in week one are designed to "stimulate [students'] interest in their own cultural identity as well as the broader concept of cultural identity" (30).

During week two, Ramsey uses cultural assessments such as the Personal Cultural Perspective Profile (Ramsey 1994, 33) to engage students in a process of discovery in which they begin "to see cultural differences as a challenging puzzle to be solved." Weeks three and four are spent in "fictitious cultural experiences" and "power simulations" such as Outside Experts (Pedersen 1994) and Powerlab (DICEL 1980).

Through these fictional simulations, students are able to experience and internalize the concepts of culture, power, prejudice, oppression, and unearned privilege without the distraction of, and prior to, connecting these concepts back to specific cultures and oppressed groups. Ramsey's research and experiences in this area have convinced her that "entry into this constructed world [of multicultural learning and change] is through the affective arena, and the cognitive follows" (Ramsey 1999, 29).

But what about the average college course in which multicultural awareness is not the primary focus? Diversity of opinions, experiences, and perceptions exists in every classroom, regardless of discipline, perceived homogeneity, or whether or not those differences are acknowledged or ignored, solicited, or denied. Preparing ourselves and our students to handle differences effectively is essential to creating "safe enough" learning environments.

Some of the primary techniques I use to create a safe environment in the classes I teach are norming, self-disclosure, de-emphasizing evaluation during practice, seating arrangements, drawing students into discussions, and cutting off or redirecting students (see Jacobs, Harvill, and Masson 2002 for more information on some of these techniques). I spend part of the first class period talking with students about what norms, or guidelines, for interacting they need from me, themselves, and each other in order to feel safe enough to risk, learn, and be successful in the course. One of the norms we typically agree to is the use of "I statements" to express opinions and feelings (e.g., I believe..., I think..., from my viewpoint..., I'm feeling...). "I statements" help us disagree with what has been said rather than argue with the person who has made the statement. They also help us own and accept responsibility for our ideas and feelings as our own rather than stating them as universal truths. Other norms have included listening to each other, one person talking at a time, and bringing issues or questions that need to be resolved back to the group for discussion.

I use self-disclosure to normalize the learning process, by sharing my successes and failures as a counselor, group leader, and teacher. This decreases perceived differences among us, creates a more genuine and realistic relationship among us, and helps the students create more realistic expectations for themselves as learners and human beings. At the end of my in-class demonstrations, I share what I thought I did well and what I might have done differently, and I ask the students for their perceptions on this as well. In this way, I try to model an openness to learning.

I try to create feedback systems that allow students to practice and learn with a reduced emphasis on evaluation and increased opportunities for mastery. For example, when students make tapes of their counseling, I ask them to determine what they consider their best tapes, based on specific criteria and expectations, and turn those in with self-evaluations including what they did well and what they would like to have done differently. I rate the tapes "pass" or "redo" (rather than fail), with specific feedback on what they will need to demonstrate on the make-up tapes. A certain number of points are lost for each redo, but if they succeed on the second attempt, they regain half of those points. Students have responded favorably to this method, although I did have one anxious student who believed the designations "pass" and "not pass" would have created less anxiety for her.

If at all possible, I arrange the seating in the classroom in a circle or u-shape to facilitate student-to-student interaction and eye contact. At the beginning of the course, I tell students that I won't always be looking at them when they speak so that I can observe other students' reactions to what they are saying, draw other students into the conversation through eye contact, and encourage them to speak to each other rather than just to, or through, me as the instructor. If students continue to respond only to me, I will redirect them to the rest of the group through hand gestures and verbal cues. When facilitating discussions in larger classrooms with fixed seats, I will move about the room as much as possible to help the students direct their communications to others. I also have them discuss in smaller groups and dyads.

I rarely single students out by calling on them individually, because I have found this can make some students feel "spotlighted" and decrease their sense of safety in the classroom. I will normally offer prompts to the entire group and use eye contact to draw students into discussions. If the same students tend to respond more often, I generally will ask for more responses from those we haven't heard from. As students gain comfort and experience with this method, they respond more often and student-to-student interactions increase.

When necessary, I use cutting-off skills to intervene and redirect statements that violate the norms we have established. For example, if a student begins to argue an opinion as a statement of fact or universal truth, I will stop the person and ask that person to rephrase what he or she is saying as an "I statement." This is difficult for many students and may require more than one intervention. My consistency in honoring this norm is essential, however, to maintaining trust and safety within the group.

A safe environment allows for diversity of opinion and confrontation of beliefs and behaviors. However, the timing and wording of these confrontations are crucial (Kiselica 1999b). During discussions, I often have observed a reaction in students (and colleagues) to move quickly into the role of "devil's advocate." This is often an indirect and cognitive response to an affective or controversial topic and usually begins with the words, "but don't you think..." In this way, the person doing the confronting is able to hide his or her opinion within a thinly veiled question. I will intervene in this situation and say to the person, "It sounds as though there may be a statement behind your question. Would you be willing to make the statement instead?" This intervention allows for more genuine and authentic communication between those in conversation and helps the "devil's advocate" identify and accept ownership of his or her opinion.

How Can Safe Environments Be Destroyed?

My experiences in the classroom have led to several answers to this question. For example, safety can be lost quickly, instantaneously, irreparably or reparably, through neglect and avoidance, through habit and assumptions, and through ignorance and fear. Palmer (1998) believes that what separates teachers from themselves, their students, their colleagues, and even their disciplines are not the institutional barriers of grading, evaluation, competition, over-specialization, or bureaucracy, but fear. He describes fear as the underlying destroyer of safety in learning environments:

> From where I stood, exposed and vulnerable at the front of the room, my students seemed enviously safe, hidden behind their notebooks, anonymous in the midst of the crowd. I should have remembered from my own experience that students, too, are afraid: afraid of failing, of not understanding, of being drawn into issues they would rather avoid, of having their ignorance exposed or their prejudices challenged, of looking foolish in front of their peers. When my students' fears mix with mine, fear multiplies geometrically—and education is paralyzed. (37)

Palmer recommends that educators explore their own "inner landscapes" in order to understand the nature of their fears. These fears may cause them to rely on power and intimidation to create environments where the teacher is the speaker and the dispenser of knowledge and students are the listeners and recipients. Palmer believes that students' fears of accepting ownership of and responsibility for their learning also can create pressure on the instructor to succumb to becoming the dispenser of knowledge. Creating awareness around these fears and establishing educational practices that contradict them can instill new life into the classroom, the content, the students, and the instructor (Palmer 1998).

A Personal Example

I wish I could say I do all of this perfectly every time I enter a classroom. A recent experience put me in awe once again of how quickly safety in the learning environment can be disrupted, if not destroyed, and how inept and humbled I can feel during and after the experience.

I made an assumption recently that all students in an advanced counseling course would be coming in with similar levels of awareness about diversity issues. I showed a film on diversity, hoping to focus primarily on the group dynamics and leadership skills demonstrated in the film and secondarily on the diversity issues. Toward the end of the period, a student who had been fairly silent during the processing of the film began to speak with obvious emotion, using the words "politically correct" to describe the film and the comments regarding it that I and other students had made.

I wish I could say I handled the situation well, that I used all of the techniques described and we were able to reach a place of resolution that evening. Palmer (1998, 5) refers to a familiar saying in the counseling field: "Technique is what you use until the therapist [or teacher] arrives." I wish I had been able to ask the student to say more, to express some of the experiences and beliefs behind the emotions that were obviously there. But in truth I was surprised and affected personally by the term "politically correct." I wanted to use self-disclosure to describe my feelings about that term and how I have experienced it as a way to shut down conversations and dialogue around diversity. I wanted to use self-disclosure, but I didn't trust myself to stay in the role of leader of the group and not slip into a member role. I knew I couldn't trust myself to keep the student's best interest first and foremost in my intervention. I was, as Palmer describes, paralyzed by my fears, which seemed to be meeting up with the fears of the student. The best I could do was continue facilitating the discussion among the students, which ended with a painfully clear lack of resolution.

We had spring break, guest speakers, and absences after that night and I chose not to revisit the discussion until we could all meet face-to-face and have the time needed to explore all aspects of the interaction more fully. There was some level of discomfort our first night back, but it dissipated. I knew we would return to the discussion in the future and I would be able to share my own reactions and even use this as an example of how I could have been a better facilitator. We would address what happened from multiple levels of learning about diversity, group leadership, group dynamics, ourselves, and our individual stories and perspectives. The resiliency of the group and its members, and our shared connections as human beings, would carry us through until we could re-enter, each from a slightly different place because of the time we would have had to think, reflect, and explore our "inner landscapes." I believe in the group process and I trusted our shared human connections.

Postscript

When we finally were able to return to this topic, I began by apologizing for how I had handled the situation and describing how I personally had been affected by the term "politically correct." I described what I wished I had been able to do that evening and asked for students' input into the discussion, reminding them to use "I statements." The discussion began awkwardly and was difficult for the group. I remember thinking that we might not get any further in our processing than we did the previous time. And then the discussion shifted to personal experiences. Students began sharing stories of their own experiences of prejudice and feelings of hurt related to being different. We found the common ground of how difficult it is to remain open to those who are different from us when we have experienced hurts and mistreatment ourselves, sometimes at the hands of those we are trying to "help." We experienced the sad reality that no one is exempted, or safe, from the effects of bigotry and prejudice, and that on an individual level we all are capable of hurting each other. A new level of understanding was achieved. We had taken the time necessary to understand a bit more completely each others' viewpoints. This did not necessarily lead to agreement on the issue, but it did lead to greater understanding. When creating safe learning environments, this understanding is the more vital element and requires that time be given to it.

References

Developing Interpersonal Competencies in Educational Leadership (DICEL). 1980, May. *Powerlab simulation: Women in leadership training program.* Boston, MA: DICEL.

Jacobs, Ed, Riley Harvill, and Robert Masson. 2002. *Group counseling: Strategies and skills.* 4th ed. Monterey, CA: Brooks/Cole.

Kiselica, Mark S. 1999a. Reducing prejudice: The role of the empathic-confrontive instructor. In *Confronting prejudice and racism during multicultural training*, edited by Mark S. Kiselica. Alexandria, VA: American Counseling Association.

Kiselica, Mark S. 1999b. Confronting prejudice: Converging themes and future directions. In *Confronting prejudice and racism during multicultural training*, edited by Mark S. Kiselica. Alexandria, VA: American Counseling Association.

Maslow, Abraham H. 1962. *Toward a psychology of being.* Princeton, NJ: D. Van Nostrand.

McAuliffe, Garnett. 2002. The heart and craft of teaching: What we know. In *Teaching strategies for constructivist and developmental counselor education*, edited by Garnett McAuliffe and Karen Eriksen. Westport, CT: Bergin and Garvey.

Palmer, Parker J. (1998). *The courage to teach: Exploring the inner landscape of a teacher's life.* San Francisco: Jossey-Bass, Publishers.

Pedersen, Paul. 1994. *A handbook for developing multicultural awareness.* 2nd ed. Alexandria, VA: American Counseling Association.

Ramsey, Mary Lou. 1994. Use of a personal cultural perspective profile (PCPP) in developing counselor multicultural competence. *International Journal for the Advancement of Counseling* 17:283-290.

Ramsey, Mary Lou. 1996. Diversity identity development training: Theory informs practice. *Journal of Multicultural Counseling and Development* 24:229-240.

Ramsey, Mary Lou. 1999. How to create a climate for cultural diversity appreciation within the classroom. In *Confronting prejudice and racism during multicultural training,* edited by Mark S. Kiselica. Alexandria, VA: American Counseling Association.

Reynolds, Amy L. 1995. Challenges and strategies for teaching multicultural counseling courses. In *Handbook of multicultural counseling,* edited by Joseph G. Ponterotto, J. Manuel Casas, Lisa A. Suzuki, and Charlene M. Alexander. Thousand Oaks, CA: Sage Publications.

Tomlinson-Clarke, Sandra, and Vivian O. Wang. 1999. A paradigm for racial-cultural training in the development of counselor cultural competencies. In *Confronting prejudice and racism during multicultural training,* edited by Mark S. Kiselica. Alexandria, VA: American Counseling Association.

Teaching the Diversity of World Religions

James W. Boyd

Introduction

How does one navigate through the diversity of "world religions" when students come to the classroom with a variety of attitudes, ranging from curiosity and existential thirst to suspicion and even hostility toward anything other than what they have been brought up to believe? My experience has been that if I can harness the emotional and intellectual energy they bring to this subject, positive or negative, I may have a chance to teach them something significant enough to touch their lives in an enriching way.

The most negative and dramatic response to my teaching occurred during a discussion of creationism vs. evolution. The Kansas State Board of Education recently had de-emphasized the teaching of evolution in its science curriculum, and I was analyzing the differences between scientific language and religious language, arguing that "Creation Science" issued from a genuine religious concern but betrayed a deep confusion about the nature of religious truth. Suddenly a student stood up and shouted "Mr. Boyd, you are Satan incarnate!" Everyone, including myself, was so surprised by this outburst that there was little time to think. My immediate response, fortunately, was one of curiosity I asked the student to explain why he had said that. Without answering he left the classroom and, to my disappointment, never returned.

The class, however, had become so energized by this interchange that they immediately plunged into an intense discussion about the nature of the *study* of religion in the university context. Were religious convictions immune from analysis because they were too personal and "no one had the right to criticize anyone's religious beliefs?" Could the study of religion be fair to religious people or would it just be a rationalistic, objective critique of all religion? This automatically led to the question: How should we define "religion?" What is it we are talking about?

The discussion brought up questions central to the course. It was a wonderful discussion, but the student who most needed to be part of it had left. I have since discovered—to my dismay—that I struggle to communicate with such students. But, more of that later. On the positive side, I have been able to engage many students in serious study of the diversity of the world's religious traditions, both Eastern and Western. To achieve this, experience has taught me that it is essential to set the tone and approach to the subject during the first week of class. For example, in my Eastern Religions class, I usually start with a personal story:

> It is my first trip to India. I have been studying the Hindi language for only eighteen days while sailing from Marseilles to Bombay, via the Suez Canal. Within a week after my arrival, I am enrolled as a foreign student at Banaras Hindu University. It was then that I decided it was high time I try to say something in Hindi to a native speaker. Seeing an empty rickshaw pass by, I called out to the driver the formal greeting I had learned: "Eh bhay, aiyee!" This was supposed to mean something like, "Hey brother, please come here." The rickshaw driver looked startled and ran off the road into a ditch. A strange response—but then I was a foreigner and probably surprised him by speaking Hindi. However, in the course of that week I also alarmed several other rickshaw-wallas. Finally, after making friends with some Indian students, I asked them to help me with my Hindi and learned I was saying "Eh bhay" when I should have been saying "Eh bhaay." I couldn't hear the difference, but instead of saying "Hey brother, please come here" I was saying, in effect, "Hey, danger (look out)!"

This is the first of many personal stories I tell as I try to guide my students through the value/thought worlds of the great intellectual traditions of the East as experienced by Hindus, Buddhists, Taoists, and Confucians of south and east Asia. Besides the sheer fun of narrating this particular story in such a way that the students get caught up in the experience of it, the reasons I tell it so early in the course are numerous.

Although it conveys an experience that happened to me over thirty years ago, this story relates to their situation as student novices about to enter another cultural world of meaning via this course. It conveys the fact that I too was once a beginner, and that I made mistakes. It lets them know from the start that this course is part of my personal journey, and that I enjoy telling the students about the rickshaw incident and, in this case, I find it humorous.

These lessons remain tacit ones, but are reinforced throughout the course as I continually tell stories to help make some point or other.

But there also are explicit lessons to be learned from my unsuccessful attempt to speak Hindi. Most of them are methodological ones. When, as students, they encounter ideas and values that are foreign or even contrary to their own, I am asking them to say to themselves, "Eh bhaay, brother come here, let me take a close look at what you are saying." I caution them not to say silently to themselves, "Eh bhay, danger, look out, this is threatening."

Mention of times when I have felt threatened by what I was learning (the Buddhists' powerful argument that there is no such thing as an individual "self") is listened to with considerable seriousness on the part of my students. I then suggest that we enter a mutual contract in which I will accept them as students and they will accept me as a teacher on the following condition: that we approach the study of each of these living traditions with *empathy*. I present them with the following quote from Carl Rogers (1985) that states clearly both my methodology and the one I am asking them to adopt in this course:

> The way of being with another person which is termed empathetic means temporarily living in their life, moving about in it delicately, without making judgments...To be with another in this way means that for the time being you lay aside the views and values you hold for yourself in order to enter another's world without prejudice...a complex, demanding, strong yet subtle and gentle way of being.

Clearly the student who called me "Satan incarnate" seemed incapable of the intellectual and emotional demands of this kind of empathy. Nor is it the case that all students are at this level of openness when they begin their studies of world religions. The encouraging fact is that I have witnessed students grow into this level of sophistication because something about this approach resonates with them. They often call it "being fair" or "being respectful."

It also helps when I state clearly and openly that I am ethically committed to this kind of approach, because the study of world "religions" is not the study of abstract systems of thought, but the study of the life commitments of people I deeply respect and to whom I remain indebted—my own teachers: T.R.V. Murti and K.N. Tiwari from Banaras Hindu University, Bhikkhu Walpola Rahula and Shanta Ratnayaka from Buddhist Sri Lanka, and Koretsune-sensei and Yamamoto-sensei from Japan. In due course, I also give the students the names of my American, Chinese, and Iranian teachers.

I name my teachers for another reason: to underscore the fact that I stand within a specific intellectual lineage in regard to each of these traditions. I want to emphasize again and again the particularity of our study, that these are real persons, committed to a specific way of constructing meaning in their lives. If anyone in the class cannot approach what my teachers have to say with the kind of empathetic openness Carl Rogers defines, then I ask that the person talk to me privately in order to decide whether he or she should continue to stay enrolled.

I also state legitimate reasons why some should drop this course: (1) It is a complex and demanding study, parallel to my attempts to understand Hindi; and (2) It may be that they are emotionally and intellectually not ready to engage in such a personal reflective journey—danger signals are too prevalent. I tell the students about one of my most capable students who, when he first met me, said he had decided not to study this subject because "it might change me." At that time in his life, he was not ready to enter what I call the "temples of meaning" constructed by the lives of my teachers. That is an acceptable and honest stance. That student later enrolled in the class his senior year. He went on to do graduate work in a Christian seminary and now unequivocally states that it was his undergraduate studies in comparative religions that deepened his insights into his own tradition.

By asking them to approach my teachers' lives with that subtle and gentle quality of empathy, I have placed myself in an interesting position in relation to my students. Because I will be teaching them what my teachers taught me in India, Sri Lanka, China, and Japan, in effect I can speak with two voices: both in first and third person.

My first-person voice is direct. I am conveying to them my own experiential knowledge—what *I* learned from my teachers. There is an immediacy, not to mention credibility, to what I am saying. On the other hand, there is the third-person voice of each of my teachers. It is their lives and thoughts I am teaching; the students realize that I am not proselytizing my own beliefs. This allows them to ask honest questions, to challenge what seem to be misconceived views or conclusions in their efforts to understand, for example, what my Buddhist teachers are saying.

I encourage questions from them that seek to understand these other worldviews. It quickly becomes apparent to everyone in the class whether a student is raising a question that is a disguised attempt to refute a new idea or that is in truth a question that seeks to understand the worldview being studied. When the former occurs, I take the opportunity to further clarify the implications of the whole methodological approach of the course. I ask pointedly, "Is there any room for critical thinking in this course, or do we have to accept as valid everything that is said?"

I open the discussion by relating one of my most important discoveries during my field work in Bombay, when I was studying with a high priest of the Zoroastrian tradition, Dastur Firoze Kotwal. Having studied the scriptural languages and sacred texts of the Zoroastrians, I came to my "informant" with a long list of questions. Over the course of six months of unforgettable conversations, I realized that I had to let go of my preconceived list of questions, and listen intently to him to learn what *his* questions were: "What s it that he wants me to know about his tradition?"

What was demanded of me, in terms of critical thinking, was to comprehend his thoughts, synthesize them in ways both he and I could understand, and then articulate them in ways that bridged the gaps between persons of different cultures. When, after six months, Dastur Kotwal said to me regarding a specific thought, "You know my heart," I knew I was beginning to understand the deepest values in his life. Only then did I feel I was in a position to evaluate, in terms of my own value commitments, whether or not he and I were in accord with each other in terms of my own personal philosophy of life. We had frank and open discussions that helped me clarify my own thoughts. Now that I look back, it is obvious that my studies with Dastur Kotwal were a turning point in my own efforts to approach persons from diverse traditions with genuine empathy.

In the context of the study of world religions, this means that initially we must approach the value/thought tradition of a person from another cultural world with the presumption that the person's perspective is of equal validity to our own. Any tradition that has sustained the lives of countless persons over the centuries is worthy of this initial respect.

However, because our studies are comparative in nature, the diversity of views among the various Asian traditions themselves offers deeply thought-out critiques of each of the other positions. Our goal is first to catch a glimpse of the existential and conceptual coherence of each tradition in its own terms, and then examine how the traditions critically relate to each other. Only after we have pursued the first two steps can we begin to formulate legitimately our own carefully thought out position, which always remains subject to change. So, although our initial approach seems to suggest a kind of cultural relativism (every tradition has equal worth), in the course of our comparative studies it becomes evident that in fact diversity means genuine, often profound differences of value perspectives.

The necessary consequence is to become responsible for one's own informed, thoughtful commitments. This is the orientation to religious diversity that I openly "profess" to my students.

What, then, of academic "objectivity?" How can I be objective if I am calling for empathy—temporarily living in the value-worlds of my teachers? I raise this question rhetorically and offer my view. If objectivity means keeping a "safe" emotional and cognitive distance from the subject matter (the personal values and thoughts of my teachers), then it is not an empathetic approach and is unsuitable for this course.

Students at this point often suggest that "objectivity" means a neutral stance, a middle ground between "empathy" and "danger, look out!" I ask them to think about that. "Neutrality" is itself a value stance characteristic of Western science and the academic establishment, but it is not a suitable stance for this subject. Why? Because we are studying the diversity of radically different *value* orientations, and few if any religious traditions privilege neutrality. If anything, they ask us not to be neutral toward life's meanings. So we need to begin to surface our own academic value commitments about what constitutes a suitable approach to the subject matter. I am committed to empathy rather than neutrality in my efforts to understand the existential realities of my teachers because this is how I successfully engaged in learning from them, and this is how I think my students too can best learn.

Although I emphasize the need for empathy, I acknowledge that "objectivity" also connotes trying to be even-handed—approaching each tradition with an equally open and balanced attitude toward the subject matter. If this is what one has in mind when speaking of an objective approach to the subject, then I heartily agree. In comparative work one must always make sure there is a level playing field. You cannot compare the philosophical thought of one tradition with the popular institutional ideas of another and consider it valid. That is why I teach the views of learned teachers of each tradition, and make clear that if students are to compare these Asian traditions with Western religions, for example, they must make sure the comparison is with the intellectual, not popular, dimension of each of the religions.

At the same time I recognize that in emphasizing the intellectual over the popular I am privileging a particular dimension of any given religious tradition that itself is pluralistic. The dominant religious institutions have been defined by men, and, indeed, I have had only male teachers. In order to better reflect the pluralism within each tradition, I have found myself over the years balancing the formal intellectual strains with, for example, the study of *bhakti* in Hinduism. Bhakti — the popular, devotional daily practices of Hindusi—s not antithetical to the philosophical tradition, but it is more infused with poetry, female images, and diverse linguistic and cultural elements.

To return to my story about learning Hindi: The truth of the matter is that this opening story is often generative of the whole preceding discussion. There are many other points that can be made as the course proceeds, often recalling the incident of my mispronunciation of Hindi terms. For example, the story indicates that we are going to enter different linguistic cultures, and that to understand another tradition means that they will be learning key terms from a number of Asian languages: Sanskrit, Pali, Chinese, and Japanese.

Likewise, the fact that I could not hear the differences between a short and long "a" in "bhay/bhaay" helps me introduce a much subtler issue—one I have not been very successful in teaching, but I keep trying It has to do with the difficulty of coming to grips with the issue of diversity itself. I have found that it is almost automatic for students to think of the diversity or plurality of religious traditions as merely different approaches to the same truth. I am speaking of the notion that there is a diversity of paths, but there is not a diversity of truths. This deeply embedded cultural view is what Diana Eck (1985, 22) calls the Western "monotheism of consciousness"; in the end it all comes down to the same thing.

If one assumes this to be the case, it is all too easy to dismiss real differences as merely incidental. One does not really hear what someone else is saying by presuming from the outset that in the end there are no real differences. In my view it is a way of not taking another person seriously. It is a failure of genuine empathy. But the ability to entertain the possibility of a *real* plurality and diversity of worldviews seems to be beyond the grasp of most of my students.

The view that differences are only superficial seems to me to be a pre-cognitive stance that is immune from reflective analysis on the part of many of my students. Perhaps it is because they have not experienced radical plurality; most have lived their whole lives seeing the world through one set of cultural lenses. For most students, at least at my university, this is a white male lens that reflects the dominant cultural paradigm of the United States. Certainly this is an argument not only for study abroad programs but for infusing the undergraduate curriculum with diverse American cultural perspectives! In my experience, it was the shock of living in a radically different culture (India) that helped me see that my own mono-vision was in need of some corrective lenses.

I try to create what is admittedly a poor imitation of being immersed in another culture by starting (and ending) each class period with the musical sounds of a particular culture. This not only reminds the students of the different language sounds of Asian cultures, but also makes them aware of the fact that these are also different sound cultures. Occasionally, I discuss the musical note "values" in South and East Asian music as compared to the taken-for-granted harmonic structures of Western music, and I give them translations of the lyrics. But more often than not, I just let the music speak for itself, a subtle reminder of the very nature of the course: a study of the diversity of a variety of value-worlds as exemplified in the life and thought of my teachers—to whom we need to listen with empathy and respect.

Despite the length of this discourse, there are two additional ideas central to my approach that I would like to mention. First, let me return to the incident when the student called me Satan incarnate. Besides the pertinent discussion it generated, there is another lesson I learned from it. My immediate reaction to his outburst was one of curiosity; I was not defensive. I have found over the years that the less ego I bring into the classroom, the more my students and I connect with the ideas being discussed. In those successful moments when I manage to weave the conceptual and emotional fabric of another worldview, there is an interesting sense in which "I" am not present. Rather, the thoughts and feelings of my teachers sustain the moment. And when this happens, each one of us in the class understands, in terms of his or her own experience of the moment, the ancient Taoist saying:

> When you're betting for tiles in an archery contest, you shoot with skill. When you're betting for fancy belt buckles, you worry about your aim. And when you're betting for real gold, you're a nervous wreck. Your skill is the same in all three cases—but because one prize means more to you than another, you let outside considerations weigh on your mind. He who looks too hard at the outside gets clumsy on the inside. (Tzu 1964, 122)

If there is any philosophical principle that guides my approach to teaching the diversity of world religions, it is this Taoist saying. In those moments when I am not invested in my own success as a teacher, when I gamble and let the subject matter speak for itself, significant learning seems to occur. In those freshly minted moments there is no self-conscious "I" who is inwardly clumsy. As I look back over the past several years, it is those moments of deep empathy with a radically different point of view that are most memorable—and that is also what my students say.

This brings me to the second idea; it is a topic that has caused me to reflect on the nature of learning for some time. Over the past few years I have been asked to videotape my courses for general distribution in order to reach a larger audience. Can the kind of teaching and learning I am talking about be accomplished through "distance education?" My thoughts on this at this point in time: I think not. At present, I am experimenting with a web-based discussion forum for each of my courses. The latter is an extension of (not a substitution for) discussions generated in class or in office hours, and it gives students a chance to *write* down what they are thinking as well as receive written responses from fellow classmates. That is all well and good.

But the weakness of classroom sessions conveyed through live TV, even if they have interactive formats, lies in the very fact that they allow for "distance" education. It is argued that distance education brings educational opportunities to those who cannot be in the classroom. That is certainly a good argument for those subject areas that largely seek to convey information—where "distance" is not a problem. However, the *distance* between me and my students, between the students and the worldviews of my teachers, and between each other in the classroom is precisely what needs to be overcome if significant learning is to occur in my field of teaching. To empathetically encounter that which is truly different requires that cognitive and emotional, and ultimately physical, distances be erased. The actual *presence* of face-to-face encounter between students and teacher allows levels of communication that are subtle and energizing, and essential for any educational endeavor that seeks to achieve that strong yet gentle empathy with each of the diverse worlds of meanings embodied in the lives of others. Consequently, I have concluded not to open my classroom to a medium that is based on distance education.

Most of my examples thus far have dealt with my Asian religions course. To prepare my students for a follow-up course that is a study of the Western religions, I usually conclude the semester with another story, which I learned from one of my Jewish teachers, Rabbi Schaalman. It is a version of a Talmudic story that, I find, resonates with my own experience:

> Rabbi Isaac lived in a desolate, cold synagogue in Krakow, Poland. His room was scarcely heated by a small fire in an old iron stove. He did not know how he, or the congregation, could survive. One night he had a dream. A voice said

to him, "Go to Prague. Go to Prague, and there you will find a treasure." Being a man of learning, he dismissed the dream time and again, until one night the voice seemed to almost smother him with its command. So not knowing what would happen, he walked to Prague, Czechoslovakia, and because the voice had said to wait by the St. Charles Bridge, he stood there silently. The captain of the guards noticed him loitering near the bridge. He went up to him and said: "Little man, what are you doing here?" The rabbi, too embarrassed to say why, excused himself and quickly walked away.

Later, seeing that the guard had gone, he returned to the bridge to wait—for what he didn't know. The guard had anticipated his move, came up from behind him, and commanded that he either explain why he was there or be arrested. Rabbi Isaac meekly confessed that he had had a dream, and that he was to come here to find a treasure. The captain of the guards guffawed and mockingly said: "Oh little man, if I believed in dreams I would be looking right now for something hidden behind an old iron stove in a dark, dank room, for that is what I dreamt last night." The rabbi said nothing, asked if he could leave, and journeyed home as fast as he could to look behind his old stove, where indeed he found a treasure of gold.[1]

I ask my students, now well-acquainted with my storytelling, what is the point? Many, upon reflection, understand the story's relevance to the study of Western religions. It took a conversation with a person from another country—a Roman Catholic culture—for the rabbi to discover the treasure to be found in his own Jewish tradition. I suggest that this also has been my experience. I first had to travel to Asia and learn from some very great teachers before I was able to return home, with fresh perspectives, to discover the richness and diversity of the religious/intellectual traditions of my own Western religious culture.

Notes

1. Many of us who have been involved in the comparative study of world religions, it turns out, know this story. Kripal (2000/2001) notes that he heard this story from Wendy Doniger while studying in Chicago, and that she borrowed it from Heinrich Zimmer, the great German Indologist, who no doubt borrowed it from someone else. I am still looking for the Talmudic source.

References

Eck, Diana L. 1985. *Darson: Seeing the divine image in India*. Chambersburg, PA: Anima Press.

Kripal, Jeffrey J. 2000/2001, Winter. Secret talk. *Harvard Divinity Bulletin* 29(4):17.

Rogers, Carl. 1985. Carl Rogers program announcement. LaJolla, CA: Center for Studies of the Person.

Tzu, Chuang. 1964. *Chuang Tzu: Basic writings*. Translated by Burton Watson. New York: Columbia University Press.

Socratic and Therapeutic Underpinnings of Self-Disclosure in the Classroom

Raymond K. Yang

Self-disclosure occurs when a person voluntarily reveals important personal information to others. As an act of moral courage or of literary significance, self-disclosure has a long history; as a psychological phenomenon worthy of study, Sydney Jourard is generally credited as having articulated its definition and characteristics, and having shown how it is encouraged or suppressed by situational elements (e.g., Jourard and Lasakow 1958; Jourard 1971a; Jourard 1971b).

Therapeutic theories have long maintained that self-disclosure is important to healthy emotional development. Harry Stack Sullivan (1953) described "chumships" as essential opportunities for adolescents to discover their similarities to their peers. From an Eriksonian (1963) perspective, the adolescent's and young adult's achievement of fidelity and affiliation arises from a growing capacity to build social relationships that are stable, mutually trustful, and intimate. Rogerian (1961) "unconditional positive regard" encourages and validates a client's self-disclosures. Maslow (1968) similarly saw the self-actualization process arising, in part, from a person's ability to be open to experience; this openness is itself closely related to the capacity to self-disclose. Through intimate and mutual self-disclosures with close friends, young people may come to realize that their feelings of isolation are common and generally surmountable.

To help achieve such ends, self-disclosure has become an aspect of pedagogy in some instructional settings and classrooms, especially in academic fields related to mental health and development. During class discussions, the sharing of personal experiences is often viewed as an important way to establish and confirm a safe, comfortable ambiance among class participants; this sharing may be used to provide concrete examples of concepts previously described on a theoretical level. Personal growth is therefore an important, if informal, aspect of the curriculum. Students must have (or achieve) some level of personal maturity. Without it, it is presumed that they cannot be effective in their professional practice. The training of therapists, for example, is infused with opportunities for the students to address personal aspects of their own development. Thus, self-disclosure can serve didactic ends while simultaneously enriching the learning environment.

Instructor Self-Disclosure

Instructors are the authoritative controllers of their classes; whatever they say is, virtually by definition, relevant. In this light, they can set an example for self-disclosure and convey a sense of openness by sharing personal information with their classes. This may be particularly beneficial when the information shared is obviously relevant to the material under study or leads students to link the material's meaning to their own experiences. But what if the students feel that an instructor's disclosures are irrelevant, or worse? Should any correction or clarification occur in the classroom, or should it occur elsewhere (as in a private discussion between the instructor and the department head)?

Student Self-Disclosure

Relevance

Self-disclosures by students can be ingenuous and cathartic. They may contribute in varying degrees to the instructor's didactic objectives, and their ultimate value may depend upon the instructor's skill in weaving the disclosure into the topic. For the student, self-disclosing can serve another important function: It may afford a sense that they have contributed meaningfully to the class. Thus, student disclosures can contribute to the education of the class as a whole as well as to the self-actualization of the disclosing student. The instructor is sometimes challenged to balance these virtues because some disclosures, while heartfelt, are not altogether relevant.

Follow-Up

Student disclosures deserve follow-up from the instructor, or, minimally, acknowledgement. Students may appreciate or desire a prompt response, which also may serve to reinforce the behavior and convey credibility to the disclosure. Without any follow-up, a disclosure may have little or no impact and may cause the discloser to feel awkward or to interpret the response as dismissive.

Another consideration is the reality that one student's disclosure may instigate another's, or that it may prompt a class discussion. This can quickly become problematic, as such discussions inevitably interfere with the instructor's prearranged class schedule. Ironically, for this reason, instructors may actively suppress disclosure or discussion if they determine that it undermines the need to address the syllabus.

Privacy

Notwithstanding their voluntary nature, there is an aspect of vulnerability and risk associated with self-disclosures. The instructor cannot presume that a student, by self-disclosing, is willing to disclose more. (Sometimes a student may even be uncertain as to why he or she made a comment, and may wish he or she had not.) Although it is reasonable to assume that some access is being granted through disclosure, a boundary for that access also presumably exists. All parties must determine where that boundary lies, and must discern the appropriateness of pursuing a topic as it unfolds.

Ultimately, the need for self-disclosure may not find a compatible outlet in the classroom; the issue of finding time outside of class for student-instructor talks is dealt with below.

Feasibility

The likelihood of quality engagements outside class time—even immediately after a class—is often quite low, due in part to the brute demands upon instructors' schedules. Students often are unaware that faculty are responsible for scholarship and research, and that their attention to a particular course may comprise only a small percentage of their total workload. To the extent that encouraging self-disclosure leads to more time and energy being spent in teaching activities, some faculty may feel that it detracts from their other duties. Indeed, if there is not a clear pedagogical basis for responding to self-disclosures, the instructor could consider it inexpedient to focus on these behaviors, even in the service of teaching.

Anxiety and Stress

Whether inside or out of class, one aim of self-disclosing is the reduction of anxiety and the creation of a socially supportive context. A desirable side effect of this transformation is the establishment of a classroom in which pedagogical goals can be more effectively met. Nonetheless, some anxiety and tension may actually be beneficial in meeting didactic objectives, and a considerable amount of attention will be paid to this phenomenon later in the essay.

Characteristics of the Discloser

Status may be assigned or acquired. Although the instructor is the most obvious example of the former, an assigned status can be applied to any group or individual. Perceived differences that contribute to the establishment of "minority" and "majority" statuses among students may cause prejudicial postures to emerge; the voices of individuals in the minority may be lost without the reciprocation of those in the majority, and these latter students may be obliged to confess, deny, or explain such postures. The fulfillment of this obligation may contribute greatly to the openness of the class environment.

Conversely, a student may acquire a status over time—one that is independent of minority/majority considerations. The basis for such a status is generally determined by the quantity and/or quality of the person's contributions to the class. This subjective assessment is constantly evaluated and re-evaluated by all the members of the class.

In both of these cases, it is imperative to keep in mind the pivotal role of the instructor in shaping class response and directing class development.

Group Development

Developmental process characterizes every group. Throughout a course, students and instructor become acquainted and get to know each other. Self-disclosing behaviors need to be placed in this time-sensitive context. For example, disclosures made early in a course may give shape to a lasting ambiance; the same disclosure made late in the term may have little or no impact whatever on the rest of the class. In addition, disclosures also may distinguish certain students from the majority and identify them as probable participants in future discussions.

The seven themes listed above—relevance, follow-up, privacy, feasibility, anxiety and stress, characteristics of the discloser, and group development— derive from our experience as instructors and are consistent with a meta-theoretical framework formulated by

Bronfenbrenner (1979) to integrate the broad and interconnected contextual influences on social development. The framework is useful here because one purpose of education is to induce socially valuable and enduring changes in individuals. Bronfenbrenner argues that socialization, in order to be truly effective, must sustain the same values among and across settings, including those that do not directly involve an individual. In the context of higher education, this would mean that among community members and representatives, faculty and students, there should be general agreement regarding the purposes of the institution and the education it provides. When such consistency exists, socialization is efficient and effective. The less the consistency, the more fractured the socialization and the more inconsistent and contradictory the values engendered.

Bronfenbrenner's colligation of socialization processes also indicates that events inside the classroom are substantially influenced by the cultural backgrounds of participants. If this is the case, then improvements in the educational process must be based in part on improvements in the interface between the institutional culture of higher education and the increasingly diverse cultural heritages of its constituents. These efforts can substantially improve the university experience for diverse student populations (e.g., Gay 2000; Ladson-Billings 1995, Marin 2000).

A Socratic and Humanistic Framework for Self-Disclosure

Whether by conscious choice or not, many teachers in the United States frequently use Socratic methods when facing their students. These methods involve an emphasis on definitions, concepts, and principles; the application of inductive and deductive modes of thought; the use of dialogue to array and evaluate various opinions; and the use of critical scrutiny as the means by which these opinions are examined. Ultimately, knowledge of the truth—not simply the accumulation of information—is the goal of the Socratic process.

From a Socratic perspective, self-disclosure can only be the start of the journey toward truth. For knowledge, including self-knowledge, to be acquired, rigorous critical examination is necessary. This includes a form of Socratic questioning called *elenchus*. Elenchus occurs when the teacher, during conversation with the student, subtly and indirectly leads the student to question his or her initial assertion. The interaction is not necessarily querulous or pedantic, but can be interrogative. The essential element is that the student seems to be carrying responsibility for the conversation and determining its direction.

Interrogatory exchanges between a teacher and a student involve some amount of tension. The tension is not personalized but is focused on the opinion or idea expressed and on its rigorous examination. Nonetheless, anxiety on the part of the student should not preclude or hinder the examination.

This is where the pedagogical issue arises: Should an instructor pursue an issue for pedagogical reasons even if it makes the student who broached it uncomfortable? Socratic pedagogy answers *yes*; a humanistic pedagogy that values self-disclosure replies *no*. Answering this question requires, we think, viewing both Socratic and humanistic objectives of classroom interaction from a psychological perspective. By using a single frame of reference that is compatible with both, comparisons can be fairly made between them and they may be integrated.

Emotional Balance in the Classroom— A Useful Conceptual Model

The pursuit of knowledge or skill has basic motivational aspects. Individuals, left to their own devices, engage in activities with no apparent reward other than to improve their skill or increase their knowledge (e.g., Bandura 1997; MacTurk and Morgan 1995; White 1959). Normatively, humans strive to learn; quiescence is a temporary and unsatisfying state. This motivational aspect of behavior is relevant to the classroom and to the ambiance in which self-disclosures can occur; an effective instructor will capitalize on students' motivation.

An effective teacher will also maintain a constructive level of tension in the room that is consistent with elenctic and interrogatory exchanges. This has implications for individual students who are considering participating in discussion or disclosing personal information. Their decisions to disclose will be based, at least in part, on the ambiance of safety in the room. So, the Socratic teacher needs to maintain a delicate balance between two elements—the constructive tension associated with critical evaluation and an ambiance of safety sufficient to permit disclosures by students.

A framework for comparison enabling the placement of tension levels and safety levels would allow the search for a context compatible to both. A model developed by Watson and Tellegen (1985) provides such a framework. With it, they summarized a substantial body of research on psychological moods and produced a model

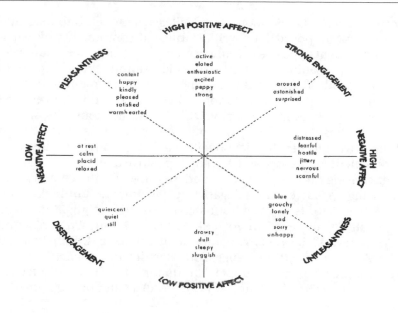

Figure 1. Model of balance between tension and safety in the classroom
(adapted from Watson and Tellegen 1985).

with two orthogonal dimensions   one representing positive affect (high to low), the other representing negative affect (high to low). Their model (see Figure 1) is useful in understanding the balance between tension and safety in the classroom.

What is notable about their model is the relationship of positive and negative affects; the emotional dimensions are not opposites but vary independently of each other. Emotional arousal is associated only with the high ends of each dimension. The low ends of each dimension represent the absence of emotional involvement. At the end of each axis is a cluster of various emotions that correlate to that particular affect. Clusters at right-angles to each other are uncorrelated, while clusters opposite each other are negatively correlated. By constructing a model that does not place positive and negative affect at the opposite ends of the same dimension, Watson and Tellegen effectively summarized a large number of otherwise seemingly contradictory studies. Their model shows how a mixture of positive and negative affects can produce a motivated engagement that would be valuable in educational contexts.

Lubinski and Benbow (2000) used Watson's and Tellegen's model to describe settings that help people develop extraordinary expertise or skill. On Watson's and Tellegen's model, Lubinski and Benbow superimposed four well-established components of learning environments: positive reinforcement and negative reinforcement (i.e., presentation of pleasurable stimuli and removal of aversive stimuli, respectively), and positive punishment and negative punishment (i.e., presentation of aversive stimuli and removal of pleasurable stimuli, respectively). The connections are simple and direct: Positive and negative punishments are associated with high negative affect and/or low positive affect; positive and negative reinforcement are associated with high positive affect and low negative affect. Maximizing positive and negative reinforcement and minimizing positive and negative punishment, Lubinski and Benbow contend, is the way to foster long-range acquisition of expertise and skill (e.g., in formal education).[1] In Watson's and Tellegen's terms, the affective components elicited in Lubinski's and Benbow's learning settings range from placidity to satisfaction to enthusiasm (See Figure 1, upper-left quadrant). That is, effective learning settings involve only low negative affect and/or high positive affect.

The Constructive Role of Tension in Pedagogy

We think Lubinski's and Benbow's (2000) emphasis on the beneficial effects of positive and negative reinforcement in learning contexts is correct but insufficient. Applied to effective learning environments, their model shows the importance of the humanistic aspects of self-actualization and maturation that were emphasized by Erikson, Maslow, Rogers, and Sullivan. But it misses the essential Socratic elements of the pedagogical process that we have argued should be embedded in classroom contexts. Self-disclosure may serve as the beginning of the educational process, but without Socratic exchange the educational process and the search for truth are cut short.

The vulnerability and risk associated with self-disclosure and the tension associated with elenctic questioning are essential aspects of classroom process. Furthermore, there are other tension- and anxiety-inducing events that are inevitable in classroom learning. For example, assessment of performance is an essential component of any course. Whether it is a self-assessment or a written examination, students need feedback regarding the extent to which they are achieving their educational objectives. These assessments are associated with some degree of anxiety for most students. The anticipation of these assessments can be anxiety inducing as well. Being called upon to answer or to make formal presentations to the class also can be tension-inducing. Indeed, the pause that some-times precedes a student's comment, question, or self-disclosure may reflect a momentary tension or anxiety. All of these aspects of classroom activity are appropriately and constructively infused, we think, with a degree of discomfort felt by the class and by individual students. Where do normal, anxiety-inducing aspects of pedagogy and classroom ambiance fall in Lubinski and Benbow's (2000) ma-trix of reinforcement and punishment and Watson's and Tellegen's model of mood? In Figure 1, the associated cluster of mood descriptors falls under "High Negative Affect"; for Lubinski's and Benbow, this is associated with positive punishment. But in the So-cratic concept of elenchus, the stress lies in the subtlety of the inter-rogator's approach. The instructor leads the student indirectly, perhaps even feigning ignorance, to a point at which the student's own logic has forced a clarification or refutation of his or her own initial premise. The instructor does not disparage or interrogate[2] (in the contemporary sense of the term), and so *positive punishment* is not an accurate description of the process. Furthermore, Watson's and Tellegen's descriptors "distressed," "nervous," and "jittery" should not be the emotions associated with elenctic exchanges.

Lubinski and Benbow (2000) associate positive reinforcement with such mood descriptors as Watson's and Tellegen's (1985) "ac-tive" and "enthusiastic." The combination of positive punishment and positive reinforcement in Watson's and Tellegen's model pro-duces "Strong Engagement" and the descriptors "aroused," "aston-ished," and "surprised."

A Possible Conflict

Because the process is one that keeps the student engaged, there must be aspects of positive reinforcement in the exchange. The problem with this ambiance is that it may not be sufficiently be-nign to encourage self-disclosures by students, who may hesitate to speak if they feel their disclosures will become a target of scrutiny. To the extent that students see assessments of their contributions and performance as potentially punishing, the anxiety associated with these aspects of classroom process must be temporarily sus-pended if self-disclosure is to be encouraged. The challenge is to do this without decreasing the affective engagement associated with positive reinforcement and positive punishment because removing high affect produces moods described as "placid," "still," and "drowsy" (Watson and Tellegen 1985). For instructors who use So-cratic techniques in their classrooms and who value self-disclosures by students, the larger challenge may be to develop a way to segue between the two or to embed opportunities for self-disclosure in the larger Socratic context. Following are two examples which help to illustrate how this may be done.

In an effort to encourage self-disclosure and engagement, I introduce new topics to my classes through case studies, which I present as narratives. I instruct my students not to take notes and reassures them that the material about to be covered will not show up on the next test. These steps establish an ambiance of safety in which students become more willing to express opinions and disclose similar experiences.

Another approach involves the discussion of stereotypes. Popular stereotypes associated with ethnicity and other physical attributes often can be used to elicit frank and open discussion. The instructor may ask students to share stereotypes with which they are familiar, while indicating that such sharing does not implicate a student's actual beliefs. However, to the extent that an ambiance of safety is established, students sometimes disclose stereotypes they actually *do* hold and self-disclosure begins.[3]

Why Combining Socratic Pedagogy and Therapeutic Self-Disclosure Is Important

Increasing Heterogeneity among Students

As students from increasingly diverse cultures and backgrounds join the higher education community, self-disclosure gains power as a tool for mutual sharing and enrichment. A common commitment to education bolsters the variety of perspectives from which that commitment arises.

Reducing Attrition

Tinto (1975, 1993) long has argued that student attrition is associated with a student's failure to become socially integrated within the college or university campus. He notes that academic integration is inescapable: Students are required to take specific courses in specific sequences, and many departments encourage students to meet with faculty advisors. But social integration, which is at least equally important in student retention, is informal and is typically proffered by auxiliary services. Not surprisingly, the attrition of ethnic minority students often occurs because they are not socially integrated into the campus environment, not because of academic difficulties.

More recently, Tinto (2000) has suggested that the classroom itself be more carefully studied as a context contributing to student persistence and attrition. He proposes that the establishment of peer "learning communities" within classrooms can contribute substantially to students' persistence. We agree and think that, additionally, the instructor can shape directly and indirectly the ambiance of this classroom learning community. This is consistent with Astin's (1993) finding that students' perceptions not only of community but also of how faculty perceive students are major influences on student success.

Increasing heterogeneity and attrition are only two examples of the many challenges students put upon college and university systems. They arguably are a result of students' increasingly heterogeneous needs being expressed in a context that remains largely homogeneous. Although increasing campus diversity is a goal of most colleges and universities, real diversification is, so far, more apparent in their student populations.[4]

In the specific context of attrition, we think that students are indirectly expressing their need for interpersonal rapport—most of all, with their teachers. Braxton, Bray, and Berger (2000) found that persistence (i.e., continuous enrollment) among college students was most strongly predicted by students' perceptions of faculty teaching skills. In a national follow-up of university alumni, Graham (2000) found that "instructional climate" had the most substantial impact on retrospective satisfaction with college education; the effect was more substantial than that generated by satisfaction with student affairs services. Thus, we argue that the needs of contemporary students highlight this aspect of teaching and show that it is of overwhelming import.[5]

We think that establishing interpersonal rapport in the classroom is of equal importance as intellectual excitement, especially in diverse classrooms. Our Socratic commitment, however, puts a limit on the establishment of this rapport; anxiety levels cannot (and should not) be reduced to zero.

Conclusion

Faculty need to respond to increasing student diversity and modify their pedagogies accordingly. It is in the classroom that students can truly be made to feel that they are full participants in the educational experience; by comparison, all other settings (e.g., administrative and student-support offices) are auxiliary. Yet, there is a connection among the students, the institutional values articulated in various institutional settings, and the overall effectiveness of the educational process. Inconsistencies among these settings fracture that process. Faculty who teach can modify their pedagogies to directly reduce these inconsistencies.

The first aspect of the modified pedagogy is a willingness to create moments of safety in the classroom so that students can speak openly, and to invite what may be irrelevant or uninformed comments.

The second aspect involves the attentive monitoring of student affective reactions. For example, a student may visibly react to some discussion or material but hesitate to share that reaction with the class. Attention and quick response to a student's body language is, in many cases, needed to properly encourage their participation.

The third aspect deals with the potential contradiction between the self-disclosing ambiance and critical questioning. Should there be a balance of self-disclosing ambiance and Socratic inquiry, with each continuously intertwined? Or is the ambiance of safety a prerequisite for constructive elenctic exchanges? Some separation seems to be called for because encouragement to self-disclose and a rigorous program of critique can strike some students as a classic double bind (Bateson, Jackson, Haley, and Weakland 1956).

Earlier, we gave one method for embedding a self-disclosing ambiance within a larger Socratic structure: Suspend the "rules of lecture" and freely discuss case studies. Unfettered from note taking, students can think freely about an issue. Doing this seems to incline them to express their opinions. Another stratagem could be to break the class into small conversation groups. If rules creating an ambiance conducive to self-disclosure have been established, students probably will participate freely, since small groups have an intimacy that is unavailable in large lectures. Furthermore, the separation of the conversation groups from the lecture session may signal to students an empowering level of involvement more akin to that of the instructor.

The strong engagement that follows the use of these techniques is similar to the components of what Massimini and Delle Fave (2000) call optimal experiences: high challenge, intrinsic motivation, and concentrated attention. Massimini and Delle Fave further propose that these components are universal; that is, these optimal experiences are composed of the same components in all cultures. If this is even partially true, we may have outlined a teaching method that is uniquely useful in classrooms with students from diverse backgrounds.

Notes

1. In a classic exchange between Socrates and one of his students, Theaetetus, about the definition of knowledge, Socrates claims to be only the "barren midwife" to Theaetetus, who is the person "in labour." Socrates' ostensible role is only to assist Theaetetus in giving birth to his own true definition of knowledge.

2. Even if they are subtle, such as Socrates' posture of deference to Theaetetus in their dialogue, at most it seems that this could only be perceived as feigned flattery.

3. Although majority students may readily accept an invitation to be "completely honest," the invitation may have a substantially different impact on minority students in a class; to them, accepting such an invitation could be fraught with risk. Also, class size and participation levels within groups may cause discussion to focus on one group's (generally the majority's) stereotypes or opinions thereof. (We thank Christina Serrano and Kimberly S. Castro for this observation.) See the chapter by Tim Davies in this volume for another example of how difficult it is to broach this issue.

4. Consider, for example, the gender ratio among students compared to the gender ratio among tenured faculty.

5. Notably, establishing rapport is different from maintaining decorum in the classroom. Recommendations regarding the promotion of civility in the college classroom are, for the most part, of a very different tenor than those regarding the promotion of rapport and an ambiance of self-disclosure. The goal of decorum and civility is to prevent emotion from overwhelming a situation. The goal of establishing rapport is to promote interpersonal understanding.

References

Anderson, James A. 1999. Faculty responsibility for promoting conflict-free college classrooms. In *Promoting civility: A teaching challenge,* edited by S.M. Richardson. New Directions for Teaching and Learning, Spring (77):69-76.

Astin, Alexander W. 1993. *What matters in college?* San Francisco: Jossey-Bass.

Bandura, Albert. 1997. *Self-efficacy: The exercise of control.* New York: W.H. Freeman.

Bateson, Gregory, D.D. Jackson, J. Haley, and J.H. Weakland. 1956. Toward a theory of schizophrenia. *Behavioral Science* 1:251-264.

Braxton, J.M., N.J. Bray, and J.B. Berger. 2000. Faculty teaching skills and their influence on the college student departure process. *Journal of College Student Development* 41:215-227.

Bronfenbrenner, Urie. 1979. *The ecology of human development: Experiments by nature and design.* Cambridge, MA: Harvard University Press.

Erikson, Erik. 1963. *Childhood and society,* 2nd ed. New York: Norton.

Gay, Geneva. 2000. *Culturally responsive teaching: Theory, research and practice.* New York: Teachers College.

Graham, Steven W. 2000. The effects of instructional climate and student affairs services on college outcomes and satisfaction. *Journal of College Student Development* 41:279-291.

Jourard, Sydney. 1971a. *The transparent self.* New York: Van Nostrand.

Jourard, Sydney. 1971b. *Self-disclosure: An experimental analysis of the transparent self.* New York: Wiley-Interscience.

Jourard, Sydney, and P. Lasakow. 1958. Some factors in self-disclosure. *Journal of Abnormal and Social Psychology* 56:91-98.

Ladson-Billings, Gloria. 1995. Toward a theory of culturally relevant pedagogy. *American Educational Research Journal* 32:465-491.

Lubinski, David, and Camilla P. Benbow. 2000. States of excellence. *American Psychologist* 55:137-150.

MacTurk, Robert H., and George A. Morgan, eds. 1995. *Mastery motivation: Origins, conceptualizations, and applications.* Norwood, NJ: Ablex.

Marin, Patricia. 2000. The educational possibility of multi-racial multi-ethnic college classrooms. In *Does diversity make a difference?: Three research studies on diversity in college classrooms,* by ACE and AAUP. Washington, DC: ACE and AAUP.

Massimini, Fausto, and A. Delle Fave. 2000. Individual development in a bio-cultural perspective. *American Psychologist* 55:24-33.

Maslow, Abraham H. 1968. *Toward a psychology of being.* New York: Van Nostrand.

Rogers, Carl. 1961. *On becoming a person.* Boston: Houghton Mifflin.

Sullivan, Harry Stack, Helen S. Perry, and Mary L Gawel, eds. 1953. *The interpersonal theory of psychiatry.* New York: Norton.

Tinto, Vincent. 1975. Dropout from higher education: A theoretical synthesis of recent research. *Review of Educational Research* 45:89-125.

Tinto, Vincent. 1993. *Leaving college: Rethinking the causes and cures of student attrition.* Chicago: University of Chicago.

Tinto, Vincent. 2000. Linking learning and leaving: Exploring the role of the college classroom in student departure. In *Reworking the student departure puzzle,* edited by J.M. Braxton. Nashville, TN: Vanderbilt University.

Watson, David, and Auke Tellegen. 1985. Toward a consensual structure of mood. *Psychological Bulletin* 98:219-235.

White, Robert. 1959. Motivation reconsidered: The concept of competence. *Psychological Review* 66:297-333.

Making Space in the Classroom for My Gay Identity: A Letter I've Been Wanting to Write

Eric Aoki

> Self-defensive lies can permeate all one does, so that life turns into "living a lie." Professionals involved in collective practices of deceit give up all ordinary assumptions about their own honesty and that of others. And individuals who feel obliged to "pass" as a member of a dominant religious or racial group in order to avoid persecution deny what may be most precious to them. Political beliefs or sexual preferences unacceptable to a community compel many to a similar life-long duplicity, denying a central part of their own identity.—Sissela Bok, in *Lying: Moral Choice in Public and Private Life,* 1989, 79.

> Liberation: not a gift, not a self-achievement, but a mutual process. It is only the oppressed who, by freeing themselves, can free their own oppressors.—Paulo Freire, in *Pedagogy of the Oppressed,* 2000.

Spring Semester 2001

Dear Ann,[1]

When you and our colleagues at the university offered me a tenure-track, assistant professor position in the spring of 1997, I was going through quite an emotionally taxing period of my career and my life. I felt a lot younger and less experienced than I do now—almost four years later—with regard to negotiating what I have learned are the private and public spheres of identity and voice.

Although I was quite successful in graduate school, I was struggling personally. I was struggling to keep myself healthy (i.e., off the booze) and above the tides of poor self-esteem and relational angst with my then-girlfriend Julianna's[2] parents. As you know, Julianna was killed in a car accident the year after I started my job. For all the love that we had shared, we were never able to overcome the barriers erected by her parents, who could not learn to accept me. In their eyes, I was a person of the "wrong" ethnicity and the "wrong" class level.

After getting myself individual alcohol counseling—thanks in large part to Julianna and my wonderful friends in graduate school —and after working to be more present in my life and with the people in my life, Julianna and I decided, while I was here in Colorado and she was doing her medical residency on the West Coast, to end the relational "us." We broke up before we risked losing the love and respect we had for each other. Sometime thereafter, before I came "out" on campus and before Julianna died, she and I were working to move on with our romantic lives as well as with our independent careers. We still were linked emotionally, but now as very close friends. Before her death, and after almost six years of being in each other's lives, Julianna knew how much I loved her despite our relationship not working out. And Julianna also knew that in moving on with our own romantic lives, I had begun a new relationship with my first boyfriend, Joshua.

As a diversity teacher, and having just finished a whirlwind first year and a half at Colorado State, I recognized how fortunate I was to have found in you both a friend and a department chair who not only talked the diversity talk but actually walked the diversity walk. I had heard several stories from colleagues in different institutions about the challenges of being out on campus. Katherine R. Allen, in her article "Opening the Classroom Closet: Sexual Orientation and Self-Disclosure," highlights the importance of departmental support when she states, "Faculty members and department chairs can recognize that homophobia and heterosexism affect everyone, not just people who are lesbian, bisexual, or gay" (140). Although I'm aware that support is not found in every department, I was confident that you, Ann, would be an ally on campus as I opened the closet door.

In the summer of 1997, prior to starting my new job, I read Kent Ono's (1997) piece, "A Letter/Essay I've Been Longing to Write in My Personal/Academic Voice."[3] I now use this essay in my graduate research methodology seminar, but back then the essay resonated strongly with the predicament I found myself in with regard to the personal and public pieces of my identity.

Through the years, my mentors, colleagues, and peers always had encouraged me to share with students personal elements of myself.[4] Now, I had to figure out how, or even if, I wanted to share this seemingly more problematic "gay self" with my students. I also had to evaluate the impact of this sharing on their learning.

Over time, I had internalized and critically examined many of the voices I had heard or read in my lifetime, and I was able to reconcile many of the voices I wanted to share. In the process of coming out to my classes, I realized the importance of support from my boss, support from administration, and the need to hear these voices of support, out loud, in the context of the university.

I see this letter to you, Ann, as a way of thanking you for your support in helping me reconcile the tensions between my personal and academic voices. I also see this letter as a space to talk out a very important diversity issue of cultured society, to give a voice to a still heavily stigmatized identity, and to remind my colleagues who hold positions of power in the academy *not to become complacent* in their support or to voice only silence about these issues. So again, as I discuss in the pages to come some slices from my life as a teacher who came out to his students, I want to thank you for being central to my connection with my students, so many of whom have in turn become great sources of inspiration and strength. Annette Friskopp and Sharon Silverstein (1995), in their book *Straight Jobs, Gay Lives: Gay and Lesbian Professionals, the Harvard Business School, and the American Workplace*, state: "[C]ompanies that are consistent in stamping out discrimination on every front are the most likely to have loyal employees" (112). With your commitment to diversity in the workplace, Ann, I believe my loyalty to my students and my job has been able to shine. I share this letter with you because I'm confident that through *your* voice, the lessons of diversity found within it will reach broader audiences.

In your own book you state:

> The metaphor *voice* is widely adopted as a way for groups and for individuals to express their search for identity, for connection to others and to a shared past, for their own particular worldview, and for their place not in the margins but in the center of society. (Gill 1994, 232)

These are words I try to bring into practice so that I can be *present* in life and encourage others to do the same. So here is the story of how I came to negotiate a personal and cultural space of gay identity in my university classrooms, and what that has meant for my teaching.

My relationship with Joshua began to intensify over the summer of 1998. In the fall of that year, before coming out to my students, I stood present with Joshua at a candlelight vigil for a young man I had never met named Matthew Shepard. Joshua and I stood hand in hand outside a hospital in my new hometown of Fort Collins, where this twenty-one-year-old student from a university just north of my own lay unconscious. On the following Monday, I heard the news that Matthew had died. Joshua called me at work that day and related to me the details of the horrific pain and torture this young man had apparently suffered. The world soon learned that Matthew Shepard had been gay, and the attention this brought to the issue began weaving its way into my consciousness.

Despite its respectable size, Fort Collins can feel like a small town. Joshua and I became more and more aware of the consequences of coming out as we grappled with the longing to do so. Joshua knew that being out at the school where he taught (he now teaches in another state) would be highly problematic, so he remained closeted. As for myself, after discussing the situation with a good colleague and friend, Brian Ott, I felt strongly about coming out on campus. Having spoken with numerous colleagues throughout the campus and with friends in the local community, I learned that I would receive a lot of support; but I still had reservations about a decision to come out in the classroom. I would try saying things as though I were in class, making an announcement—"As someone who is gay,"or simply, "I'm gay"...I remember practicing these words. Even though most of my concerns revolved around sharing this piece of my identity with a young (i.e., first year) audience, these folks happened to be the ones I felt *safest* coming out to that fall. So I did—in what seemed like a casual mention, I noted to the class that my *boyfriend* and I had been at the hospital vigil for Matthew Shepard.

That day in class, I had what I believe to be a transformational moment in teaching. I felt honest and connected with all the theory and concepts I spouted off in class; I felt myself *being* with my students. Over the course of the semester, one student in particular—Samantha—became for me a source of inspiration. Her voice of acceptance (a step beyond tolerance) and diversity advocacy kept me smiling throughout that entire course. (As it happened, several years later Samantha became my senior-level teaching assistant for a co-cultural communication class. She was then preparing to graduate, and she was a constant reminder to me of my having negotiated and survived the "first wave.")

The same semester, it remained for me to come out to my upper division students. Toward the end of the course I came out to my senior-level interpersonal and intercultural communication classes, this time with more nervousness. Overwhelmingly, the response was supportive. Some students told me they felt a little uncomfortable or uncertain, as they had never met anyone who was openly gay. And later that day, one of the students, Rilee, sent me an email that I carry in my wallet to this day. He wrote:

> I didn't get a chance to speak with you after class, so if you care, here are my thoughts on your statement. I commend you for doing what you did. I know that took lots of thought and lots of courage and bravery simply to be who you really are. I hope that over the course of your career you are able to use your position as an "instructor of the human condition" to teach people that diversity is a good thing. I hope that society, in learning from professors like you, will not require bravery as a prerequisite for individuality...I don't feel like you need to hear my judgment of you or your statement or anything else, but I would like you to know that I hope we can continue growing in what I feel is a positive relationship. I can learn a lot from you not only as an instructor but as a person...

As you know, Rilee is now in our graduate program, preparing to take the final steps toward an M.A. degree. I can't stress enough how fortunate I feel to have had students like Samantha and Rilee speaking on my behalf these past four years.

I also feel quite fortunate that every semester, students try to obtain an override into my courses because they have heard such positive comments from former students. Whether initially comfortable or not (and I've never guaranteed to my students a feeling of comfort, particularly when discussing diversity issues), many students have participated in and finished the class with open minds. I know that with your support and the support from my students, my colleagues, the administration, my family and friends, and many encouraging parents, I have experienced a wonderful boost to my holistic self-esteem. I also have acquired an enhanced awareness of my students and their views on diversity, tolerance, and acceptance.

Still, there have been some challenges. On an evaluation, one student wrote that he couldn't believe he had spent his college money only to take a class from a professor who wanted to convert people into homosexuals. Nonetheless, in time, I was able to recognize that most students did not read my inclusion into the classroom of my gay identity as a threat to their own identities or as part of some "conversion mission." In fact, what really helped me put that one negative evaluation to the side was another interaction I had with a different student.

Without my knowledge, the university had required this student to take my class on account of his involvement in a homecoming parade float that carried words and images disparaging of Matthew Shepard and of homosexuality in general. After a while, this student and I developed a friendship. When I found out about his role in the parade I felt betrayed, but this was tempered by his regret and humility and by the ideological changes he was making regarding diversity. Over several years, this student returned to my courses by his own choice, and today he speaks out against hate in all its forms.

Again, Ann, I am thankful to you for standing behind me in my decision to share my voice of diversity in the classroom. As one of my students once reassuringly quipped that he and his "brothers" "got my back" when I'm confronted with hate or injustice you, Ann, in a parallel sense, have always "had my back" as my boss. I can't imagine being openly gay in a context where this support did not exist.

Of course, I should mention that I am not special in my decision to come out in the classroom; many before me have opened that door and laid the groundwork. Martin Duberman's (1999) *Left Out: The Politics of Exclusion/Essays/1964-1999* is a good way to get up to speed on the many histories of exclusion in the U.S. I also believe it is important to recognize that one can't just open his mouth and expect a cogent voice to come out. I've mentioned some people in my life who have been influential in the development of my voice, but I also have gained strength from a number of books, notably: Paulo Freire's (2000) *Pedagogy of the Oppressed;*, Eduardo Galeano's *(1998) Upside Down: A Primer for the Looking-Glass World;* Claudine Chiawei O'Hearn's (1998) *Half and Half: Writers on Growing Up Biracial and Bicultural;* Tracy E. Ore's (2000) *The Social Construction of Difference and Inequality: Race, Class, Gender and Sexuality;* Alberto González, Marsha Houston, and Victoria Chen's (1997) *Our Voices: Essays in Culture, Ethnicity, and Communication;* Beth Loffreda's (2000) *Losing Matt Shepard: Life and Politics in the Aftermath of Anti-Gay Murder;* Andrew Sullivan's (1998) *Love Undetectable: Notes on Friendship, Sex, and Survival;* Virginia Cyrus's (2000) *Experiencing Race, Class, and Gender in the United States;* Thich Nhat Hanh's (1976) *The Miracle of Mindfulness;* Judith Martin and Thomas Nakayama's (2000) *Intercultural Communication in Contexts;* and Jean Vanier's (1998) *Becoming Human.*

Vanier (1998), in *Becoming Human,* tells us:

The excluded, I believe, live certain values that we all need
to discover and to live ourselves before we can become
truly human. It is not just a question of performing good
deeds for those who are excluded but of being open and
vulnerable to them in order to receive the life that they can
offer; it is to become their friends. If we start to include the
disadvantaged in our lives and enter into heartfelt relationships with them, they will change things in us...They will
call us out from our individualism and need for power into
belonging to each other and being open to others. They will
break down the prejudices and protective walls that gave
rise to exclusion in the first place. They will then start to affect our human organizations, revealing new ways of being
and walking together. (84)

And I suppose that, in the end, with my students and with society, this feeling as though we can co-exist, participate together, and
walk together is what creates that sense of belonging. I know that
when negotiating diversity, particularly sexual diversity, the walk is
not an easy one. I also have come to realize that the identities we
bring into the classroom can have an effect on how our relations
with our students develop or can develop. Although my path toward
identity in the classroom has hardly been what I'd call easy, I do realize that while my sexual orientation and ethnicity have brought
challenges along the way, being male may have given me privilege
in my role as a professor. Celeste M. Condit's "Theory, Practice,
and the Battered (Woman) Teacher" (1996, 167) is a reminder that
identity negotiation between students and teachers occurs within a
context of "specific constraints." She provides a necessary caution
about relying too stringently on theories to pigeonhole our teaching
practices; she reminds us to use theories but also to foster a "critical common sense about teaching [that] is garnered by experience
in the classroom, discussions with other teachers, feedback from
students and administrators, and reflection on teaching in comparison to available theories of communication and social structure" (168). In addition to this approach, I afford for the inclusion
of democratic principles that provide students a voice in making
decisions about the framework of the classroom (Campbell 1999).
I also integrate cooperative learning skills that promote listening
and empathy in the classroom (Johnson and Johnson 1994), and I
work to foster an environment grounded in respect (Belenky et al.
1986).

There is a great book by Rebecca Solnit (2000) *Wanderlust: A
History of Walking*, which I picked up in Cambridge, Massachusetts

last year. In reading this book, I have become more aware of how my emotional and physical health are affected by walking, as well as how walking is so much a part of the history of social movements (e.g., walking for awareness, walking to protest, walking to "take back the night.") As you know, I returned recently from a Fulbright-Hays project in India conducted with other academics from Colorado State University and the Fort Collins and Poudre high schools. In Delhi, we walked along a city route to a historically significant mosque, the Jama Masjid. I have never taken a more emotionally difficult walk. We saw people, many of them children, some missing limbs, all with dirtied faces, living in diseased conditions, lying on the ground or walking about asking for handouts.

Now, I don't want to essentialize India as a "sacred land" or a "land of poverty," for there is a thriving mass commercialism and abundant wealth there as well; but this walk, because it was so uncomfortable and so out of my experience, affected me so strongly that my humanity tried to "shut down" in order to cope. We walked almost robotically to get beyond the scope of this human condition.

I wonder, in retrospect, if that is how people who are racist, sexist, and/or homophobic respond to people like me. I do realize the differences between these two cases, but the reminder is that I have to speak up with regard to negotiating my sexual identity and other difficult issues in the classroom. Taking this step helps the identity be *known*, for to remain silent is a setback for diversity. Keeping the channels of communication open, however, is no easy task. I learned through the works of Hans Georg Gadamer (1989) that prejudices are a naturally occurring aspect of personal development, and that sexual prejudices remain some of the most stigmatized, emotional, and political in the world in which we live. The hardest obstacle to overcome, I tell my students, is diversity of the *mind*.

Just under four years ago, I opened a door that for many years I tried to ignore. I have enough common sense, and the privilege of a wonderful education, to know that I had kept this door closed for many reasons. But now, having opened it, I have a much clearer view as to how and why we need to live for the moment, and how to help others share in this joy of living. And I know without doubt that this passion and joy has transferred into the energy of my classrooms and into the wonderful relations I have with my students and with colleagues.

The view is great from where I now stand. I realize that I have allies who will support me regardless of my sexual orientation. I've learned, as an educator and learner, that sometimes those allies come in the form of a boss or a friend. Thank you for being such an ally.

My love and respect,
Eric

Note: An earlier draft of this letter was presented to the Intercultural Interest Group, Western States Communication Association, Coeur d'Alene, Idaho, February 2001. The author would like to thank the panel participants, respondents, and attendees as well as the co-editors of *Teaching Diversity: Challenges and Complexities, Identities and Integrity* for their invaluable feedback. Eric can also be reached at Eric.Aoki@colostate.edu.

Notes

1. Ann is Dr. Ann Gill, former chair of the Speech Communication department, Colorado State University.

2. With the exception of my academic colleagues and previous professors/mentors, I have changed the names of individuals in this essay for reasons of confidentiality.

3. Kent Ono's "A Letter/Essay I've Been Longing to Write in My Personal/Academic Voice" had a significant influence on my conceptualization and understanding of *voice*. The decision to use Ono's essay as a model for sharing my voice on this particular issue was based on the Western States Communication Association's theme for 2001—"Turning Scholarship into Practice."

4. If someone asked me to describe myself presently, I would avow to the following identities: Ethnically, I am Japanese American and Mexican American; I am American in nationality; I am a non-practicing Catholic though I consider myself to be spiritual and I have Buddhist leanings; I come from working-class roots; I speak English and a fair amount of Spanish, but due to its stigmatization during the Second World War I have forgotten the Japanese I learned as a child; I am gay/bisexual; I am an alcoholic (sober for six years); I am "mostly" vegetarian, though fish remains a dietary staple that connects me to ethnic roots on both sides of my family.

References

Allen, Katherine R. 1995. Opening the classroom closet: Sexual orientation and self-disclosure. *Family Relations* 44:136-141.

Belenky, Mary F., Blythe M. Clinchy, Nancy R. Goldberger, and Jill R. Tarule, eds. 1986. *Women's ways of knowing*. New York: Basic Books.

Bok, Sissela. 1989. *Lying: Moral choice in public and private life*. New York: Vintage Books.

Campbell, Duane, and Delores Delgado Campbell. 1999. *Choosing democracy: A practical guide to multicultural education*. Upper Saddle River, NJ: Prentice Hall.

Condit, Celeste M. 1996. Theory, practice, and the battered (woman) teacher. In *Teaching what you're not: Identity politics in higher education*, edited by Katherine J. Mayberry. New York: New York University Press.

Cyrus, Virginia. 2000. *Experiencing race, class, and gender in the United States*, 3rd ed. Mountain View, CA: Mayfield.

Duberman, Martin. 1999. *Left out: The politics of exclusion/essays/ 1964-1999*. New York: Basic Books.

Freire, Paulo. 2000. *Pedagogy of the oppressed*. New York: Continuum.

Friskopp, Annette, and Sharon Silverstein. 1995. *Straight jobs, Gay lives: Gay and lesbian professionals, the Harvard Business School, and the American workplace*. New York: Scribner.

Gadamer, Hans Georg. 1989. *Truth and method*, 2nd rev. ed. New York: Crossroads.

Galeano, Eduardo. 1998. *Upside down: A primer for the looking-glass world*. New York: Metropolitan Books.

Gill, Ann. 1994. *Rhetoric and human understanding*. Prospect Heights, IL: Waveland Press.

González, Alberto, Marsha Houston, and Victoria Chen. 1997. *Our voices: Essays in culture, ethnicity, and communication*, 2nd ed. Los Angeles: Roxbury.

Hanh, Thich Nhat. 1976. *The miracle of mindfulness*. Translated by Mobi Ho. Boston: Beacon Press.

Johnson, David, and Roger Johnson. 1994. *Learning together and alone*. Needham Heights, MA: Allyn and Bacon.

Loffreda, Beth. 2000. *Losing Matt Shepard: Life and politics in the aftermath of anti-gay murder*. New York: Columbia University Press.

Martin, Judith N., and Thomas K. Nakayama. 2000. *Intercultural communication in contexts*, 2nd ed. Mountain View, CA: Mayfield.

O'Hearn, Claudine Chiawei, ed. (1998). *Half and half: Writers on growing up biracial and bicultural*. New York: Pantheon Books.

Ono, Kent A. 1997, Winter. A letter/essay I've been longing to write in my personal/academic voice. *Western Journal of Communication* 6(1): 114-125.

Ore, Tracy E. 2000. *The social construction of difference and inequality: Race, class, gender, and sexuality.* Mountain View, CA: Mayfield.

Solnit, Rebecca. 2000. *Wanderlust: A history of walking.* New York: Viking Penguin.

Sullivan, Andrew. 1998. *Love undetectable: Notes on friendship, sex, and survival.* New York: Alfred A. Knopf.

Vanier, Jean. 1998. *Becoming human.* New York: Paulist Press.

Reaching the Congregation, Not Just the Choir: Conquering Resistance to Diversity Issues

Val Middleton

Introduction

Diversity courses in teacher education present a unique set of issues for instructors as well as for preservice teachers in training. As an instructor highlighting diversity issues, I often have to evaluate my own preparation and ability to deliver such issues. I must be able to process both the students' issues and my own as they are revealed throughout the course. Anger, fear, silence, vehemence, avoidance, guilt, passion, enthusiasm, and many other constructive and unconstructive emotions and reactions can erupt as we construct, deconstruct, and reconstruct our attitudes and beliefs about diversity.

The assumptions informing this chapter are that (a) diversity enriches the United States (Manning and Baruth 1996); (b) a better understanding of people and their differences leads to unity rather than segregation (Manning and Baruth 1996); (c) diversity education is critical in retaining the democratic ideals of the United States (Campbell 1999); (d) understanding diversity is fundamental to the education of all learners (Bennett 1995; Davidman and Davidman 1994); and (e) schools play a major role in teaching acceptance and respect for diversity, and are logical places to reinforce and celebrate diversity (Manning and Baruth 1996).

The theoretical framework for this chapter highlights cognitive dissonance (Festinger 1957), intimate and equal status contact (Allport 1935, 1979), and logical thinking (Pate 1982) as methods for constructing, deconstructing, and reconstructing beliefs and behaviors associated with diversity issues. In short, involving individuals in equal status experiences in which they are not of the "privileged status" (McIntosh 1988), either in worldview or physicality, promotes a state of dissonance that then can be deconstructed and/or reconstructed through a productive process. Additionally, this chapter offers some suggestions for educators committed to supporting diversity issues in the curriculum and in the classroom.

"The Shepherd and the Sheep"

Relying on eight years of public school teaching experience in the Chicago area, I smiled confidently upon entering my first university classroom as a teacher educator, in spite of the fact that nearly every preservice teacher in the room sat before me with mouth agape. I turned my back to them to write identifying information on the board while I subtly checked to make sure I was appropriately buttoned and zipped. Upon realizing that I was appropriately secured, I assumed that the shocked expressions were a result of my being a Black female in a classroom of all White students. When I had finished writing and turned to face the class again, everyone had corrected their posture and awaited my delineation of the syllabus for a course on diversity. That was the first and last time I entered a course on diversity with self-proclaimed assurance.

When I reflect on that day, I sometimes miss the naivete that came with that false sense of confidence. My previous teaching experiences had been in Chicago-area, K-12 public schools where students came from a variety of racial, ethnic, religious, and socioeconomic backgrounds. In contrast, my current teaching experience is in a university setting with predominantly White, Christian, middle-class students who are in training to be teachers. I, a Black American female college professor, am an anomaly. Typically, I am the only teacher of color many of my students have had, the only Black teacher they have had, or the only Black professor they have had. As a result, I find I must carefully and purposefully establish a level of credibility and authority that would typically come with the position as it does for many of my White American male counterparts (Condit 1996). Additionally, I must be *extra careful* when challenging students to recognize their ethnocentricity; their self-centric attitudes, beliefs, and behaviors; and their privilege associated with dominant-culture status and upbringing. Failing to do so puts me at risk of being negated for having a "minority agenda."

Before meeting each new group of future teachers, I wonder how my blackness will affect the process of teaching for diversity. Will my blackness stifle students' honesty and create an atmosphere of deceit, under the guise of political correctness? Will my femaleness cause individuals in the class to take a stance of defense because they assume the course to be a course on "male bashing?" Will my preservice teachers deny their roles as perpetuators of institutionalized "-isms"? Will they voice the opinion that teaching about diversity is part of a politically correct minority agenda? Will they shut me out or actively engage in not learning from me? The answer to all of these questions is a qualified "yes." That is, each semester, at some point in time, these concerns have been raised by some of the preservice teachers through face-to-face contact, in their writing, or anonymously via student evaluations. Making sense of student's verbal and nonverbal responses to my diversity and the diversity issues I present thrills me, baffles me, and frustrates me in my attempts to help students focus on the issue of unintentional perpetuation of oppression based on race, gender, class, ability, sexual orientation, etc. Moreover, this intellectual and emotional struggle helps me to keep in mind how the preservice teachers may be experiencing my presence and the class content.

In addition to keeping the above questions circulating in my mind, I participate in many of the learning experiences I ask of my preservice teachers. One such activity requires involving oneself in an experience that is ethnically or culturally different from one's own. This perspective-taking activity often takes the form of being put in the position of being a numerical minority among a majority of others who may be physically, behaviorally, or ideologically different from oneself. The goal is to be gently forced outside of one's comfort zone in order to gain a conscious awareness of one's own values, beliefs, ethnocentricity, and/or privilege. Boundary-crossing activities such as this support the theoretical principles for prejudice reduction identified in Allport's *Social Contact Theory* (1935, 1979) and Pate's *Defense Against Prejudice Theory* (1982). This boundary-crossing activity encourages intimate, equal-status, inter-group contact (Allport 1935, 1979) and logical thinking (Pate 1982) through reflective participation, journal writing, and in-class discussions.

A "Religious" Experience

In an effort to "walk my talk," I wanted the experience of silently listening to someone else share values and beliefs that could likely be in opposition to mine. After thoughtful, but fretful, consideration, I decided to go to church after years of avoidance. Growing up in the Pentecostal tradition, I was told to listen to the voice of God or there literally would be "hell to pay." Once I had made the decision to go to church, there was no turning back, for any argument against going was a direct affront to God's will. Eventually, I found comfort in my decision based on the rationale of this experience being a research project on culture.

Upon arrival at the church, the individual members of the culture smiled at, greeted, and welcomed me as they do all newcomers. My early years of conditioned responses took over as I participated in the opening ceremonial traditions of clapping, praising, and praying. I easily acclimated to this part of the culture. When we were finally allowed to sit, I knew it would soon be time for the sermon. I immediately became guarded, assuming that a barrage of condemnation would soon follow. After realizing how defensive I had become in just a few moments, I purposely shifted my thoughts to my preservice teachers and how they might react when I begin my lessons.

My mind replayed several opening scenes of the first day of past diversity classes in which I was the instructor. I saw myself smile and greet my future teachers as they walked through the door, all the while wondering where each individual would fall along the continuum of interest or detestation of learning about diversity issues. On occasion, I would ask the preservice teachers to anonymously share with me their thoughts on my presence and on learning about diversity issues. On occasion, I was brave enough to read the written responses to my queries. Those memories began to dissipate as I contemplated methods of decreasing defensiveness in myself as a listener and as an educator.

I soon heard the musical accompaniment fade to the background as the pastor began speaking. The power of the sermon began to take hold of the people around me as members increased their verbalizations through call and response. Pastor's words, accented by the beat of the music, came faster and with increased power. The words and the rhythms began to capture me. Pastor descended from the pulpit and mingled with the people; he used their names, told personal stories, touched their raised hands, and talked about personal power. He made me feel empowered and included. I soon noticed that my defenses were gone.

After the service, I found myself longing for the power and charisma the pastor had in helping the members hear that as individuals, they could make a difference. I posed rhetorical questions and assessed my capabilities. How did he do that? How did I do that in my public school years of teaching? Was it the music? I have used music. Do I need music? Was it the personal connections? I try to do that. They laugh at my stories and sometimes nod positively, but not as much as my public school students did. Maybe I need more work on my comedic delivery? I left church that day reflecting on ways to improve the delivery of my "message" and methods for helping my preservice teachers as they struggle with issues of diversity.

I found myself less resistant to going back on subsequent Sundays, due to an increased sense of comfort in getting to know the culture, the members, and the rules. However, I remained somewhat on the defensive because experience told me that at some point my beliefs would conflict with the cultural norm. In comparison, I find this pattern of interest and apprehension to be consistent with my preservice teachers' verbal expressions of both interest and fear in their nonverbal behaviors as well as their written responses.

After a few weeks of church attendance, I felt that my immersion experience was helpful in gently forcing my comfort zone to expand, but I did not feel I had learned much about negotiating the toughest issues. Church-going had become part of my routine. Presumably, a few weeks of diversity class also had become routine. It was time for me to push my students' comfort zones to another level.

One succeeding Sunday I walked into the church at the same time I always had, but I noticed that the "meet and greet" time was not occurring as usual. I stopped at the door to analyze what was happening but found myself carried inside by the members who arrived after me. As I was forced into an empty space by the rushing crowd, I noticed the absence of the pastor and his replacement, the assistant minister. I felt myself become upset at this violation of the pattern to which I had become accustomed. As I tried to analyze my reaction, I was launched into a childhood flashback in which my grandmother was pulling me along with her into the church. Once we had made it to the seats bearing the indentations of our frequent use, she leaned over to me and said, "Child, you know that's the devil. Don't bring the devil into God's house." By the time I came back to the present I was standing in the pew clapping along with the same song we sing every week to get us in a "praising" mood. At the subliminal insistence of my grandmother, I regained my composure and relaxed my defenses.

The assistant minister started his sermon with a story that progressed to talking about various occupations within the plumbing and medical fields. In every instance, he used the pronoun "he" unless he made reference to a more female-dominated position such as nursing. I could feel my feminist temperature gauge rising as I shifted positions to regain some level of comfort. I looked around to see if anyone else looked visibly uncomfortable, but no one's body language gave a sign of the type of distress I was feeling. Soon, I began to mentally remove myself from the situation. My mind conjured up mental pictures of women in every verbalized occupation. I rationalized that I was still listening because I had to be listening in order to match my female depictions with his male-centered declarations. At the very least I expected him to follow the lead of Pastor, who often used "he" but usually caught himself and added "she" as an afterthought or quickly thought up another example that included women. Unfortunately, my wishes were not strong enough to influence the assistant minister's thoughts or words, so I began deflecting his words and ultimately his message.

Upon conscious awareness of my actions, my thoughts turned to my preservice teachers, who likely use similar tactics to regain their sense of consonance. I took a mental inventory of the language I use and the possible effects it may have on my audience. I recognized that I purposely try to use examples, nouns, and pronouns that are inclusive and diverse. I explain that I usually refer to myself as Black, rather than African American, because I grew up in the era of "Black Power" and "Black Is Beautiful." I ask them if it's OK for me to use the term "White," although I do intersperse it with European American. I often use "dominant culture status" as a term because the issues of diversity are so much broader than skin color. It also is important for me to let them know that it is not "me against them," because I too, at times, have dominant-culture status as an educated, middle-class, able-bodied person.

During my mental diversion, the minister's topic changed from gendered occupations to homosexuality, and the words "wrongness of homosexuality" pierced my consciousness. A condemning voice regarding various issues was one of the reasons I had left the church earlier in my life. I unfolded my arms and stretched my fingers that had somehow become clenched around my biceps. Needing no more pretense, I was gathering my things to leave when I again remembered my purpose for sitting on that pew—"How do I help preservice teachers hear a message on diversity when it affronts their current belief system?"

"The Struggle for Redemption"

My personal struggle to understand the resistance I get from the preservice teachers and my desire to make diversity issues an integral component of their teaching repertoire keeps me participating in, reflecting upon, and analyzing my own continuous journey as I monitor and analyze their verbal, nonverbal, and written reactions. Each semester I go through emotions similar to those my preservice teachers do, such as fear, guilt, passion, and feeling overwhelmed. We traverse the semester-long course with some level of fear when embroiled in the fight to maintain values and beliefs that we assume right, the guilt that sometimes comes with the initial acknowledgement of privileged status, and the feeling of being overwhelmed with the amount of work toward diversity there is to do. We sometimes react with anger, silence, vehemence, avoidance, and passion. Addressing these emotions and reactions in a safe and empowering way is critical to working on our journeys into the "diversity zone."

Reflective journal writing is one method I use to help my preservice teachers and myself analyze our journeys toward understanding and managing diversity issues. Following participation in course activities, I require the preservice teachers to analyze their experiences using the following guidelines: (a) state your and/or your instructor's objectives for the activity/experience; (b) describe your participation in the activity; (c) personally react to the activity, (d) interpret the activity as it connects to the literature and other media (i.e., guest speakers, videos, novels, etc.); (e) apply the learning to your personal and professional responsibilities; (f) identify whether or not you met the original objectives and/or discovered any unforeseen outcomes; and (g) commit to a plan for improving future interactions with diverse others or diversity issues.

The aforementioned religious experience addresses the above reflection guidelines. These guiding statements generally help writers get into the flow of their reflective activities in a structured or focused way while also allowing for the freedom to describe the experience in their own words. Additionally, it gently forces writers to examine their levels of awareness, knowledge, and commitment to an issue. Overlaying my religious experience with preservice teachers' reflections on the course's inclusion of homosexuality issues further illustrates these components.

Interpreting the "Scriptures"

I invited a panel of lesbian and gay individuals and allies to share their educational experiences with my preservice teachers. The preservice teachers expressed a variety of reactions and emotions to the topic; however, most were uncomfortable and fearful. Below are quotes from two preservice teachers that give the majority reaction to the issue of homosexuality and its inclusion in the class.

One of the two preservice teachers identifies the following reaction: "Homosexuality is probably the most difficult issue for me in this class. I am strongly against the lifestyle choices of homosexuals.

My beliefs are founded in evidence and information that is too involved to discuss, but nonetheless I am not very understanding when it comes to this issue."

While some preservice teachers do not believe sexual orientation is a choice, many of my preservice teachers do support this belief system and/or believe that, regardless of the cause, homosexuality is "sick" or "wrong." As a result, this issue is one that makes understanding difficult for those on any side of the issue. The second preservice teacher identified his difficulty with the issue of homosexuality; however, he was able to hear and receive the panel's presentation in a different way. His reflection follows.

> I found today's discussion to be very practical. I thought the discussion about what we can do as future teachers was very beneficial to me. For me, this situation was the first one for me where I was exposed to the homosexual lifestyle without negative interference (hostility, closed-mindedness, stereotypes, etc.) They suggested that by being open and affirming toward all students, I can be most effective and supportive of homosexuals. They also suggested some resources for information about homosexuality. I think this is the best way for me. Since my own values and beliefs conflict with those of homosexuals, it would be best for me to refer such students to a better source. I will do my best to create an atmosphere in my classroom that will be inoffensive and inclusive for homosexual students. Although having a student confide in me about their sexuality will be uncomfortable for me, I want my student to trust me enough to do so. Establishing the trust and respect of my students is one of my personal goals. Being hateful or discriminatory toward homosexuals or any other students only hinders this goal.

The reflection components can clearly be seen in the above quote. In addition to describing and reacting to the presentation, this preservice teacher was able to: (a) add to his knowledge base on diversity issues because he was "exposed to the homosexual lifestyle without negative interference;" (b) analyze the objectives as creating "an atmosphere in my classroom that will be inoffensive and inclusive for homosexual students;" (c) apply the new learning to his professional responsibilities by referring "such students to a better source;" and (d) commit to a plan for "establishing the trust and respect of students." The hope is that his future interactions with diverse others or diversity issues will involve the stated changes in his behavior.

While there is no single method that will be successful for conquering every individual's resistance to diversity issues, analysis of the successes and failures in addressing diversity issues can lead to insights for conquering resistance at the level at which individuals are responding.

"Altar Call"

A qualitative analysis of preservice teachers' verbal and written reflections identified key elements in combating resistance to diversity issues (Middleton 1997). These elements were: (a) the circumstances by that the issues were approached; (b) the authenticity of the speaker and the message; (c) the accountability for practicing behaviors which affirm diversity; and (d) the level of awareness and assessment capabilities of the individual. Each theme is interconnected, delineated with descriptors, and supported at its core by the constructs of safety and empowerment. A visual representation of these elements can be found in Figure 1.

A non-threatening approach aided both the preservice teachers and me in the initial stages of combating our own resistance. As I returned to church each week, my fears began to subside and I felt the

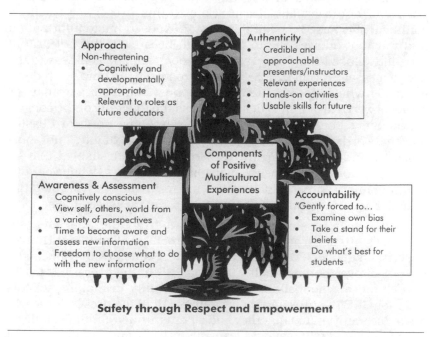

Figure 1. Thematic framework for facilitating positive multicultural experiences.

levels of safety and empowerment increase. I was welcomed each week with smiles and opportunities to get to know the pastor and the congregation through the pastor's words and the congregation's responses to his words. In contrast to the assistant minister, Pastor used words that were not condemning or threatening, but thoughtful and compelling. His life scenarios and advice for change were put before us as offers rather than orders. He offered up a scenario, invited us to find our reality within that scenario, and encouraged us to make a change or adapt a new belief system. This invitational delivery offered the safety and empowerment needed to stay tuned in and the assessment time needed in order to make an informed decision.

In comparison, the preservice teachers expressed that they were more likely to remain receptive to a "questionable" or "challenging" presentation if the presenter was approachable and made it safe for them to express their thoughts, concerns, fears, and biases in an honest manner and without negative repercussions (Middleton 1997). The preservice teacher quoted above stated, "For me, this situation was the first one for me where I was exposed to the homosexual lifestyle without negative interference (hostility, closed-mindedness, stereotypes, etc.) They suggested that by being open and affirming toward all students, I can be most effective and supportive of homosexuals." I can relate to this preservice teacher's comments because I too felt that Pastor exposed me to information in a way that allowed me to "hear" him because it did not deal in "hostility, closed-mindedness, or stereotypes." The goal was to deliver a message for all people. Pastor often uses the phrase, "It doesn't matter what color you are, whether you're a man or a woman, or how you were raised" in order to address the diversity of the congregation. Since I began attending this church, I have not heard Pastor use the words "sexual orientation" or "homosexuality," nor purposely include this group in his sermons, and I suspect that he never will; however, he uses other phrases such as "whatever your family configuration," which allows me to include gay, lesbian, bisexual, and transgendered individuals in the messages I hear.

After hearing stories of harassment from the panelists and learning statistics from the U.S. Department of Health and Human Services—such as, 30 percent of all teenage suicides may be linked to conflict over homosexuality (Gibson 1989), the preservice teachers felt more responsibility and accountability in making schools safer for GLBT youths and their families. All of the preservice teachers in the study stated that they had a better understanding of the issues associated with gay and lesbian students and families, and of the prerequisites for making an environment safer for all students and families, regardless of their own perspectives on homosexuality (Middleton 1997). Comparatively, the level of commitment and methods espoused by the preservice teachers to make their classroom environments safe differed. Some preservice teachers only felt comfortable stopping physical harassment and name-calling, while others felt comfortable enough to discuss the topic and include gay and lesbian people as role models. Recognizing their responsibility and accountability for student safety was critical in helping this group of preservice teachers absorb, rather than deflect, the message from this panel. One preservice teacher stated, "Now that I know, I am accountable."

The authenticity of the panel created another level of awareness and amplified the need for safety and engagement to ensure their message would be heard. The panel's participants told personal stories of coming out, being harassed in hallways and classrooms while teachers did nothing, and being rejected or accepted by peers, family members, and teachers. In comparison, Pastor frequently interspersed his sermons with personal stories and anecdotes of his failures and triumphs. The personal authenticity helped us realize that we all had many experiences and beliefs in common, and that none of us lacks the ability to make change in our present beliefs and behaviors if we desire to do so. This level of authenticity and a non-threatening approach allowed us to stay tuned-in or become tuned in even after some initial discomfort. Being tuned-in provided the opportunity for conscious and purposeful assessment of the message in order to incorporate the knowledge into our belief systems and our interactions.

"The Benediction"

In summary, approaching individuals in a respectful, empowering, and relevant way encourages listening, hearing, and responding to messages that otherwise might be tuned out. In reflecting upon my religious experience as well as my initial queries as to how preservice teachers perceive me and the course content, I realize that I must not be perceived as a "preacher of diversity doctrine," condemning those with belief systems differing from mine, but as a messenger delivering content while allowing time and space for dissonance and attitude adjustment toward a broader worldview. I must also remember that ideological change takes time, and that my interaction with preservice teachers often comes at the beginning of the process. However, in the time I am with my students, I can offer them a message on diversity that is delivered in a non-threatening and authentic way that takes into account their assessment needs while keeping them accountable.

The suggestions for "reaching the congregation" include but are not limited to: (a) approaching multicultural content as a positive and necessary component of the curriculum; (b) providing qualified instructors; (c) providing authentic diversity experiences; (d) assessing and addressing students' current levels of comfort and understanding of self and diverse others; (e) providing opportunities for self-reflection and dialogue regarding the strategies, rewards, and difficulties of teaching diversity; and (f) holding teachers accountable for pluralistic attitudes and behaviors. Guidelines such as these can help students realize what this preservice teacher acknowledged: "I learned tons from this class. I'm sure I will take it into the classroom with me. It was very beneficial to me both as a future teacher and for my own personal growth."

References

Allport, Gordon W. 1935. Attitudes. In *Handbook of social psychology*, edited by C. Murchison. Worchester, MA: Clark University Press.

Allport, Gordon. 1979. *ABC's of scapegoating*. New York: Anti-Defamation League of B'Nai B'rith.

Bennett, Christine I. 1995. *Comprehensive multicultural education: Theory and practice*. Needham Heights, MA: Allyn and Bacon.

Campbell, Duane, and Delores Delgado Campbell. 1999. *Choosing democracy: A practical guide to multicultural education*. Upper Saddle River, NJ: Prentice Hall.

Condit, Celeste M. 1996. Theory, practice, and the battered (woman) teacher. In *Teaching what you're not: Identity politics in higher education*, edited by Katherine J. Mayberry. New York: New York University Press.

Davidman, Leonard, and Patricia T. Davidman. 1994. *Teaching with a multicultural perspective: A practical guide*. New York: Longman.

Festinger, Leon. 1957. A *theory of cognitive dissonance*. Stanford, CA: Stanford University Press.

Gibson, P. 1989. Gay male and lesbian youth suicide. In *Report of the Secretary's Task Force on Youth Suicide*, edited by M. Feinleib. Vol. 3. Washington, DC: U.S. Department of Health and Human Services.

Manning, M. Lee, and Leroy G. Baruth. 1996. *Multicultural education of children and adolescents*. Needham Heights, MA: Allyn and Bacon.

McIntosh, Peggy. 1988. *White privilege and male privilege: A personal account of coming to see correspondences through work in women's studies*. Wellesley, MA: Wellesley College Massachusetts Center for Research on Women. (ERIC Document Reproduction Service No. ED 335 262)

Middleton, Val. 1997. *Preservice teachers: Beliefs about diversity and multicultural commitment.* Unpublished doctoral dissertation, Colorado State University, Fort Collins.

Pate, Glenn S. 1982, November. *The ingredients of prejudice.* Paper presented at the College and University Faculty Assembly of the National Council for the Social Studies, Boston.

Using Dialogue Discussion Groups When Addressing Sensitive Topics

Mona C. S. Schatz

Introduction

At the university, many of us feel an imperative to be alert to issues involving diversity. We are expected to pursue our work without prejudice or bias. Steinberg (1999, xiii) suggests, however, that in addition we also must think in more systemic terms, that the "mandate for social inquiry...is that ethnic patterns should not be taken at face value, but must be related to the larger social matrix in which they are embedded." Some encourage caution that in an era of "political correctness," we should avoid analyses that examine social and cultural difference[1]. Yet, universities must promote rigorous inquiry. We can offer a diverse array of courses that require critical thinking so as to produce our society's leaders and innovators.

As a way to understand diversity as a construct in American society, I embrace Fuchs' (1990) description of a "civic culture" and "voluntary pluralism in America." He suggests that voluntary pluralism supported immigrant Europeans, giving them the freedom to maintain affection for and loyalty to their ancestral religions and cultures while also claiming an American identity. Further, Fuchs (1990, 5) states that civic culture provided citizens the opportunity to participate in public life, free to differ with each other in areas of religion and other aspects of private life in a civil, non-threatening manner. When these new Americans walked out their door, they cloaked themselves in this aura of civility. This idea became more prominent for me after my 1990s travels to Russia and former USSR countries, as I witnessed the resurgence of old ethnic disputes/ conflicts/prejudices. Re-reading Fuchs during these years helped me consider what is actually different in the social structuring of cultural groups in the United States. Fuchs' civic cultural model is the foundation of my thinking. I have come to believe that one of my responsibilities as an educator is to motivate students to engage in sensitive dialogue within this civic culture.

Educators worry about how far to push students in discussions that explore sensitive issues. For example, students may not select those courses where they are asked to work "too hard" or "pushed" in ways that are not comfortable. From the faculty member's perspective, classes must not be a negative experience, as class evaluations are generally a portion of the measure of a teacher's effectiveness. There are many times when an instructor is rated poorly on standard class evaluations if his or her ideas are "too radical" or "too different." Students may indicate that a professor is "rude" or "unwilling to listen" to others' ideas when students view the faculty as smart and culturally different. From some of my colleagues, I have learned that these comments often are directed toward professors who are culturally or ethnically different from the students.

The question must be posed, however: Are academic institutions succeeding at teaching critical thinking skills if students do not "dip into murky waters?" Topics such as oppression, political disenfranchisement, and discrimination are outcomes of economic, social, and political studies in all types of communities and societies. Course curriculum and class discussions must address sensitive issues of diversity, marginalization, and oppression to prepare students to be effective and, importantly, productive citizens.

A goal of this book is to consider how educators approach their teaching in these sensitive areas. A part of this goal is to examine how our teaching approaches and strategies influence our successes or failures in exploring issues of diversity, marginalization, and oppression. In this chapter, I discuss aspects of my teaching framework as they relate to areas of cultural and spiritual diversity—dimensions that can be examined through explorations of ethnicity, race, gender, age, ability, and sexual orientation as well as spiritual and religious perspectives and practices. This chapter has been challenging for me, in part because "my personal is my professional." This is a typical quote among feminists, who came of age in the 60s and 70s. I am unable to offer any prescription to readers if I am unable to introduce my own context, struggles, and accomplishments. I am required, therefore, to place this discussion into some context.

Contexts: Current and Personal

Events of the recent past contribute to why I now am writing about my experience of being stalked and harassed. I see relationships between my personal context and a more global context as I try to make sense of my own experience.

A Current Context

In the 2000 national election, Joe Lieberman was nominated to the Democratic ticket. He is a practicing Jew, meaning that he adheres to a wide range of religious laws in his daily life. Lieberman became a national figure, signaling an opening for Jewish people in the national dialogue—a positive sign for growing cultural inclusion.

Then, the bombing of the World Trade Center in New York happened on September 11, 2001,. Americans witnessed a tragedy of such major proportions that our sense of well-being was shattered. The terrorist attacks of September 11th did challenge our very existence. But they also forced us to listen to how others on the globe view us—others who suggest that our way of life is damaging to their very existence and that our support of Israel is wrong. Painful as that may be to hear, it suggests that, at least on the surface, Americans might be at a point in time when we can accept and try to understand people whose lives and perceptions are very different from ours.

Unless pushed, Americans rarely spend time learning about smaller, often marginal cultural groups. Today, however, there seems to be a new interest among Americans to better understand Muslim people, as well as Arab peoples generally—their religious views, their social structure, and their growing influence on American life. Universities are among the best institutions to provide this cultural education. Universities also are well placed to help different communities relate to each other more harmoniously.

Personal Context

I myself am an educator in the field of social work and social welfare. I have been in academia since 1981. I identify as a Jew and maintain a Jewish home life. However, my spiritual and religious education is broader than Judaism. I have had teachers with very different religious and spiritual traditions. I have also taught myself. I walk around the university without any apparent outward manifestation of my cultural identification. Yet, whether teaching, doing research, or providing service, it's clear to me that what I call my "cultural or ethnic landscape"—Judaism—continues to influence my daily life.

I often talk with colleagues and students about the varied landscapes we all have. In that sense, my cultural/ethnic landscape is apparent, as is my "gender landscape" and my "professional landscape." To those landscapes, I also add my landscape as "mother." As are most others, my own context is, therefore, multidimensional. Beginning with my undergraduate work, my education contained a great many courses that examined ethnicity. Throughout work on all my academic degrees, I have kept a clear focus on multiculturalism. My years working with families and children kept me involved with a broad range of ethnically and culturally diverse people as well as those differences that reflected family make-up, such as families headed by single parents, blended families, and multigenerational families. A central question I ask about every family or individual is, "What is unique here?" It is my contention that uniqueness provides an important sense of individuation.

Mentors Teach More Than They Are Aware Of

Whether I have ever met them or not, my mentors have been very important to me. They include Gisela Konopka (1966, 1988) for her important work on girls. Carlos Castaneda (1968, 1971), storyteller and teacher of Yaqui spiritual ways, opened my mind to new ways of viewing both the physical and non-physical worlds. Castaneda also helped me understand another way of walking and thinking in the world. In the 1960s and 1970s, political leaders such as John Kennedy and Martin Luther King, Jr., were icons of cultural and social transition for me—their dreams became my ambitions.

In my early days as a worker in a youth work agency, I had the privilege to study with Gisela Konopka and her project team at the University of Minnesota, where she studied ways to teach youth workers how to better meet the needs of young people. Dr. Konopka is short in stature but large in presence. Her foreign accent cloaked her English just enough so that you knew she did not begin her life in America. Her approach stressed the importance of working collaboratively with other, more traditional social agencies. Listening to her descriptions of girls' problems and youth problems in general, I remember I asked her whether I would ever have the deep compassion she had. I wondered if her experience in the Nazi camps helped her to feel for others as deeply as she did. She said to me that she hoped no one would have to ever again experience the levels of humiliation and human degradation she had lived through. Today, I realize more fully that my question to her reflected my beginning awareness of the many social transitions that were occurring in our own society as I was entering adulthood. Somewhere in that question was my concern for whether I could handle all these changes.

I was then working in a new program designed to help girls who were at risk of delinquency or developmental problems. Working with girls and women during the 1970s reinforced my political efforts for women. I could see how feminist writings influenced feminist social and political events in such a way that social programs for women and girls benefitted as well.

I decided I would become a social worker and someday teach social work to others. I wanted to spend my life helping others. I completed my undergraduate studies, then my master's education and then my doctorate. I continued to work while I pursued my formal education. I even spent a few years working in youth programming at a national level. Throughout those years, I retained my high regard for Konopka. It was during my first teaching post, after completing doctoral course work, that I decided to invite her to the university where I had accepted a teaching position. The school was in the Ozarks region of the United States. I taught social work classes in child welfare, social work with women, and general social work practice. I wanted these social work students to meet and experience this very special social worker!

Her visit had a mixed outcome. On the one hand, I was able to achieve some of what I had hoped for—namely, having students meet this extraordinary person, this important social work practitioner and educator. She had many stories and insights about working creatively and compassionately with youth in institutional settings. Her deep commitment to those who are oppressed or violated comes across powerfully in her talks, which combine her personal experiences of vulnerability with the experiences of her clients.

However, because of the publicity that surrounded Dr. Konopka coming to speak, my family and I became a target for hatred. One of the employees at the university where I was working began coming to my classes and expounding his anti-Semitic attitudes and beliefs. Over a period of several months, both before and after Konopka's visit, this person wrote hateful letters to me about Jews, referring to the unfinished work of the Nazis. He also included in these letters his views on feminist writers and Christianity. He physically threatened me on several occasions. Eventually, my husband drove me to the door of my office building each day so that this stalker could not follow me from the parking lot or corner me outside my office building when there might not be anyone else around. This man was never formally enrolled in any of my classes. His job at that university was to deliver audio-visual equipment when requested by an instructor. When he came to run the equipment for my classes, he often came early, clutching textbooks and articles written by leftist feminists and Christians. He would then insist on proving to me how erroneous these authors were, how their writings were not Christian. This was very disruptive for my classes. Students became very concerned for my safety as well.

Though I had lived as a Jew in predominantly Christian communities throughout my life, I now felt singled out. I was scared and my husband was outraged. He is not Jewish. Not having any strong cultural connection made this entire experience confusing. Mostly, he was angry at someone attacking his family. He had no understanding of why anyone would be anti-Semitic and hateful. When more letters arrived at our home, my husband hid them from me. He took each one to the university police. Since I also was pregnant at the time, he became especially vigilant and protective of me.

I (more truthfully, we) asked for protection from the university police. In our several meetings with police officers, we were very discouraged. We were told that little could be done by the university in this situation. We also were told that we could file a complaint with the local city police force. We then were told that a complaint of this nature would probably not achieve our desired end, and might actually open the door to heightened threats and escalated retaliation. We were horrified at the lack of support by the university. We were equally angered when confronted with the reality that the legal system would not be a solution but rather a stopgap measure at best. As I recount this situation, I think it was resolved in three or four months, in part because the university police did question this man and indicate to him that he could not continue to deliver equipment to my classes. I learned later that year that this man did go on to harass another female faculty member and actually caused damage to her home. I began looking that winter for a new teaching position. I left that summer.

Taking Time to Heal and Teach about Religious Freedom(s)

I tell this story not to garner sympathy or shock. Rather, I have come to realize that this experience pushed me into a period of silence about it. When I took my new position at Colorado State University, I decided I would not talk about this experience to anyone. My fear overtly played out as anxiety and spilled out into my teaching. This is a common effect in response to oppression. Trauma survivors often use silence as a coping mechanism, though that may appear maladaptive to some. In addition, I chose not to teach in areas that might have been construed as politically left of center. Assaults on either side of the spectrum seemed potentially dangerous. I stayed in "middle-of-the road" territory, even when addressing issues of prejudice and oppression.

I found it interesting that at my new university post, all faculty were required to attend a short training session on the new policies and procedures regarding sexual harassment. I never shared my own "fresh" experience, even though I wanted to lash out at the trainers for suggesting that the university would actually "protect" people—students or faculty—who were sexually harassed!

The 1980s and 1990s were years in which colleges and universities throughout the country were creating faculty development programs to help their instructors bring diversity into their classrooms. At Colorado State University, the College of Applied Human Sciences received a grant from the U.S. Department of Agriculture to support faculty development in multicultural education. Faculty were asked to consider bringing into their courses the perspectives of non-majority scholars in their fields. For example, in textile courses, faculty worked to introduce content identifying the contributions of African American designers.

Having an extensive academic background in ethnicity and cultural difference allowed me to navigate these development programs well enough. But I also knew I had to retrieve the silent parts of my self in order to create an atmosphere that encouraged deeper learning about diversity and difference. My experience of being harassed and stalked had left me angry and scared. In retrospect, I can see it was nearly impossible for me to foster effective discussions on these issues since I was harboring this kind of emotional baggage.

A New Entry Point into Diversity Work

My experience of being stalked is almost twenty years behind me. I now have had many opportunities to re-find myself, reclaim my sense of comfort, and heal. Among the ways I used to move through and beyond this frightening experience were reading and workshops that used multicultural perspectives. At times, I also began to talk about my experiences. This book project has been one of the "places" where colleagues listened and supported me. Though slowly at first, I also began to focus more class work on areas of socially sensitive topics and multiculturalism. Social work education requires significant focus on multiculturalism, whether working individually, in groups, with families, or in communities.

One aspect of my own process of reclaiming that became clearer for me was how important it was to build safety for students and myself when teaching in these arenas. Perhaps the best experience I created for my "coming out of fear" involved a training contract for a project in which I facilitated discussions about religion in foster care homes. A colleague and I designed the program and wrote the accompanying training manual (Schatz and Horesji 1996). We wanted to improve the placement process and case monitoring for foster children and their families. This training allowed for in-depth discussions with groups of ten to twenty participants. It examined how the religious background of the foster home might influence the identity of the foster child and challenge the emotional connections with his or her birth family, personal history, and culture. In the training, we also hoped to increase participants' awareness of differences in their religious beliefs and spirituality. At core, we wanted participants to consider what they could and could not tolerate about religious behavior in their own homes. We also wanted participants to consider how a foster child, who had one set of spiritual beliefs and practices in his or her home of origin, might feel entering a home with different traditions. We wanted to model clear and honest communication so that foster parents and caseworkers could openly discuss these issues of religious and spiritual beliefs and practices.

This program took me to every nook and cranny of Colorado, and eventually to other states and other countries. I was talking to primarily Christian audiences, fostering very interesting discussions and, I think, getting very positive results. I learned, for example, that talking about religion in foster care is not much different than talking about sex with young teens! It's not easy! Everyone's nervous! I also learned that these audiences were neither adequately prepared nor equipped with the language necessary to effectively discuss these issues.

Being non-Christian actually afforded me a level of objectivity and detachment. Everyone in attendance seemed to have issues that posed real challenges. I felt it appropriate to identify myself as a Jew early in the training experience so that participants did not have to wonder. Over and over, participants told me that I fostered a safe environment for the process to unfold. I also was able to facilitate honest and at times emotional discussions about very personal matters. I was able to move the process along without anyone feeling threatened or intimidated. One of the outcomes of these programs was a new sense of "okay-ness" among foster parents about the choices they made about their religious life as foster families.

Importantly, I was not facilitating this program in order to determine which Christian religion was "better," "best," or "worst."

Nor were these experiences organized with a set of "right" answers. I was, however, asking the participants to consider how a non-biologically-related child or teen, in a temporary custody situation, might feel when immersed into their religious culture. Should their religiously oriented home be considered a cultural experience? Equally important, were there civil rights issues embedded in this situation? Or were there simply issues of basic human decency and dignity? The stakes could have been high for these participants. I learned that most, if not all, of these foster parents had never talked with anyone about their religious or spiritual practices prior to entering foster care work, nor had they addressed these issues since working with children in their own homes[2].

My own spiritual journey through many of these orientations supported me as I designed and conducted training workshops. In addition to my own Jewish background, I also had studied Hindu practices, Buddhist meditation techniques, Christianity, Sufi, and New Age literature along with various eco-spiritual ideas. I found that I was again able to risk identifying myself publicly with labels such as Jew, feminist, mother, social worker, and teacher. I also undertook a research study in this area (Schatz 1996) and agreed to discuss how learning about the Holocaust and its survivors can help others better understand the importance of efforts that contribute to global peace (Schatz 1998). I presented findings from my research in social welfare classes, in part because these issues of cultural and religious identity have significant impact on social policies and civil rights.

Principles Central to Teaching Topics of Diversity and Sensitive Social Areas

There are several key principles that guide my teaching when examining topics of diversity and sensitive social areas. These principles are based primarily in adult learning strategies (see Knowles 1989 and Knox 1986) and principles of reflection in action (see Brubacher, Case, and Reagan 1994). Each of these principles is addressed briefly below.

Getting Students Prepared for and Involved in Their Learning

Students in the university classroom must be prepared for the issues that impact our own communities as well as those elsewhere on the globe. I continue to believe that getting students prepared for and involved in their own learning is essential for effective central learning experiences. Being available to students, including outside the classroom, is equally important. Understanding that everyone learns differently, I hold a deep appreciation for individual learning processes and expectations.

I teach adult learners at the university and in the community. I usually try to start *where the learner is*. Five pillars represent my teaching philosophy here:

1. Cultural lenses (i.e., the windows that we look through) exist in all learning situations—i.e., there are particular lenses for the learners, the broader community, and the university.

2. I try to blend research-based material with prevailing ideas, thereby sharpening the experience for students and giving them an "edge" in critical and creative thinking and doing.

3. I try to include innovative tools that aid students in demonstrating their competence—tools that go beyond traditional pencil-and-paper testing methods.

4. For me, teaching is also a process of sharing that requires me to explain my own connections to course content.

5. Teaching means I am simultaneously a learner, a facilitator, a creator, a de-evolver, and, at times, a mentor to my students.

Culture and Learning

Learning is influenced by culture; learning generally reinforces cultural identity and cultural development. When I teach adults in other parts of the globe, I have to ask about how they were taught in their formal institutions. I often ask, "What was valued in your educational process?"

Beyond a dominant cultural learning model that exists, every university has its own cultural environment for learning. In social work, there is also a set of cultural "maps." Faculty must gain experience in multicultural environments in order to bring effective diversity discussions into the classroom. Some of my own work in multicultural education came through a special university project and with my own research (such topics as Holocaust survivors, sexual trafficking, and religion in foster care). I feel fortunate because other members often say their fields do not have much information on cultural diversity. In the sciences and mathematics there may not appear to be much that requires a multicultural perspective. Yet, I also am aware of how often we minimize cultural experiences, particularly in schools and colleges. I'm convinced that faculty and researchers in every discipline must be willing to examine their specific areas in search of diversity issues.

Dialogue

One of the specific tools I use in the classroom is the dialogue model (see Schatz, Jenkins, and Furman in press). Dialogue through group discussion offers opportunities for transformative experiences and valuable networking, both professionally and personally, when used in the classroom or at multicultural conferences. Dialogue has been referred to as an experience of shared exploration toward greater understanding, connection, or possibility (Co-Intelligence Institute 2001). When engaged in true dialogue, the main objective is to move toward greater understanding and the sharing of meaning. Dialogue does not seek any tangible outcome. Most importantly, ideas, beliefs, and attitudes are not seen as inherently right or wrong. Dialogue groups are used to create a sense of community and wholeness. Bohm and Nichol (1996) and others (Krishnamurti and Bohm 1986) believe that if a process is created that leads to the development of true understanding of meaning, people will be transformed. The processes of dialogue groups can move members away from competitive ways of being in social interactions and toward more egalitarian and caring relationships (Schatz et al. in press).

When introducing a learning area that will examine multiculturalism and other sensitive topics, I begin by discussing how I define "learning" at the university and in social work specifically, how I intend to bring both the profession's and the university's values and principles into the classroom. I ask students to listen for and examine different perspectives. I may ask students to read texts and articles written by authors of diverse backgrounds. The dialogue process I use is summarized in Figure 1. Let me review some of the central points of this model.

Contracting with Students in the Learning Environment

Contracting with students is one way to share the learning experience and flatten the academic hierarchy somewhat. A written contract is not necessary, yet working out the needs students have may require some brainstorming. Some consensus-seeking process is important, and restating agreements made is vital. Often, when I ask students to build a contract—a conscious agreement for the

---

Guidelines to Consider when Developing Dialogue and Group Discussions for Sensitive Topic Areas

1. Contract for and work to establish an atmosphere of trust, respect, and safety.

2. Model what you expect.

3. Use varied learning approaches, particularly approaches that enhance student participation, as well as, their ability to express difficult opinions, ideas, and questions.

4. Promote student abilities to support other class members, validating and respectfully questioning each other.

5. When a class has been discussing a sensitive topic, watch the time so that there can be a 5-10 minute closure process. This allows the teacher/facilitator time to tie together what has occurred.

Figure 1. Dialogue guidelines.

learning in this class—they will stare at me, befuddled. I have to start with some basic suggestions such as "we will all respect each other's opinions" and "everyone must listen respectfully." Once I help students see that we are creating a safe learning environment with this kind of contracting process, they start to introduce ideas that are important to them.

Building a contract for the learning process allows students to examine related implications. Sometimes a particular idea may be vague or unworkable in a discussion process. For example, a student may ask that no role-play exercises be used as part of class. Though this suggestion may reflect an individual student's concern, it also may set an unreasonable limitation on instruction. In response, I can validate this person's wish not to participate, yet allow others to do so. Contracting helps to clarify these kinds of ground rules.

Contracting is a beginning point for the learning experience. Getting students more comfortable using dialogue and discussion as a mode for learning in sensitive areas requires some practice. The instructor must develop class dialogue exercises that allow students to build their competence over time. A beginning exercise might ask students to read the first paragraph of the U.S. Constitution and imagine how people who are among the newest immigrants to the United States would understand that paragraph, or how that paragraph would be understood by death-row prisoners.

Comfort in discussions that examine sensitive topics and issues develops over time for any group. If a class or group is not addressing sensitive topics, we should temper our expectations as instructors. To help enhance the quality of sensitive dialogue, we can discuss terms such as opinions and biases, facts and knowledge, moral standards and norms, etc.— terms that address the difficult terrain traveled when talking about sensitive topics. Serving as facilitator of this dialogue group process, the instructor also must take a lead role for managing the contract once it has been agreed upon. This requires checking in with students often about how the process is going and whether any adjustments are needed.

Modeling What We Expect

Modeling what we expect seems self-explanatory. It really is not. Modeling appreciation for the contributions of another person may not be something that an instructor is used to doing. Saying "thank you for sharing your own ideas and experiences" indicates to students a sense of your genuine regard. Every teacher has his or her own impulses or emotional responses when topics are difficult. I myself have said, "What you have described is very interesting—information I was not aware of before."

Modeling appropriate self-disclosure also is part of modeling what you expect. If instructors are uncomfortable talking about their experiences with discrimination, it is less likely that students will be willing to talk about their own experiences. We can help students by disclosing our own discomforts, ambivalences, and concerns when talking about sensitive topic areas. At times, we may also want to shift to a different course by introducing a personal bias, something we believe and prefer but for which we have no factual justification. Bias is part of how we all operate. An instructor could introduce personal bias by using a phrase such as, "I know my bias will be evident as I say ...." This models how another member of the discussion group also can contribute ideas even if he or she has not researched the issue. Most important to promoting successful group discussions is to be consistent and inclusive in supporting and validating group members. Students like to know that their ideas are valued; students also want to know that they are valued as individuals. This may be the most important role for any instructor.

Using Varied Learning Approaches and Strategies

Using varied learning strategies such as dyads and triads also can help students build confidence as discussants. Short video or movie clips or news stories can be useful as jumping-off points. They can portray some issues quickly and allow students to engage fully in a topic that may be difficult to introduce otherwise. By using case studies—for example, a depiction of someone who is harassed in the workplace—you can externalize a sensitive topic and provide a useful concrete context.

Promote Students along the Way

To promote full participation from students, you can also employ other strategies. You can have the group take short breaks in order to summarize the learning that has occurred and identify the range of expressions that have surfaced. In the process of recapping, you can seize the opportunity to acknowledge any emotional content that was expressed. You can also congratulate each class member for his or her part. As the discussion process unfolds, I have also found it essential to acknowledge the support that group members are giving to each other. In this way, I can work toward a shared group management of the learning process.

Bringing Closure to the Learning

Groups have a beginning, a middle, and an end. Managing the end process is as important as the other two. The last part of the discussion provides an opportunity for final summarization of key learnings that have emerged. During the last five to ten minutes of the group's time, it can also be helpful to ask if anyone has emotional "rumblings." For example, during a discussion around the need for gay and lesbian bars, one of my students became very angry about this kind of segregation. During the ending time period, the group returned to this issue and the emotional response in order to provide some reflection for all the group members. In the ending stage, there also may be a need to restate the importance of retaining confidentiality about any self-disclosure that occurred. If discussion runs right up to the end of class, there is a risk that some students may still have strong feelings, hurts, or concerns that require attention.

Final Thoughts

Providing some of my own story in the early part of this chapter was my way of illustrating how important *context* is to education, especially for this new millennium. Assuming we all think alike and experience our environment alike is naïve. Our schools, colleges, and universities need to loosen their grip on traditional pedagogical approaches. We cannot just "force feed" learners. As I re-read Knowles' (1989) early principles on adult teaching, I am sure that he, too, is one of my longtime mentors. We must also require adult learners to engage in discussions that go beyond polite and trite expression. Using a dialogue discussion approach has been very effective in my own teaching at the university and in various public programs.

Ultimately, I believe that effective citizenry requires effective teaching on our part. Moreover, none of us stops learning when we graduate. How we learn *with* others and how we value the ideas and opinions of others are critical to American society and all those societies that embrace democracy.

Notes

1. Recently, after a student's presentation, I asked the student why she had not taken a more directive point of view on the topic of her study. She responded that "it was not good to be opinionated in public."

2. I did learn that if a foster parent became too forceful around religious issues in his or her home, more than likely that home would be "black-balled" from future foster child placements. This approach supports a kind of oppressive authority that institutions can exact when there is no oversight in matters of this kind.

References

Bohm, David, and Lee Nichol. 1986. *On dialogue*. New York. Routledge.

Brubacher, John W., Charles W. Case, Timothy G. Reagan. 1994. *Becoming a reflective educator: How to build a culture of inquiry in the schools*. Thousand Oaks, CA: Corwin Press/Sage.

Castaneda, Carlos. 1971. A *separate reality: Further conversations with Don Juan*. New York: Simon and Schuster.

Castaneda, Carlos. 1968. *The teachings of Don Juan: A Yaqui way of knowledge*. New York: Pocket Books/Simon and Schuster.

Co-Intelligence Institute. 2001. *Dialogue*. Taken from the World Wide Web on February 27, 2000. http://www.co-intelligence.org/P-dialogue.html.

Fuchs, Laurence H. 1990. *The American kaleidoscope: Race, ethnicity, and the civic culture*. Hanover, NH: The University Press of New England.

Knowles, Malcomb. 1989. *The making of an adult educator: An autobiographical journey*. San Francisco: Jossey-Bass, Publishers.

Knox, Alan B. 1986. *Helping adults learn*. San Francisco: Jossey-Bass.

Konopka, Gisela. 1988. *Courage and love*. Edina, MN: Burgess Printing Press.

Konopka, Gisela. 1966. *Adolescent girls in conflict*. Upper Saddle River, NJ: Prentice Hall.

Krishnamurti, Jiddu, and David Bohm. 1986. *The future of humanity: A conversation*. San Francisco: Harper and Row.

Schatz, Mona S., Lowell E. Jenkins, and Rice Furman. In press. Space to grow: Dialogue for multicultural/ multinational learning. *International Journal of Social Work.*

Schatz, Mona S., and Charles Horejsi. 1996. The importance of religious tolerance: A Module for Educating Foster Parents. *Child Welfare* LXXV(1):73-86.

Schatz, Mona S. 1997; 1987. Teaching adults to learn: Andragogy versus Pedagogy. In *Teaching Resources Manual* edited by F. Vattano. Ft. Collins, CO: Colorado State University Office of Instructional Services.

Schatz, Mona S. 1998. How does teaching about the holocaust create opportunities for building understanding about the importance of global peace? Second Annual Social Work Conference, Advancing Diversity through Human Rights, Colorado State University.

Schatz, Mona S., and Charles Horejsi. 1996. From moral development to healthy relationships: The role of religion in out-of-home placement. Presented at the 24th Annual Child Abuse and Neglect Symposium, Keystone, CO.

Steinberg, Stephan. 1989. *The ethnic myth: Race, ethnicity, and class in America*. Boston: Beacon.

Majority as Minority: Transferring Lessons Learned from Teaching K-12 Inner-City Students to the University

Suzanne Tochterman

Introduction

Before I came to CSU, I spent ten years teaching in the inner-city neighborhoods of Washington, DC. A white woman in my twenties, I devoted myself to helping kids whom the district had deemed most challenging. I worked in classrooms filled with juvenile offenders and children who had been labeled as emotionally disturbed, conduct disordered, or behaviorally challenged. These students ranged in age from four to fifteen years. Most were illiterate, most were poor; most had experienced many years of academic setback and struggle. Many had never before known a White person.

The schools in which I worked were overcrowded, and support services were limited. Supplies were short, standards were low, and accountability of student achievement was abysmal. Conditions were basically deplorable. One school was infested with roaches. Another was filled with the stench of backed-up toilets. In another, I had to borrow coats and mittens from my friends to warm students using a classroom in which the windows had been broken out. Violence, both on school grounds and in the surrounding neighborhoods, was common; we were frequently warned over the P.A. system not to go outside because of gang activity. Most of the students knew someone who had been shot. Survival, not excelling in school, was the priority. In this milieu, I often wondered if I could make the slightest difference.

I now realize that I was a student in the DC system myself. The students with whom I worked taught me far more than I ever can measure. They taught me life lessons about ethnicity, identity, privilege, power, and culture. My experience working with the neediest students in some of the most impoverished schools in our nation's capitol also taught me a great deal about what it's like to be a majority-race person in a minority status. Never before had I questioned my status so critically.

I now am teaching at the college level, helping prepare future public school teachers. Thus far, my charge has included courses on instructional methods, standards, assessment, foundations, classroom environment and management, and diversity and communication. The beginning of my career in academia finds me in a large, predominantly White, middle-class, land-grant institution in the western United States.

On my first day as a university instructor, I looked out at my students and saw a sea of white. I panicked; what could I have to offer these students? How could I share my teaching experience so that it would relate to their lives here? How would I begin to make that connection for them?

Fortunately, it did not take me very long to realize that many of the lessons I had learned in DC were transferable to my new environment. And whereas at first I had assumed that a background filled with homogeneous white classes would have better prepared me for my new career, upon further reflection I decided that my decade in the District of Columbia had afforded me an invaluable perspective for diversity content teaching.

This will be a personal piece. The stories of my work with inner-city students will interweave with the more recent stories of my engagement at the University. This will be both vignette and commentary, both reflection and analysis. It will illustrate the lessons I have learned from my past, how I apply them today, and how I hope to pass them on to the future through my students.

Programs Are People Committed to Constructive Change

I will never forget my very first week of working in the Washington, DC school system. Each teacher in our building was required, every morning, to sign a logbook in the main office. I remember going into the office those first few days: Smiling, I would greet the staff, my face beaming with anticipation and excitement. The women behind their desks would snicker and keep their eyes on their paperwork. The principal—a stately, commandeering woman who had been in charge of the building since the 1960s—would peer over her reading glasses and stare at me unblinkingly.

One day, after a few weeks of this same routine, the principal followed me out of the office. She called my name and I turned. She lowered her glasses to the bridge of her nose and said, "Miss Tochterman, why is it that you come in here every morning with a big grin on your face, as though you are the happiest person on Earth to be working in a place such as this? Why are you here? Are you a reporter for *Time* magazine or something?" She seemed to be telling me I did not belong there. She was telling me she did not trust my desire to work in her building. She was warning me.

On another occasion, I was working as an administrative intern at a school in Prince Georges County, Maryland. Over the summer, the principal of eight years had been replaced. Although I had predicted some change, I could not have anticipated the intensity of the upheaval. Although the new principal had worked in the system for some time, she was new to this staff. Undoubtedly this increased the opposition she met when she began to make much-needed changes. These changes began with a reform of the crisis support system.

In the then-current system, children deemed too unruly for class were locked in isolation closets, sometimes for hours on end. There were days when the majority of the middle-school children spent time in such closets. When the decision came down that such measures should no longer be taken, teachers resisted, staff resisted, social workers resisted; and during the holiday break, the new principal was quietly relocated and replaced.

I was devastated. The staff returned to their old ways and the children returned to theirs. If a program's accomplishments are reflective of the people who endeavor to implement it, how was this reversion to a failed system reflecting upon us? Systems that are neither dynamic nor reflective run the risk of not meeting their students' needs; here I was facing a dramatic manifestation of this fact.

Attitudinal Set and Perceptual Style

One of my very first students, Shakita, was a fixture in my classes for three years. Being young and inexperienced, I naively assumed that she could readily learn to love school. I assumed she would soon value learning and believe deeply in the power of education. But I soon found out that this little twelve-year-old had spent the majority of her school days doing anything she could do to avoid going to school at all: She stole, she hid, she ran away, she hit her mother, she ran drugs for young men, she played watchdog at a local crack house. Probably the last thing on her mind was schoolwork. Despite all this, or perhaps because of it, I made it a goal to see this child fall in love with school. And she did. With a relevant curriculum, a strong interpersonal connection, a commitment based on trust, and a *lot* of hard work, Shakita made strides in every area of study.

At the very outset, it had become evident to both me and Shakita that we had very different value sets. To me, knowledge of the importance of an education seemed like instinct, the belief that schooling opens doors a simple fact of life. And after such an experience as mine and Shakita's, I now feel personally insulted when comparatively privileged college students skip classes, turn in late papers, or don't study for exams. *We must have differing value sets.* But instead of casting blame or shrugging my shoulders, I have found it helpful to explore the value set that governs their actions. Understanding the intricate web that ties together values, thoughts, attitudes, and behaviors is key to a student's construction of reality. And by developing this understanding together, relationships develop—relationships that are critical for any lasting change.

Assumptions

A young student actually asked me once if I knew the president of the United States. I suppose that since I was White and lived in Washington, DC, this somehow seemed plausible. Maybe this student assumed I knew all White people.

More recently, while walking the path to the university student center, I saw Dennis, a man much my senior, who was one of my students in an intensive six-week summer course. I greeted him as he passed, and when he asked me if I had a minute to talk I said "Sure!", thinking, *"What is it that this student wants with me?"*

Dennis began, "I have two daughters—both older than you— and the first day of class I was a little put off. You see, I have been in the business world for many years, and I have run across many young women like yourself—women who have been successful at a young age, women who set the expectation so high that it is unreasonable, women who speak *at* you instead of *with* you. I saw your East Coast suit and your business-like demeanor and I thought: *I should drop this class.*"

He went on: "But I want to tell you that my perception has changed. Over the last six or seven class sessions, I've felt a growing sense of relief. You're not like that at all. Your syllabus is indeed challenging, but your approach is such that I believe we'll all learn a great deal with you. I am truly looking forward to the next four weeks."

I thought about what Dennis said for a long time.

Identity

For several years, I worked as a teacher at an inpatient psychiatric hospital in Washington, DC Many of the young patients there were cared for with Medicare/Medicaid funds. All of the children in the hospital had been considered, upon admission, to be a threat either to themselves or others. Many had been convicted of crimes but were too young to be jailed.

Shevon had been in the hospital for about a month when we had a conversation that still rings clear for me today. I had been leaning over her table, helping her complete an essay on Harriet Tubman, when she just stopped, gently took my face in her hands, and stared into my eyes. "Miss Tochterman," she finally asked, "are you sure you're not Black?"

What I realized was that Shevon had started to trust me. She had started to like me and she wanted to learn from me, but for years she had been conditioned not to trust Whites. In her mind, if I could just be Black she could accept me and she could *relate* to me.

I have never forgotten that look in Shevon's eyes, and I often am reminded of that incident when working in the university. Although the university culture here is not that of the "hood," it does seem to offer some interesting parallels. For example, although I may now find myself a part of the racial majority, I also find myself a part of the gender minority

Our university, like many others, is governed both by a male president and a cabinet consisting mainly of male vice presidents. The director of my own program and the leaders of several degree programs and standing committees are men. Of the full professors in my department, all but one are male. Conversely, of the nearly thirty women in our department, only three have tenure. This is not to say that the administrative hierarchy at all resembles the overt male machismo of the "hood." It is merely to suggest that someday the university system may see past a faculty member's gender to the same degree that Shevon looked at me and saw past my color.

Finding the Child Within

Fourteen-year-old Nikki had been a prostitute for more years than anyone wanted to count. She was physically very well developed, and she dressed in revealing clothes that left little to the imagination. And she was bright. We were at a "Level V" school, the type to which students were transferred after they had exhausted all other public school options. Students like Nikki were sent here to receive the attention allowed by a lower student-to-teacher ratio.

An administrator informed me that Nikki would be joining my classroom of 10-12 year-olds, citing his presumption that "having her in the Upper School with the boys would be just too disruptive." He promised that this arrangement would last only a few weeks, during which he would find an appropriate place for Nikki in the Upper School. As it happily turned out, she stayed four months.

I remember those months quite clearly. Nikki sauntered in the first day, chomping on her gum, stinking of cheap perfume, painted heavily with brightly colored makeup, her hair piled high and heavily sprayed. And here were my eight students, singing songs, drawing pictures of *Old Yeller,* and practicing their spelling assignments. It was an interesting convergence of value sets to be sure.

Within a few weeks Nikki felt more comfortable in our room. She became my assistant of sorts, helping others with their schoolwork. I soon had her reading chapters of *Old Yeller* to the others and they, like I, wondered what we had ever done before without her.

I specifically remember Halloween that year. Having always dressed up for the holiday when I was a child, I encouraged my class to dress up for the school-wide party. I remember gathering costumes from my friends and family for those students who did not have the resources to buy costumes themselves. We carved pumpkins and did all the typical Halloween activities that elementary school children do. We made a haunted house and recited scary poems and just had some plain old fun.

We decided to make an impromptu parade and head down to the Upper School gym for the big school-wide party. We were all laughing together, happy at being lost in this parade. This was a rare moment. I remember unlocking the gym door and seeing that a disco ball had been suspended from the ceiling and the gym had been transformed to a dancehall. As might be imagined, all of the Upper School boys and girls clung to opposite walls. Few were actually dancing and none were wearing costumes.

Now my class entered—the clown, the astronaut, the Cowardly Lion, the vampire, the Hells' Angel wearing his motorcycle helmet, the veterinarian, the pilot, and Martin Luther King, Jr. The younger ones immediately ran to play on the dance floor and the others made a bee-line to the food table.

Before I made it to the bottom of the stairs I felt a hand touching mine. I turned around and saw Nikki. "Miss Tochterman," she said, "would you take me to the bathroom?" (This was a lockdown facility: students always had to be supervised when leaving the main quarters.) "Of course," I said, not reading her face. Once we were in the ladies' room, Nikki started taking off her devils' ears and her red devil costume. She asked me to help her remove the red paint we had put on her face. She took off the tail that was pinned to her shorts. She looked at me and said, "I don't want to dress up."

I helped her from her costume and loaned her my cardigan. I watched as later she danced and talked with the boys, her new maturity and confidence, as well as the kid in her, showing through.

At the university, I still think of Nikki. My students will be at rapt attention, sitting upright, taking notes, preparing questions for discussion, staring forward expressionlessly, taking everything from a safe distance. The seriousness of it all sometimes can be daunting. But I try pushing them to vary their perspectives, to reorder their thinking, and to behave in different ways so they can learn how to express and understand their weaknesses and vulnerabilities.

Navigating New Waters

Navigating new territories requires the instructor to make a dynamic exchange. Recently I had an experience that illustrates this point.

The teacher licensure committee, of which I am a member, received a mandate from the state legislature that we restructure our program. An argument ensued between faculty of opposing camps. Some simply wished to finish the task as quickly as possible and get on with life; others saw fundamental problems with the state's approach and wished to maintain what they saw as the committee's integrity by resisting some of the recommended changes. I searched for my voice in the process and attempted to engage my colleagues in critical examinations of schooling and teachers. I expressed my sense that we were going to need to change our approaches to accommodate the new curriculum, despite the fact that we were not prepared for its implementation.

The program was eventually approved and implemented, and many teachers on the front lines continue to struggle with the impact of the changes. I believe that the essence of our training has suffered, but I continue to encourage everyone to engage in critical reflection on the process so that we may be better prepared in the future. This preparation is a dynamic process that requires dialogue and reflection, and as a junior member of the staff I believe that mobilizing others has been more effective than shouting about my own ideas.

Systems and Codes

While working in the schools of our nation's capital, I learned one thing in particular: It is imperative to know who is in charge. In Washington, DC, most of the African American people with whom I worked focused initially on understanding the hierarchy of a system. Equally important was finding out just where I fit into that school structure. Knowing this helped me avoid a lot of headaches, but figuring it out wasn't always easy.

At the university, I try to help my students think about the unwritten codes of behavior they may encounter when teaching. I ask them to examine systems and what makes them sustainable. Thinking back on my own experiences, I advise students to beware of isolating themselves in their future classrooms. I tell them that a shared vision with others will act as a life preserver when times are tough. I encourage them to plan interdisciplinarily, and I assure them that working with support personnel and curriculum specialists will strengthen them and help their students. It is my experience that shared governance, collective decision making, and joint goal setting promote success in any system.

Teaching can be very isolating, even in a college setting. Much like teachers in the public schools, academics tend to retreat to the confines of their own offices. I have come to think that academics are not used to openly discussing the art and craft of their own teaching. Although I make every effort I can to initiate dialogue with my colleagues, I find that few share what it is that they do in the classroom. Instead, people will tend to talk primarily about policies and procedures. Often, when I share my strategies, I will notice that some seem to see this as threatening. I believe that if we can get others in the department to know us and our work—if we truly have a network of peers—we will feel far more empowered to act individually as well.

Power and Pedagogy in Educating

Lisa Delpit's *Other People's Children: Cultural Conflict in the Classroom* (1996) opened my eyes to my situation in DC In the book, interviews Delpit conducted with Black, White, and Native American teachers indicate significant differences among the groups in classroom pedagogy and discipline. However, they universally reported that their teaching styles were influenced mainly by their own experiences as learners and their sense of relation to their students and the community at large. Delpit discusses this silent dialogue of power and pedagogy, shares teachers' voices across cultures, and sheds light on their different approaches and attitudes.

Meeting Students' Needs

In DC it was not unusual for students with emotional disorders or special needs to go without current textbooks. Many of the students in my class were not only ridiculed for being placed in the Special Ed section, they also received further taunts because they weren't even provided with books. I had no math or reading books for my class, and the social studies texts we used were outdated, worn, and written at a level far beyond what my students could hope to read. So when I heard from a friend that one of the most exclusive private day schools in the area had just discarded hundreds of textbooks to make room for new editions, the news sent me running. I wound up filling my trunk with books (with the help of two police officers who had stopped to check me out, thinking I looked rather suspicious emptying the contents of a dumpster into my car) and returning to my school with the materials my students so desperately needed.

The situation at the university often can seem startlingly similar. Recently, an advisee with whom I was working was denied financial assistance. After the student completed the forms necessary to contest the financial assistance office's decision, the grievance committee supported the student's petition, and so this student has been able to remain enrolled. In another, very different case, a student (I will call him Evan) in one of my courses approached me after class and told me his religious faith led him to decide that he should not read a passage about homosexuality that I had assigned. He explained his belief that in life, one must wear "filters" to guard from that which one finds unhealthy for one's spirit.

I began to search for a course of action that could accommodate both this student and my goals for the class. I supplemented the normal class readings with additional texts that exemplified inclusiveness; I urged these teachers-in-training not to outwardly condemn people's lifestyles; I encouraged them to provide a safe place for their students, one that promoted tolerance.

I cited the high suicide rates among gay students and suggested that by maintaining an attitude of acceptance, my students, in their future roles as teachers, might someday actually save a student's life. I brought in panels of gay students who candidly told their stories and reflected upon the horror of their high school experiences; each could remember teachers who had made a positive difference.

I believe that I too made a difference that semester. On his final evaluation of the course, Evan wrote, "I do not believe in homosexuality—for that my students will have to face their maker. Yet, I want to offer a safe harbor for all in my classroom. That is the key. When students know you care about them they will want to learn. I have learned this from this class. For this, I am grateful."

Standards and Expectations

District of Columbia students are enrolled in first grade at the age of five. The intention is basically to keep them in school as long as possible, seeing as nearly 60 percent of them won't make it past the tenth grade. Students with behavior disorders drop out of school at an even higher rate. This emphasis on retention has helped create a system in which many "teachers" simply let their "students" glide through school, not demanding much of them and consequently not creating any discipline problems for the administration. I witnessed many principals rewarding teachers who had quiet and seemingly well-ordered classrooms. In a system that had become more day care center than school, many of my junior-high-aged students had not been taught to read or write. I continued to believe that it was my responsibility to ensure student learning, and I continued to act on that belief.

Similarly, at the college level, I find that struggling students benefit most when standards and expectations are emphasized and supported, not lowered or ignored.

Brentro, Brokenleg, and Van Bockern (1990) write about empowering students through a focus on values traditionally associated with Native American culture. They stress the importance of communal interdependence and collective learning, whereas so much modern thought deals primarily with independence, individualism, and competition. This Native American approach considers generosity to be one of the greatest of virtues. The authors want school to move from alienation to belonging, from inadequacy to mastery, from egoism to generosity. These values can be the unifying themes for a positive school culture. Reclaiming children and youth is central to what they describe as the "circle of courage." Meeting students where they are and providing environments in which all young people can grow and flourish are my core values.

White Privilege

I now work with students who are training to be teachers. Although the environment on and around campus is predominantly European American, there is considerable ethnic diversity in addition to a great diversity of ages, socio-economic statuses, sexual orientations, political affiliations, and religious beliefs.

I have my students read Peggy McIntosh's (1988) "Unpacking the Invisible Knapsack," which highlights the importance of recognizing the relationship among ethnicity, history, and privilege. I also have them read Nate McCall's (1993) short stories "The Elevator" and "Babies." In my opinion, McCall captures the frustration and angst of people in a minority position.

I also invite students of color into my classrooms as panelists for discussions and questions. My students hear their stories of status and their experiences in high school and college classrooms. (Memorably, one Hispanic panel member told a disconcerting story about a former professor of his who had recommended that he "study with the other Mexicans in the class" if he needed help.)

Spokesperson

Teaching in a predominantly Black environment in DC, I often was asked what White people thought or felt, as if all European Americans had a common experience. I am thus careful not to repeat the mistake by saying or implying that someone can speak for all members of his or her ethnic group.

I recently had a student of Native American decent in my class, and he was talking about life on the reservation. I encouraged him, for the sake of the class, to preface his remarks with the fact that this was *his* story and did not necessarily reflect the experiences of any other Native American.

When introducing new material, I frequently will remind my students of any competing theories, perspectives, interpretations, or ideas. All too often, they may otherwise be inclined to think that there is one final authority on some matter or another.

Closing Thoughts

The lessons I learned teaching in Washington, DC have shaped my perspective as a college professor. Having been part of the minority has helped me examine my place in the majority. There are parallels between my White identity as it affected me in DC, and my junior faculty identity, as it affects me in the university. In both instances, thinking about power or privilege has helped me find my place within the structure. Navigating this path has proven difficult, however; stepping out of my comfort zone has forced me to examine my own values, attitudes, and behaviors. This has led me to consider the influence I have on those with whom I interact, and to realize that my students have taught me at least as much as I have taught them.

Postscript

We learn through practice, study, reflection, and discussion. When we connect with humans through teaching, we also learn. And when we read further about this connection, we uncover additional meaning. For me, separating the concepts of teaching and learning has been most difficult. This is true of teaching young students in the inner city of Washington, DC, and this is true of teaching students in college. As I am driving home from a day at school I often think about the line where teaching begins and learning ends. I have come to the conclusion that neither starts nor ends. As in the process of life itself, these two are connected. I found it very challenging to be a minority person. However, it has also proven to be a source of many lessons and of great growth.

References

Brentro, Larry, Martin Brokenleg, and Steve Van Bockern. 1990. *Reclaiming youth at risk: Our hope for the future.* Bloomington, IN: National Educational Service.

Delpit, Lisa. 1996. *Other people's children: Cultural conflict in the classroom.* New York: New Press.

Gilligan, Carol. 1993. In a different voice. Cambridge, MA: Harvard University Press.

McCall, Nathan. 1993. *Makes me wanna holler.* New York: Doubleday.

McIntosh, Peggy. 1988. Unpacking the invisible knapsack. In *Working Paper 189: White privilege and male privilege: A personal account of coming to see correspondences through work in women's studies.* Wellesley, MA: Wellesley College Center for Research on Women.

E Pluribus Unum:
Teaching Diversity in Rural Colorado

Angela V. Paccione

Introduction

I wasn't eager to travel one hundred miles from Colorado State University to rural Colorado to deliver a graduate-level course. However, the School of Education had made a commitment to deliver the master's degree and secondary principal license to a group of educators in the northeastern corner of the state. As a faculty member in the Educational Leadership program, I was expected volunteer to teach some of the courses. I was involved in discussions to determine precisely *who* would teach *which* courses offered in this distance program.

At some point, it became clear that we would offer a course entitled "Multicultural and Special Populations." As faculty names were being suggested for the diversity course, I worried about the consequences of that decision on one of the most sensitive courses we offer. I was convinced that without the requisite knowledge base in multicultural education and issues of diversity, those teaching these courses could do more harm than good. Since I felt we had an obligation to provide the students in rural Colorado with the equivalent preparation to that they would get on campus, I agreed to take on the travel and extra teaching load to teach the course. Multicultural education is a central focus of my own preparation, teaching, and research.

Preparation

I am a bi-racial woman (half White and half Black) who grew up in the South Bronx, New York. I spent most of my childhood with my mother's family (Black) in the city. During my teen years, we moved north of the city to an environment that was mostly White. It was in this environment that I experienced the rejection often felt by children of mixed races. I was not "Black enough" for one group; I was not "White enough" for another. Since I was an outstanding athlete and student, I managed to preserve my self-esteem and earn a scholarship to Stanford University. I struggled for a long time to make sense of my own ethnic identity. By the time that I began my career as an educator, I was secure in my identity as a bi-racial woman. Being *both* Black *and* White gives me a unique perspective and unique insights into relations between people of differing ethnicities.

As a high school teacher and later as a dean of students, I often was involved in issues of diversity training. I served on advisory committees and generally kept my finger on the pulse of race relations in the second-largest high school in Colorado. Most of my work during this time was based on my own experiences and not on any particular research/knowledge base. When I was enrolled in graduate courses at CSU for the master's degree, I took the course "Multicultural and Special Populations" and was introduced to the theoretical perspectives that help to construct the knowledge base of the academic discipline of "diversity."

It was this experience that led me to become more interested in the research on multicultural education and issues of diversity as an academic discipline. After completing the master's degree, I was recruited to CSU to act as an instructor for an experimental teacher preparation program (Project Promise) while I worked towards a doctoral degree. I immersed myself in the research of the scholars in multicultural education (e.g., Banks, Bennett, Gay, Grant, Ladsen-Billings, Nieto, Sleeter). As the research broadened to include issues of educational equity, activism, transformation, and identity development, I saw more clearly the direction I would take in my doctoral work.

In my doctoral research, I sought to understand the process of developing a commitment to issues of diversity. After identifying a population of individuals who were committed to diversity (by virtue of their membership in the National Association of Multicultural Education [NAME] and their attendance at the 1997 NAME National Conference), I performed a content analysis on one hundred surveys of these individuals and interviewed fifty of them. The research indicated that many individuals demonstrated a developmental approach to becoming committed to diversity (Paccione 1998). This finding helps to explain why some students become resistant or even hostile when presented with issues of diversity while others fully embrace the issues.

Using a developmental approach to teaching about diversity, a colleague of mine offered me yet another perspective by structuring her classes on diversity around three ideas: knowing self, knowing others, and making the connection (McWhorter 1995). In this approach, students spend roughly the first third of the course discovering issues about their own diversity and understanding the nature of their biases and perspectives. In the next third of the course, students discover the world of other nationalities, ethnicities, races, and perspectives. There is considerable immersion into the world of others for deeper, more meaningful understanding. Finally, the last third of the course is devoted to discovering how to engage in "border crossing" and "bridge building" between oneself and others. Making the connection between self and others may require understanding white privilege and power structures that perpetuate inequity. In addition, students begin to understand how to make the connection between self and others as it relates to the teaching and learning process.

Having been solidly grounded in the research of the leading scholars in the field of multicultural education, educational equity, race relations, and racial identity formation, I felt very well equipped to deliver the course "Multicultural and Special Populations." In addition, my own research as well as my colleague's theoretical perspective helped me solidify a developmental approach that I thought would help students better respond to issues of diversity.

Presumptions

I am no stranger to rural Colorado. I have lived in Colorado for sixteen years and have traveled to and through its rural locations on numerous occasions. I have delivered commencement addresses for three rural communities and have spent one week in each of the past six years immersed in rural environments with Project Promise. Still, I approached my commitment to teach the diversity class with some trepidation. After all, I *am* half-Black and it is very rare to see *any* Blacks in rural Colorado. Nearly all minorities in rural Colorado have a history with incidents of discrimination, racism, and persecution. Although current demographics show a large Hispanic/Mexican population in most parts of rural Colorado, many Hispanics/Mexicans hold jobs as ranch hands and farm workers on lands owned by European Americans. Ownership confers power—economic, social, and political. It is clear that those in power in rural Colorado are White.

Native Americans, who were the first inhabitants of the eastern plains of Colorado, were driven off these lands between 1850 and 1900. The Sand Creek Massacre of 1864 was one of many atrocities perpetrated on the Native Americans in this state.

It also is no secret that in 1924 politics, the Colorado Republican party was dominated by the Ku Klux Klan. In elections held that year, Colorado elected a pro-Klan governor and U.S. senator. While this state helped to lead the way for women's suffrage and child labor laws, it was not a place that embraced diversity. Knowing the history of Colorado and of rural communities, I anticipated that I would face tremendous difficulty and resistance in teaching a course on diversity.

As a very fair-skinned bi-racial woman, I often have been mistaken for White. I imagined that this would be an asset while teaching in and traveling to and from the rural community. I had a new car so my fears of breaking down in what used to be Klan country were alleviated. With those fears aside, I began to construct a curriculum that I thought would be developmentally appropriate for individuals immersed in White privilege and with little, if any, significant experience with people of color. I wanted to begin with a diagnostic activity with which I would be able to ascertain their level of readiness to engage in the *work* of diversity and self-reflection. At our first class meeting, I used an activity developed by McWhorter (1995) for use in a prejudice reduction workshop. This activity involves reaching consensus on working definitions of terms frequently used in this work. The terms included words such as *race, racism, discrimination, oppression, ethnicity,* and *culture.* Students worked in pairs to define a word, then presented their definitions to the group for feedback and discussion while trying to achieve a consensus definition. I had made the assumption that because this group of students had already taken two classes together and knew each other very well, deep discussions would occur. I was wrong!

Using the definitions activity as a diagnostic tool was not such a good idea after all. The discussions became heated, and two students became visibly frustrated and withdrawn. This was obviously a topic and a series of terms that this group had never discussed before. Many students resented having to participate. One student in particular appeared very angry throughout the activity. He suggested that discussing these terms helps to perpetuate issues like racism and discrimination. His idea was that if we don't talk about these terms, we won't think about them and subsequently won't act them out. It may sound good in theory, but it is just this sort of denial that I believe enables White privilege to flourish. While these students (all White) have the option *not* to think about these terms, most people of color face these issues every day. They do not have the option *not* to think about them.

On the long drive back to the university I had plenty of time to reflect on the class and on the task ahead. I muttered to myself, "What have I gotten myself into?" I knew the course would be a difficult one but I steeled myself for the challenge. It was back to the drawing board to reconstruct the curriculum. I had to suppress the urge to make assumptions about the students' readiness, closeness, openness, and experiences. I fell back on the basic triad that forms a foundation for diversity work: knowing self, knowing others, and making the connection.

Students and Stories

At the next class meeting, I introduced an activity called "The People Bag." This activity had been used in Project Promise for many years to have students introduce themselves. It involves presenting three features of one's self: cultural, personal, and professional. Students select a bag to carry artifacts that are representative of their identities. In the past these have included pictures, diplomas, tools of their trades, mementos, and heirlooms. Each student is given ten minutes to tell the group about the items in his or her "people bag." I always do the first one as a model. It was at this time that I told the class that I was bi-racial. In our discussion afterward, I asked if any students were surprised to know that I was half-Black. Many students indicated that they had assumed I was White. We had a lengthy discussion about the complexities of mistaken racial identity. This was a significant step in the direction of disclosure, vulnerability, and learning. I have found that demonstrating a willingness to self-disclose and be vulnerable helps others take those steps as well.

The next few class sessions were spent having students present their "people bags" and discussing race, ethnicity, nationality, and culture. Students were given assignments to help them explore their own heritage and history. They wrote a cultural autobiography that proved difficult for some and enlightening for others. Many if not all of the students were descendants of European homesteaders. Nearly every student had a relative who had come from Germany, England, Scotland, Wales, or Ireland. Many of their relatives had answered the call for homesteaders to Colorado. Some traveled down from German enclaves in Canada, some from the northern territories of Minnesota, and others kept traveling west from their initial arrival in New York. While most settled on the plains of Colorado to ranch and/or farm the land, few of my students knew of their ancestors' having had any contact with Native Americans. It was during this same era that the skirmishes between the Plains Indians and the homesteaders were rampant. It appears these stories were not handed down in the cultural heritage of those who settled here.

As their stories moved to their own experiences with diversity, many students explained that they had virtually no contact with people of color other than the Mexican workers on their property. Because this contact was so limited, the students confessed that they knew little of the Hispanic/Mexican culture. However, it was when many of the students went off to college that they had their first encounters with African Americans and Asians. Most students told stories of being silent observers, of being fascinated and enamored but reticent to engage.

One student told the story of how a sibling went off to college and had married someone from Arabia. She told of the turmoil this marriage caused in her family. The family had no resources with which to embrace this new culture, and when the sibling converted to Islam it sent the family into a spin. It was clear to me that when it came time for "knowing others," this student would do well to begin a process of understanding the Islamic culture.

One perspective that kept repeating itself was the overwhelming assumption that the students made regarding Hispanic/Mexican culture and education. All of the students were educators and all had had Hispanic/Mexican students in their classes; still, nearly all sounded the refrain that Hispanic/Mexican families do not value education. This was used repeatedly to explain why Hispanic/Mexican students do not do well in school. I waited until the last third of the course to address this issue. It was apparent that these teachers would have to reconsider their assumptions as we talked through White privilege and made attempts at "making the connection." My students would need tremendous assistance to see beyond the easy assumption that "Hispanics/Mexicans don't value education." I would have to work to help them see how economics influence values.

E Pluribus Unum—A Rural Perspective

When the Founding Fathers chose the phrase *E Pluribus Unum* as our nation's motto, they envisioned a country where, out of the many nationalities of origin, one nationality would arise—American. As a country that welcomed individuals from all nations, the

United States was a place where national origins would be forfeited for the sake of the new nation. Rural Colorado during the 1800s exemplified this theory. Homesteaders from England, Wales, Germany, and other northern European nations intermarried and adopted the nationality of "American."

After working with the descendants of these homesteaders, I became much more aware of the meaning of *E Pluribus Unum*. The people of rural Colorado truly exemplified the motto, "Out of many, one." When asked to describe or explain their culture or their ethnic origins, many of these students struggled with frustration. "I'm American," they would assert, "just American." When encouraged to explore their "roots," some were able to trace their ethnic origins to combinations of northern European nations. Students would refer to themselves as "mutts." Because of the multiplicity of nations in their heritage, they were more comfortable identifying as "Americans" rather than sorting out their backgrounds.

From one perspective, the identification of "American" has come to symbolize *White* Americans. Since European Americans owned the land of America, owned the corporations in America, and possessed nearly all of the wealth and power in America, the nation of America could be seen as a *White* nation. In this context, it is easy to understand White privilege, i.e., those unspoken, unwritten rules of conduct by which Whites are treated by others. Too often, white privilege confers freedom to select any place to live, to shop without being followed, to write checks without showing identification, to secure bank loans with no collateral, and to be offered employment on the basis of one's family or friends rather than one's résumé.

When I consider what it means to be "American" in this new century, I see a different face, not just a white one. Just as individuals from northern European nations came here, intermarried, and became the earliest "Americans," many more recent immigrants also have intermarried. There are now a plethora of multiracial and multiethnic individuals who call themselves "Americans." As this number rises, perhaps the definition of "American" will change as well. Many multiracial individuals are often mistaken for being White. If the meaning of White becomes clouded, then how will White privilege prevail? Today's Americans are much more than White. Although the Founding Fathers had it right when they envisioned the *idea* of an "American," in their day they omitted people of color from that category. Today's "Americans," however, must be inclusive of all who call the United States their home. Rural Coloradoans have tremendous pride in being Americans. I would be thrilled if tomorrow's Americans have that same degree of pride.

Final Thoughts

My rural adventure turned out to be a learning experience for me as well as my students. I was able to make a human connection through my teaching style, my sense of humor, and my authenticity. My course's developmental approach enabled the students to explore issues of race, privilege, and diversity in a safe environment. Although many of the students had never examined these issues, I found that they were willing to take a hard look at themselves. In their course evaluations, many used the term *transformed* to indicate the level of change they had experienced. While the power structures of rural Colorado are far from being transformed, perhaps a few educational leaders can begin to make a difference by adopting a different view of power and privilege.

I don't know whether knowledge without action produces much change. My course fell short of promoting social action. Developmentally, it wasn't yet appropriate. Some students chose to focus their final investigative project on issues around the education of Hispanic/Mexican students in their schools. I believe those students will help promote educational equity for Hispanic/Mexican students. Other students focused on redesigning the curriculum to be more culturally relevant. Although the structures of power may not be directly affected in rural Colorado, important changes may take place in the schools.

I have agreed to teach another class for the rural cohort of students. I will have the same students who were in my "Multicultural and Special Populations" class. This will give me one last chance to encourage them to make a sustained commitment to issues of diversity and equity.

References

Lawrence III, Charles R., Mari J. Matsuda, Richard Delgado, and Kimberle W. Crenshaw. 1993. Introduction. In *Words that wound*, edited by Charles R. Lawrence III, Mari J. Matsuda, Richard Delgado, and Kimberle W. Crenshaw.

McIntosh, Peggy. 1990. White privilege: Unpacking the knapsack. In *Working Paper 189: White privilege and male privilege*. Wellesley, MA: Wellesley College Center for Research on Women.

McWhorter, B.A. 1995. Personal communication.

Paccione, Angela, V. 1998. Multicultural perspective transformation: Developing a commitment to diversity. Unpublished doctoral dissertation. Colorado State University.

U.S. Census Bureau. 2000. Census 2000.

Wah, Lee Mun. 1996. The color of fear. Lee Mun Wah, producer.

A Native Perspective on Teaching Law and U.S. Policy: The Inclusion of Federal Indian Law and Policy in a College Curriculum

Roe Bubar and Irene Vernon

The purpose of this essay is to discuss the challenges and methods used in teaching a course that is focused on a particular marginalized group of U.S. citizens—Native Americans. We believe there are numerous issues associated with multiculturalism and diversity in the classroom. What we want to share are our experiences in teaching "against the grain," i.e., that our course contradicts (and adds to) the traditional approaches to the study of law and Native peoples. Mainstream law and policy courses rarely address issues facing tribal peoples, and few include any discussion of Indian/White relations or the richness of American Indian law and policies. Moreover, a course on federal Indian law and policies is rare in colleges and universities. We recommend its adoption into college curricula because the study of the country's first inhabitants can expand and deepen a student's understanding of U.S. history.

Multicultural education has emerged in academia as a fairly recent movement. Sometimes it has not been perceived as "academic" enough, yet we believe that multicultural education is as "academic" as it is taught. By this we mean that, historically, what was often taught about Native peoples is that they lived in tipis, roamed the land for food and water, shot bows and arrows, and wore feathers in their hair. Many courses also have been quite static, focusing on primarily the Plains Indians in the 1800s. Native peoples have a much richer and fuller history than that, and it is the inclusion of a course such as "Federal Indian Law and Policy" that can broaden student knowledge and understanding.

In a recent study on the impact of diversity in college classrooms Alger, et al. (2000) found both direct and indirect positive educational effects for all students that

> cannot be duplicated in a racially and ethnically homogeneous setting...It was learned from faculty members and students themselves that cross-cultural interaction and overall satisfaction with college are higher at more racially and ethnically diverse colleges and universities, and that racial and ethnic diversity has a direct positive impact on students' outcomes and students' beliefs about the quality of education they received. (3-4)

For example, a number of the respondents in this study "agreed that classroom diversity broadened the range of perspectives shared in classes, exposed students to different perspectives, encouraging them to confront a range of stereotypes, including racial, ethnic, social, political, and personal experience" (14). More than two-thirds of the faculty members surveyed indicated that students benefit educationally from learning in a diverse environment,

> both with respect to exposure to new perspectives and in terms of their willingness to examine their own personal perspectives....Faculty members strongly believe that racially and ethnically diverse classrooms enrich the education experience of White students. (15, 4)

According to this study, when faculty members view diversity as "unimportant or irrelevant to learning, they are more apt to ignore diversity in their classrooms" (12). Furthermore, when faculty members ignore diversity within their classrooms, students do not benefit from diverse classroom settings. We, on the other hand, view diversity as important and attempt to identify subject matter that is itself diverse. We also try to show our appreciation for the diverse perspectives that the students bring. Consequently, we believe our students leave our classes challenged, reflective, and oftentimes more aware of the different human and cultural issues around them.

A class we both have taught, and one that we believe imparts critical cultural concerns and ideas, is Colorado State University's "Federal Indian Law and Policy." This class is a required course for obtaining the Native American Certificate from CSU's Center for Applied Studies in American Ethnicity. Through an examination of our own teaching experiences, we have found that focusing primarily on indigenous peoples when teaching about diversity can be an effective cross-cultural learning experience for students if it involves the interaction of a number of variables, i.e., a meaningful subject matter, a supportive classroom environment, and appropriate pedagogy.

Subject Matter

As a course that addresses Native issues, Federal Indian Law and Policy is critical because it includes a discussion of history, the sovereign status of tribes, the federal trust responsibility to tribes, the role of the federal government in Indian affairs, and current tribal issues. A federal Indian law and policies course addresses the past, the present, implications for future generations. For example, although old and perhaps broken, treaties are still valid and enforceable unless specifically abrogated by Congress. The "founders" of this country signed treaties in exchange for land and those promises still must be honored, legally and ethically. We have also found that when students understand what Native people have lost and others have gained through the courts and federal policy, they begin to develop a deeper understanding of what is at stake for indigenous people in the present legal and political arenas. The study of law and policy can focus on issues of power, survival, colonization, and cultural continuance, which then become avenues for cross-cultural learning. Students come to understand how fairness, honesty, and responsibility are important in the development of both law and policy for all people in the United States.

A text we find useful for those who have just begun to learn about Native American subject matter is *American Indian Life Skills Development Curriculum* (LaFromboise 1996). This book was developed in conjunction with a diverse group of academics, educators, and tribes. Zuni school district personnel and the Cherokee Nation were lead contributors. While *American Indian Life Skills* was developed for American Indian students, its relevance and applicability can cross cultural boundaries. While the text was developed to help prevent suicide among Native youth, it is about empowering students more generally and providing them with real life skills. LaFromboise provides several interesting and useful suggestions for teaching sensitive and critical topics. She has a specific lesson plan for reviewing Native American history and examining Indian rights and oppression. This knowledge is critical in a federal Indian law and policy class. The introduction of Native American history allows students to understand fully what tribal people have experienced over the years and the pressures that continue to surround them today because of that history. As trained lawyers, we have discovered that the study of legal opinions provides an especially authentic reference for what we are trying to do.

We begin our course by laying a historical foundation that is fundamentally tribal in perspective, but that speaks to the interactions between the colonized and colonizer. We then begin to examine court cases and federal policies to concentrate on the legal discourse that defines tribal sovereignty, their right to self-determination and governance. We focus on how Indian nations in this country never have been afforded the ability to assert their sovereignty in its fullest extent within the confines of the judicial system. The sovereign authority of tribes as well as their political autonomy have been constrained over the years by both courts and Congress. The Supreme Court and Congress no longer uphold fully the promises of past generations, and *stare decisis* (to abide by or adhere to decided legal precedence) has given way to the political or economic wishes of the majority. We also spend a great deal of time discussing how the legal (and racist) discourse that underlies land ownership in this country was born out of a medieval, Christian-based "doctrine of discovery," helping to explain the theft of tribal lands and sovereignty.

In the face of this kind of (in)justice, it becomes a real challenge for us to get students to learn this history and to then empower them to think about the law in a more ethical and equitable manner. The quasi-sovereign status of Indian Nations, as reflected by the phrase "domestic dependent nations," was first announced by the Supreme Court in 1831 in *Cherokee Nation v. Georgia*. While tribes have asserted their sovereignty over their members, internal governance, membership, justice, domestic issues, taxation, and property within Indian Country and Alaska Native communities, tribal governments nonetheless remain largely crippled by their constitutional status as "domestic dependent nations" and the plenary power of Congress.

For myriad reasons, certain Native groups in the U.S. have been unable to rely upon the doctrines of federal Indian law to protect their land, acknowledge their status as indigenous peoples, and uphold their sovereignty. In particular, the contemporary struggles of Alaska Natives and Native Hawaiians mirror the historic struggle of all Native people in this country. For those reasons, we have developed the syllabus for this course on federal Indian law to include an analysis of Alaska Native communities and Native Hawaiians. Our broader discussions, then, extend beyond U.S. borders to include international references to similar indigenous issues. Specifically, we incorporate indigenous legal cases and policies from Australia, New Zealand, and Canada.

For example, in the *Mabo v. Queensland* case, Australia looked to U.S. federal Indian law for leadership on how it should deal with aboriginal land rights in its own country. The issue of Native rights becomes very sensitive when we look across these cultures and see how the U.S. system was built upon a "doctrine of discovery" where *non-Christian savages and infidels* have diminished rights to their aboriginal land and, therefore, were forced (by conquest or purchase) to surrender their lands to Christians. The Pope in Rome was divinely designated by some colonial powers as the Shepherd of Christ's universal flock and vested with spiritual jurisdiction over all of humankind (Williams 1990). While Australia's high court eventually acknowledged and rejected the cultural racism inherent in the doctrine of discovery, the United States still recognizes it as law. Originally bestowed by the Pope and later delegated to European sovereigns, these Christian entitlements elicit a wide spectrum of student opinions and questions in our class. The contradictions and complexities associated with issues of prosperity, honor, religion, and equity are very challenging for students who themselves struggle with questions of religion and justice.

Coupled with our examination of court cases is our look at the role of the U.S. Congress and its legislative authority to further divest tribes of their political autonomy and sovereignty. Students quickly learn how many of the United States' legislative policies and Supreme Court cases reflect underlying roots of cultural racism. Looking at specific federal Indian policies like allotment, termination, assimilation, and relocation, our students are able to see their devastating impact on Native land holdings and traditional lifestyles as well as the resulting poverty, poor health, and underdevelopment still found on Indian reservations today.

The subject matter found in a federal Indian law and policy class provides us with a wealth of information to challenge, engage, and teach students about cross-cultural boundaries and the fairness of our laws in the treatment of North America's first inhabitants. It is through this study of history, religion, and culture that students learn to broaden their understanding. They learn to think more critically and ethically about the difficult issues. We think they become more aware and involved in the world around them.

The importance of incorporating ethics within this course is also key. George Gadow (1995, i) says it best; "When we are ethical, we no longer use force against each other, and we take responsibility for how we affect each other's lives. We begin to be ethical when we strive to be respectful, understanding, and reasonable." It is the combination of teaching federal Indian law and policy with a careful examination of how the United States has made its legal and political decisions that challenges students to examine the institutionalized nature of racism within the federal system.

Classroom Environment

In teaching federal Indian law and policies, it is important for the teacher to note the class composition because many students of color will respond differently to the content of this course. In our experience, students of color, women, gays, lesbians, bisexuals, transgendered students, and students with disabilities often will have more experience with cultural oppression. Thus their participation can add much to understanding what it means to be marginalized. Generally, the ethnic composition of the "Federal Indian Law and Policy" class is predominantly white. However, many bring other aspects of diversity into class and, often, discussions. Informed of Native issues and concerns, they can add their own experiences with oppression. Yet, many students also come with preconceived, idealistic, and romantic notions about Native people and reservation life. They often carry with them emotional baggage that can range from guilt to historical apathy. Over the years, we have found that encouraging self-awareness is important. Structuring activities and assignments to facilitate this self-awareness helps students examine their own attitudes. It also motivates them to master the law content of the course. Noting these other aspects of diversity among our students permits us to create a teaching environment that encourages growth, empowerment, and openness for all students.

In our classes, we see a variety of students. The diverse perspectives they bring add much that is positive to the classroom environment. For example, since the Indian law and policy course emanates from an academic center (CASAE) and not a department, its students come from a variety of disciplines. Many students take this course as an elective; hence, they come to us at different times in their educational careers. We have seniors mixed with freshmen, eighteen-year-olds with fifty-year-olds. In addition, this course typically attracts students from diverse geographic regions, from the east to the west, as well as urban, rural, reservation, and international communities. The inclusion of Native students in this course has proven critical because the contemporary lives of many Native students are impacted by the laws and policies implemented in the past. It is this lived experience that the Native students bring to the class and share with others. It is hearing their stories in the classroom that can contribute to a powerful educational experience. Some Native students may not know the federal policy, history, or case law, but they then find their life experiences reflected in the readings. Students who represent worldviews that differ from the majority challenge others to re-examine their perspectives and ideas that most simply take for granted as true. All of our students seem to benefit from the introduction of other paradigms and diverse worldviews.

On the first day of class, we form a circle and fill out a personal questionnaire that helps students explore their unique experiences, hopes, and plans for the future. This is often a helpful way to start the class with an atmosphere of openness, introspection, sharing, and community. Because we tell the students that the personal questionnaire will be shared in the larger group, students can opt to share as much or as little as they feel comfortable doing. Once we know the composition of the class, we next want to begin creating an academic environment that is supportive, safe, and honest, one that will facilitate the study of law and cultural differences. This type of milieu allows for students to fully engage intellectually without feeling guilt, anger, or frustration. Studying law in an unsupportive environment can be overwhelming. Reading case law that is in small print and drenched in legalese is an intimidating process for most students so we begin by making them comfortable in the decisions that have led them to this class. That is why we begin with an exercise to encourage the students to reflect on their career goals and how this course can help. This serves as a baseline for individual conferences at the beginning of the course and a midterm check-in on student intentions. We also offer comfort by telling the students that "there is no stupid question," and that the study of law often makes people feel dumb.

We want to create a sense of safety and encourage students to voice their opinions so they may effectively talk with others—especially those different from themselves. Others have shown, and we agree, that learning how to work effectively in diverse settings can be critical to the development of leadership (Maruyama and Moreno 2000). We help students develop leadership skills by collectively creating ground rules about honesty and respectful communication. We also talk about the powers of persuasion, argument, and compromise. Concurrently, we are firm in our approach and firm in our boundary setting about what is and is not acceptable classroom behavior.

A challenge we confront in the development of a safe and open classroom environment seems to exist in many academic institutions. Too often, instructors encourage only those most willing to raise their hands or those who think quickly on their feet. To counter this effect, we make it clear that everyone in class should partici-pate and everyone's ideas or comments are worthy. In many ways, we conduct class in the same manner that tribal groups have made important discussions. Open tribal council meetings have been an integral part of tribal life from time immemorial. Both women and men are allowed to speak in an effort to give everyone voice and op-portunity in the decision-making process. We respectfully call on quiet students and provide smaller-group work to encourage the participation of those students who are reluctant to speak up in the larger classroom environment. Classroom activities and a support-ive environment for broad student participation can bring a balance of perspectives that includes all students. We are convinced that stu-dents learn best when they feel supported, heard, and safe, and when they are learning something of value.

In many Native communities, traditional teachings are used to encourage and remind people of how important it is to speak their truth and be authentic. Then people are seen as powerful. As Native women, we agree that much of our teaching is from the heart, a pro-cess whereby both teacher and students learn together. To get to this point in class, we try to overturn what we term "academic dis-tance," which defines an environment where students view teachers as privileged. This can happen when teachers do not value students, and where the teaching process is seen as a "one-way street." In this environment, students can lose confidence in themselves. When teachers are content to simply lecture, there is no acknowledgement that the students and their interactions with one another merit any academic value. We believe we must also be honest with and open to our students. We must listen and value students as people if we are to gain their respect, confidence, and appreciation.

Academic distance is what we ourselves experienced in law school. We both found it to be ineffectual. In contrast to academic distance, we try to develop a supportive relationship with students (one that encourages honest and open dialogue), an open-door pol-icy, and one-on-one student visits. We think these approaches send the message that students are valued, important, and heard. In many ways we follow the approaches of tribal groups such as the Ir-oquois Nation, whose principles of democracy predated the found-ing of the United States and permitted men and women to have an equal voice in decision making.

One of the great difficulties in teaching federal Indian law is coming to terms with our own legal education and the indoctrina-tion process we ourselves endured in the study of federal Indian law. Colonization, boarding school policies, assimilation, and relocation policies were largely glossed over, and the underlying cultural racism that is pervasive in our laws, policies, and court decisions was not addressed. When we began to teach federal Indian law, we both found it was difficult to reread certain cases because we began to experience again the anger we felt over what we did not learn. We were forced to remember all those academic conversations about a justice system that demeaned Native American beliefs and histories. We now can see clearly how much our law school experiences have impacted us as teachers. For example, one day a student came to Roe's office and asked if she was mad at him. He said he felt she often had an expression of tension on her face in class when he spoke up, and he wondered if it was personal. In response, Roe shared some stories from her own legal education, how she herself was struggling to read the casebook, and the difficulty she was now having in teaching the material. She assured the student that it wasn't personal. Later, she shared with the entire class how her law school experience impacted her and her teaching, and why she thought it was so important to examine the underlying policies, laws, and ethics that federal Indian law is built upon.

As the class struggles with issues of ethics and justice, we encourage free, honest, and open discussions and insist on responsible language. We encourage students to support their statements with logical arguments, and to take responsibility for what they say. This helps them master the complexities associated with learning and speaking intelligently. Students are taught that they must be able to explain how they come to their conclusions. They must examine their thought processes, including their own preconceived notions and biases. We delve deeply into their reasoning and teach them the importance of using their intelligence and honesty in a tactful manner, whether in the classroom or in the courtroom. To encourage students to speak in class and present cases in front of their peers, we support them in finding their voices. We have also noticed that issues that come from the heart have been the ones that students are able to speak about with ease. When students are able to identify issues that stir their soul and consciousness, we find that their confidence to speak out increases.

For example, in helping students express their ideas better, Roe uses a creative writing process to get to those "heart" issues. She passes a teacher/student response envelope around the classroom to encourage students to ask about or discuss any issue that has come up in class. She then provides students with a written response to their questions or concerns. Irene requires weekly response papers that are due at the end of a week. The response paper must address the assignments, class lectures, and/or guest speakers. In her reply to student responses, she always finds the positive in what they are saying while challenging them to think more deeply. We both have noticed that after receiving their replies or notes, students become more confident in their class discussions. When support and safety have been established with these kinds of teacher-student interactions, we have found that students become more open to and engaged in the issues under study.

Pedagogy

We also have found that student support, safety, and openness are that much more critical when we are attempting to teach about a group of Americans not regularly included in college curricula —group that has been surrounded by stereotypes, historical misunderstanding, and ignorance. First, we begin teaching by helping students understand the "study of law." Law is a difficult subject matter, with an "elitist" jargon that typically requires students to purchase a separate legal dictionary to complete reading assignments. It involves a new way of thinking. We both have extensive legal training, and despite the academic distance we experienced in law school, we both have found this legal knowledge extremely useful in helping to provide structure for our own teaching. We have drawn on these experiences to design our classes and sustain high expectations. We expect students to learn this new legal language, to brief legal cases, and to participate in moot court arguments.

The difficulty students face in our class begins at the introduction of their class text, *Federal Indian Law: Cases and Materials* (Getches, Wilkinson, and Williams 1999). The text has been used to teach federal Indian law in a variety of law schools, and we were confident our students would be able to use it, particularly if given the tools to succeed. We know this text is challenging, but we do not think it is insurmountable, and all our students have been successful to varying degrees. To facilitate student learning in the first several weeks of class, we empathize with their struggle and remind them they are not "stupid." To help them gain confidence, we tell them they are learning a new language and developing a new way of thinking that is a long and hard process, but a process they can master. This threat of perceived "inadequacy" is revisited throughout the semester as a way to deal with these issues. Mastering the law is presented as a tool of empowerment, and the course culminates in the oral argument each student will present in a district court courtroom with lawyers who practice Indian law serving as appellate court judges.

One pedagogical tool we both gained as law students is the Socratic method. The true spirit of the Socratic method of teaching, prominent in law schools everywhere, is found in dialogue, questioning, and responding. We both believe this method of teaching can be effective when used responsibly. We incorporate it into our own teachings because we find that it helps develop critical thinking. It also assists in cross-cultural learning by providing a rich structure for challenging traditional perspectives and assumptions. When the Socratic method is used to study the law in a supportive and responsible manner, it can be very powerful. It also can be used effectively to address related issues involving social class, oppression, and the like. For instance, to embrace, articulate, and question the other side of an issue that you strongly oppose invokes empathy that, in turn, can encourage greater openness to new ideas and perspectives.

Student empowerment is at the heart of our pedagogy because it allows for a more engaging and authentic exchange. As the class begins to grapple with controversial topics such as colonization, cultural and spiritual oppression, land theft, water rights, and diminishment of tribal sovereignty, students begin to express a variety of feelings and raise concerns about a variety of issues. There are a number of students who find sensitive issues silencing. Some non-Native students feel "guilty about what their ancestors did," while others assert that "they had nothing to do with what their ancestors did so why should they pay" for their transgressions? Concurrently, many Native students assert "they are owed for the wrongs done to their ancestors," and that "they [whites] are silently continuing that oppression by doing nothing." These kinds of responses in class can cause stress and anger. It is at these times that we have found our ground rules so important. Often, we set these at the beginning of the course, and always with student input and agreement. We want students to really listen, to focus on issues and ideas but not the people, to keep an open mind and to empathize with others. As teachers, if we can control the climate in class, anger can be an acceptable emotion. However, anger must be directed in healthy ways that contribute to deeper learning. We must help students direct their anger at the source of perceived problems—i.e., policy-makers—and not at each other.

Teacher facilitation is always important. By encouraging students to reach out beyond their own ethnocentricity and culture, beyond their own sense of worldview, we try to encourage students to develop a better understanding of each other. For example, when a student says she herself did not steal Native lands and does not see why tribes should have any right to get those lands back a hundred years later, we pose questions for the class about the ethics and values of our society, world opinion, and our own justice system. We often refer to the first day of class, when we wrote on the board the famous words of Supreme Court Justice Black: "Great men, like great nations, should keep their word." We ask, "Is it still important for our society to uphold such lofty ideals?" Irene may respond by asking, "Even if treaties are old and broken, should they still be enforceable a hundred years later?" Both of us "bring the issue home" by asking, "What if someone goes to your house and removes you and your family because they believe you are not utilizing it correctly? Should you have a legal right to have it back?" Regardless of how the colonials and Founding Fathers chose to act, we encourage our students to consider how legal decisions could have been decided, how society should conduct itself, and what values and morals we should advocate.

The struggle we face in this course is similar to what many others who teach a nontraditional course face—the content can cause polarization. The class may devolve into standoffs between students of color versus whites, or women versus men, young versus old, and/or Native Americans versus others. If this type of polarization occurs, we reassert control over the class to ensure a classroom environment where everyone can speak about and explore the issues at hand. With open discussion, students can reflect on their own biases, understandings, and histories as well as the biases, understandings, and histories of others. For some Native students, it does matter when a friend they have been sitting next to expresses deepfelt sorrow about actions taken against them by their ancestors. It is the linking of "student discussions to everyday life" that we have found to be most useful. Everyone has a home, family, history, etc., and it is the linkage with these factors that can bring students together and prevent polarization.

For us, the most difficult aspect of teaching this class is our being able to discuss topics that directly confront the continuing colonial domination of tribal people and the institutionalization of cultural racism found within the judicial, congressional, and executive branches of our government. Addressing these issues is fraught with difficulties because this information often contradicts U.S. law and policy courses, where the focus is on the experiences and histories of the dominant society, not the silenced and marginalized. Yet, we have discovered that as we struggle with issues related to discrimination and oppression, we help lay the intellectual foundation for decolonization and resistance. Students themselves then begin to struggle with questions about critical cases and, more importantly, the legal theory that could have led to different decisions. In many ways, this class teaches a form of Native resistance in an academic milieu. It allows all students to challenge the way things are and to actively seek deeper, more meaningful, hopeful solutions to contemporary Native/White relations.

To some, this can look like a "political agenda." To us, it is about democratic ideas and basic principles of fairness. We do understand that our teaching of empowerment can lead some students to be activists for social justice, and we certainly hope it does. But there is a larger issue: What we teach is the recognition of rights and how they are important to any group's cultural, physical, and spiritual health. Although we focus on tribal rights, we believe that understanding rights in general and the importance of rights in the lives of all people are fundamental to maintaining them. By studying Indian law and policies, students are able to make the connections to the values, rights, and choices we all share and enjoy. For years, federal Indian law was not taught at all. When it was, any underlying cultural racism in the North American judicial system was ignored. For those students who are resistant to learning new information that contradicts earlier teachings, we focus on those structural sources embodied in U.S. law and policies that have permitted and maintained inequalities for tribal peoples. We are convinced that a more responsible teaching of this course requires us to address the cultural racism that underlies Supreme Court decisions and government policies about Natives. Just as it is not acceptable today to leave Natives out of history books or to portray Native people as one dimensional "savages," it should not be acceptable to teach federal Indian law without a critical look at the cultural racism that underlies U.S. laws and policies.

Empowerment comes in a variety of ways. We think it is imperative for students to recognize their rights, how precarious those rights may be, and how easily they can be taken away. Another way to build student empowerment is to encourage them to speak out at public meetings and represent themselves and others effectively. For example, Roe has worked extensively in Indian Country and Alaska Native communities and incorporates cultural competence from real case experiences and investigations. Providing training on how to work respectfully and ethically with Native people is important for many students, whose future careers, at one point or another, may be impacted by federal Indian law. Encouraging dialogue on current issues in Indian Country, Alaska Native communities, and Hawaii also is an important part of Roe's classroom environment, providing an opportunity to openly discuss issues like "political correctness."

Over the years of speaking with people in a variety of venues, we have seen how some people, particularly students, will tell us only what they think we want to hear. While some might view this as "political correctness," we also see it as the beginning of intellectual commentary. For us, political correctness is a double-edged sword. If students speak to us openly and directly using the language we want to hear, we think it can be a positive. However, some may fear that they do not have sufficient safety to truly speak their minds, and that they may be ostracized by other students if they do, especially if their opinions are viewed as not being "politically correct." Speaking from the heart is critical. Once students are given that right, they may say things that are not "politically correct." A student once said in class that in his experience, all Indians are lazy and drunk. Is this "politically correct"? No, but the positive aspect is that this student was articulating his perspective and others were able to challenge, agree, or respond in an environment where open discussion can be a powerful vehicle for learning. It is our responsibility as instructors to guide students toward understanding the source and impact of their language. We teach students that they must be careful with their words; they must claim them and take responsibility for them. For us, "political correctness" in the classroom demands respectful language and active listening so that we can challenge ideas and not the person.

We believe that respectful language, in conjunction with professionalism, builds knowledge and student skills. For example, Roe provides a moot court experience as a significant part of the course. She has incorporated an oral argument requirement, and she prepares students in a more traditional legal setting. In some ways, this class activity is grounded in traditional Native teachings that emphasize preparation through practicing arguments and watching others. By participating in an oral argument, each student acquires the skill and ability to experience a courtroom simulation that demonstrates how community partnerships are created with court administrators, judges, and practicing attorneys. Through observation, students learn to articulate their ideas, opinions, and arguments in a coherent and effective way. There are, however, a lot of safeguards built into this experience to ensure that students are able to successfully complete their arguments, for example, using mock arguments in class, pairing up with peer partners, and dialoging with the teacher by phone and email. The instructor also serves as a back-up partner in the oral argument itself by helping any student who requests her assistance or who is struggling in the courtroom setting. The oral argument is structured around a contemporary issue and encourages an in-depth study of a real case. In recent years, the oral argument has centered on Alaska Native and Native Hawaiian issues given the recent Supreme Court opinions impacting these communities. The oral argument is videotaped for each team of students who would like a copy. Most students report that the oral argument is one of their most important learning experiences in college.

Empowerment for the students also comes from how they develop their own thinking and, for some, how they then take political action. Historically, the law has been both an instrument for empire building as well as a vehicle for personal empowerment. When students are empowered, when they can experience their own internal sense of mastery, their intellectual horizons can widen. They can move on with a sense of hope, a positive vision of what the future can mean for themselves and others. In mastering and learning federal Indian law, students can find a renewed sense of justice. They better understand the contemporary issues of Native peoples in a context that promotes a different outcome. Students also can emerge with a renewed sense about learning when they see how people can change the world. As teachers, we desire a wider vision of the world. We believe in the words of Mahatma Gandhi: "Our ability to reach unity in diversity will be the beauty and test of our civilization."

References

Alger, J.R., J. Chapa, R. Gudeman, P. Marin, G. Maruyama, J. Milem, J. Moreno, and D. Wilds. 2000. *Does diversity make a difference? Three research studies on diversity in college classrooms.* Washington, DC: American Council on Education and American Association of University Professors.

Appel, M., D. Cartwright, D.G. Smith, and L.E. Wolf. 1996. *The impact of diversity on students: A preliminary review of the research literature.* A report commissioned for the Fifth Annual Ford Foundation Campus Diversity Initiative.

Carrillo, J. 1998. *Readings in American Indian law: Recalling the rhythm of survival.* Philadelphia: Temple University Press.

Cherokee Nation v. Georgia. 1831.

Gadow, George.1995. *Ethics in everyday life.* Denver: University of Denver.

Getches, D., C. Wilkinson, and R. Williams, Jr. 1999. *Federal Indian law: Cases and materials.* St. Paul, MN: West Publishing.

Johnson v. McIntosh. 1823.

LaFromboise, Ted. 1996. *American Indian life skills development curriculum*. Madison, WI: University of Wisconsin Press.

Mabo v. Queensland. 1992.

Maruyama, G., and J. Moreno. 2000. *University faculty views about the value of diversity on campus and in the classroom*. Washington, DC: American Council on Education and American Association of University Professors.

Milem, J.F. 1997. *Key educational outcomes of diversity for college and university faculty*. A paper commissioned by the Harvard Civil Rights Project for the conference Diversity and Higher Education, Cambridge, MA.

Milem, J.F., and K. Hakuta. 2000. The benefits of racial and ethnic diversity in higher education. In *Minorities in higher education: Seventeenth annual status report*, edited by D. Wilds. Washington, DC: American Council on Education.

Smith, D.G., G.L Gerbick, M.A. Figueroa, G.H. Watkins, T. Levitan, L.C. Moore, P.A. Merchant, H.D. Beliak, and B. Figueroa. 1997. *Diversity works: The emerging picture of how students benefit*. Washington, DC: Association of American Colleges and Universities.

Williams, Robert A., Jr. 1990. *The American Indian in western legal thought: The discourses of conquest*. New York: Oxford University Press.

Disability as Part of the Diversity Curriculum

Rosemary Kreston

Introduction

Disability often is overlooked as part of diversity curricula. There-fore, when asked as an instructor for a class on disability, to con-tribute my reflections to this text, I was delighted. I also was some-what intimidated by this prospect. I am not the typical university instructor. By trade, I am a director of support services for students with disabilities. My reflections do not stem from a traditional aca-demic venue, nor am I as versed in the various theories of teaching. My reflections on the experience of teaching about disability are likely to be different from those outlined in other chapters in this book. Still, having taught what I consider an introductory "disabili-ties studies" course for a number of years, my experiences do seem to be similar in some respects. This is especially true when it comes to student reactions and personal/professional issues. When differ-ences do appear, they may be more related to how disability itself differs from other aspects of diversity.

I believe that, when taught from a perspective outside the more established (medical) viewpoint, a study of disability lends itself well to diversity curricula in several ways. However, this perspective is also one that challenges the traditional underpinnings of several "helping" professions and, hence, challenges many students who en-roll in the course. As a result, resistance, rage, and fear from stu-dents are not uncommon reactions—a reflection of a student's ego identification with their professional canon. Being a person with an apparent physical disability, I further challenge the students as an atypical instructor. As with other diverse instructors, the accep-tance of my authority is highly influenced by how I present myself and how I am received. While self-disclosure is integral to teaching about the disability experience, I have to be careful to ensure that specific information does not become interpreted only as opinion and, therefore, invalidated. In addition, students with disabilities themselves may find taking the class to be both enlightening and frustrating as they come face to face with the realities of their own experiences, of which they may only have been vaguely aware.

Disability as a Diversity Dimension/Experience

While many courses offer content regarding disability, as part of the *diversity* curriculum the inclusion of disability is still relatively new to the academy. Various disciplines (the majority of helping professions) often highlight disability but tend to filter information through the traditional medical perspective (i.e., pathology or deviance) of a professional (or expert) in the field. This approach sees disability, both physical and mental, as a personal experience with distinctions based on type, or diagnosis, of disability. In contrast, a *disability studies* approach tends to be more closely aligned with more common diversity curricula. The approach is centered on the disability experience as an experiential (socio-political) phenomenon. The filters are through societal, or cultural, parameters; it is seen as a group experience, with its foundation informed from the viewpoint of people with disabilities (Hirsh 2000). Distinctions between and among physical and mental conditions are subordinate to the experience of living and interacting within society. In this context, the challenges to teaching about the disability experience are similar to those faced by other instructors of diversity (e.g., cultural or ethnic studies).

When disability is examined through a diversity or sociological framework, it is no longer an individual experience but a collective one, and it undeniably creates an identity for a group of people influenced by specific societal constructs. This sociological framework is manifested in a variety of ways. For example, the symbols used to designate accessible entrances, the medical diagnoses that give meaning to specific disabilities, the premise that disability equates with inability, and myriad rules within the disability service delivery systems are social constructs we take for granted, but that clearly divide one group from another. Qualifiers used to distinguish programs specifically designed for people with disabilities, such as "special" education or recreational "therapy," further illustrate how society isolates those who are different. When describing cultures, Philipsen (1992) refers to this as "codes of speaking" and one of the qualities that delineates cultures.

However, what is most convincing about this line of reasoning are the socially constructed and historically transmitted attitudes and behaviors related to people with disabilities (Philipsen 1992).

As with other groups, when society first deemed this particular human characteristic as deviant, the response was to isolate, segregate, even exterminate or otherwise exclude people because they were viewed to be outside a restricted ideal image of "normal." A leading British scholar in disability studies, Oliver (1990, xiv), notes:

All disabled people experience disability as social restriction, whether those restrictions occur as a consequence of inaccessible built environments, questionable notions of intelligence and social competence, the inability of the general population to use sign language, the lack of reading material in Braille, or hostile public attitudes to people with non-visible disabilities.

Society's response to disability (as deviant) has ranged from such atrocities as infanticide and the holocaust (i.e., first groups for the Nazi gas chambers) to relatively benign habits of designing facilities with only one accessible restroom stall per floor or protesting group homes in neighborhoods. As a result, people with disabilities have experienced systematic oppression, discrimination, isolation, and devaluation from those who are non-disabled. The consequences are lack of opportunity and disenfranchisement from the benefits of our citizenship. It is from this framework of ideas that I teach a course entitled, "The 'Handicapped' Individual in Society."

The quotation marks I added to the title are significant. The title of the class sets the direction of the course; it also provides an initial discourse on how language and identity are intertwined and the effect it has as we conceptualize our world. As explained to the class, the course explores how society *handicaps* a person with a disability. The *experience* of having a disability in society is the focus, not disability itself. This is a subtle but significant shift since the terms "handicap" and "disability" often are used interchangeably, even by those with disabilities. Yet, critical to the discussion of disability as a diversity experience is identification and language. *Disability* is embraced as a personal identifier by disability rights leaders. As other groups have claimed their naming rights (e.g., African American, gay/lesbian, etc.), leaders in the disability community have proudly reclaimed disability as their "marker of identity," defining it simply as a human characteristic (Linton 1998). *Disabled* becomes an acceptable descriptor, not a noun, for the constituency group, while *non-disabled* refers to all others. The term *handicap*, in contrast, refers to how individuals are further limited above and beyond a physical or mental condition. It signifies the effect attitudes, policies, and practices have on individuals who are defined as deviant due to disability.

A Class on the Disability Experience

The course, "The Handicapped Individual in Society" (sans quotation marks around "Handicapped") was introduced by and continues to be offered through the Occupational Therapy Department in the College of Applied Human Sciences. Although designed by an occupational therapy instructor, the course has been something I have been involved with from its inception. I first volunteered as a co-instructor and then served as the sole instructor for the past fifteen years. The initial intent was simply to expose students to a more non-medical perspective of disability. When the course was first offered, students in occupational therapy were predominantly enrolled, although the course has been and continues to be open to all majors. Over the years, enrollment of students from a variety of majors has increased; it now includes students from Human Development, Social Work, Recreational Resources, Psychology, Education, and Interior Design.

The original outline of the course highlighted both the *barriers* and *bridges* created in society for people with disabilities. A major emphasis naturally was on the role individuals (non-disabled) have in creating the bridges. The concept of interdependency (as opposed to independent living) was introduced through a requirement to volunteer with individuals with disabilities.

As the course has evolved under my direction, more emphasis has been given to society's role in creating the barriers, including a more critical look at the systems designed to help bridge the gaps. An emphasis on advocacy has replaced the volunteer involvement, and an introduction to the philosophy of independent living, from the disabled community's point of view, is now pivotal and more closely aligned with a disabilities studies philosophy.

I explain this in order to put into context the various reactions from students taking the course as well as the challenges I face in teaching about disability as a human experience. As mentioned, the informed disability viewpoint or perspective is not the common one in the traditional disciplines. Many of the "helping" professions—education, psychology, social work, occupational therapy, and human development—filter disability through a medical model perspective:

> The medicalization of disability casts human variation as deviance from the norm, as pathological condition, as deficit, and, significantly, as an individual burden and personal tragedy...to keep it a personal matter and "treat" the condition and the person with the condition rather than

"treating" the social processes and policies that constrict disabled people's lives. (Linton 1998, 11)

As pathology, disability often is portrayed as personal affliction, underscoring individual differences and "special-ness" that marginalizes rather than integrates the experience as human phenomenon. Many of the systems created for disabled people and supported by the helping professions are in direct response to this marginalization. Students who enter particular helping fields are often motivated to "help" those less fortunate than themselves. This driving force is valued as admirable and tends to give self-worth to the person as "helper."

What often is unexamined is how the pathological perspective continues to perpetuate isolation and separateness. Students who enroll in my class are required to examine their perceptions as well as question concepts they may have taken for granted. It can be quite a shock to realize one's career choice is to join a system that, under the guise of support may add to an imposed isolation. What information I present and how I present it—especially when, at times it is antithetical to their major disciplines—are challenging aspects of teaching this course. If the criticism is too negative, students tune out.

While a few students come with little experience with or exposure to, disability, many begin the class with specific notions about disabilities and about those who have them. Some either have had a disabled friend or family member while others may have some care-taking experience working with disabled individuals (e.g., Special Olympics or providing personal care). For the very few disabled students who enroll—one or two at most per semester—their experience or knowledge may be more direct but it is often limited to a specific disability group. It can be a challenge for students to give up what they think they know and accept a different, and sometimes oppositional, perspective without some resistance, rage, or fear.

Challenges and Reactions

Because content is often contrary to mainstream concepts about disability, even for those with disabilities (e.g., many limitations are imposed by society), I begin the course by explaining that my intent is to give students an opportunity to "think" about disability differently. The students are invited to be open-minded and to contribute what they know from their own experiences, recognizing that each person may have a somewhat different familiarity with disability but a piece that can contribute to a more complete understanding. I stress that I am not the sole authority and neither are the guest speakers. The whole of the disability experience is both theoretically based as well as personally perceived. Students are encouraged to contribute even if their perspectives may not seem to fit easily with others. While some perceptions may be misconceptions, interpretations of specific experiences can help to illuminate a broader understanding for everyone, including the instructor. For example, hearing about what it is like to have a sibling with a disability can add much to discussion of family and attitudes. Contributions from disabled students also help to reinforce specific concepts through firsthand accounts and interpretations.

It is often difficult to gauge how effective I have been at encouraging participation, as some groups of students have been less talkative than others and the pace of the course (one day per week) does not lend itself well to opportunities for feedback. However, there are indications that the intent of the course has been realized for most students. As one student commented on a class evaluation:

> Thanks so much. I really enjoyed this course and learned a lot from listening. It was the best to get a different perspective. Really enjoyed all of the guest speakers. (Spring 2002)

For those in helping professions, especially those closely aligned with the medical model, confrontation with a socio-political perspective may feel like a personal attack at first. This may be one reason why some students find it uncomfortable to speak up. With "disability is normal" as a basic tenet, students may be faced with something different from what they have learned in their chosen major. In addition, students are faced with the assertion that their profession may be perpetuating isolation and separatism. These conflicts are often interrelated for students on a very personal level. Their feelings of wanting to "give to" and "help" others may be the primary motivation for their career choice. It may be difficult to accept that one's kind-hearted efforts to help another who is less fortunate (less able) could be seen as oppressive. Understanding oppression based on kindness can create a great deal of dissonance, both intellectually and emotionally.

To work with students who may be personally challenged by the concept of "oppression of kindness," I present specific systems through an historical lens to emphasize how the systems were created to be of help. However, a rigorous examination of systems also calls for a critique through the eyes of people with disabilities, which reveals barriers. Students hear that a person can have a range of views and still be effective within a system. In other words, if they become part of a system, they may have an opportunity to initiate change. This approach has proven valuable in retaining the interest of students who are not yet ready to fully recognize the oppression within a system. As with White students coming to grips with their privileged status, students in the helping profession often need time to examine their own motives and understand the bigger picture before they are able to give up on the status quo and accept responsibility as a potential change agent.

Like non-disabled students, students with disabilities must struggle with the dissonance created when their personal experiences and knowledge bases are analyzed within a more global context. For disabled students, however, the realization is not identification with the oppressor but with being oppressed. One instance stands out as an illustration. When a male student (early twenties) took the course, he had been a wheelchair user since the age of thirteen. For all practical purposes, this student appeared adjusted and well adapted to his experience. Yet, when presented with the idea of being normal, he struggled with the concept. He had only defined himself as a disabled male, not as a normal male with a disability. While he could see his normalcy within "disability," he had difficulty seeing himself in the broader context of "normal." Unconsciously he had come to accept his role as deviant; to acknowledge this meant he also needed to recognize his oppressed status.

As with others who finally come to realize their oppressed state, his reaction evolved from denial to anger. To constructively channel that response, he became the TA for the class and brought a new dimension to the course for several semesters. Not only did he bring his new passion for independent living and disability rights, but he also his rage at the full realization of his oppression. The challenge was to keep a balance within the class so his intensity did not evoke resistance from the students. This was not always easy. Yet, having a very passionate viewpoint was also stimulating for the learning environment. One particular class discussion illustrates how resistance to this TA's perspective by non-disabled students provided an important opportunity for expanding awareness.

Leading the class in a discussion, the TA complained about a small business that was inaccessible to him as a wheelchair user. He argued that it was unacceptable that the business owner was not prepared for his needs, especially since the Americans with Disabilities Act (ADA) had been in practice for nearly ten years. Several members of the class, however, were reluctant to hold the owner accountable—excusing the owner's ignorance of the law and giving her the benefit of the doubt for lack of action. Some students had difficulty understanding the perspective of a person using a wheelchair who simply wanted, and expected, to use the facility as would anyone else. It was easier to see the TA as unreasonable in his expectations rather than hold the business owner accountable. As non-disabled people, they may have found it easier to relate to the business owner than to the TA.

My response to this at times heated exchange was to direct the discussion toward a more sociological interpretation rather than one that was only personal. Some wanted to focus on the lack of awareness of the business owner. I pointed out that the ADA had a great deal of media coverage when first implemented and the symbols, signs, and other information in public spaces provided extensive notice that people with disabilities existed. Other students then suggested that awareness on the part of the business owner might have been a result of a devaluation of the disabled population as potential consumers. We discussed how people with disabilities can remain invisible despite being out and about, and how they still are forgotten in part of the marketplace. Two significant insights emerged: (1) disabled people are left out of the mainstream of society regardless of the laws (as exemplified by the TA's perspective); and (2) whether or not a person pays attention to symbols and other indications is often a personal choice. All of us are accountable for our own learning and awareness about important social issues, the laws of the land, what is required of citizens in a democracy, etc.

While supporting the TA's position as important for the class, I also was able to reinforce the notion that awareness was everyone's responsibility and not simply the business owner's. Taking responsibility for our own knowledge and awareness is not always easy, especially for younger students. The direction of the discussion we had may not have eased the personal feelings of guilt among the non-disabled students, but it did permit me to see their reasons for taking the class. While promoting this sense of self-awareness and self-responsibility is one level of challenge, for me, changing their emotional response from sympathy to empathy is quite another.

Between the Heart and the Head

Perhaps the greatest struggle for me in teaching about the disability experience is normalizing it both intellectually and emotionally while minimizing defensiveness or distancing. A focused examination of public forces helps to deconstruct the social construct of deviance as it applies to people with disabilities. At the same time, it is also necessary to understand the various emotional reactions to the experience. Individual attitudes and beliefs are the foundations upon which any social construct comes into being. Students in my class tend to distance themselves from an experience they do not understand. At the same time, taking self-responsibility for their own reactions calls for a self-examination that can be painful for some, as much as it may be enlightening. Once a level of comfort is established in class, however, students are better able to question each other, the behavior of others, as well as, understand their own responses, and identify what they need to further their growth.

Unfortunately, typical emotional response to disability seems to be rooted in sympathy, a "feeling sorry for," as opposed to empathy or an understanding of how someone might feel. The former tends to distance people while the latter tends to connect. One of the central goals of my class is to help students develop empathy for the disability experience, to understand it as a human condition and not an abnormality. This is one of the more challenging aspects of teaching this course.

Often, students are able to identify specific sympathetic tendencies in others while thinking their own reactions are empathetic. Challenging a student who is well-meaning (sympathetic) to examine his or her feelings can elicit a defensive and resistant reaction that is difficult to overcome. It may feel like a personal criticism to the student, as illustrated by the following comment from a class evaluation:

> Some of my papers were asking for how I felt and then I was told not to feel that way and given poor grades. (Spring 2002)

How students feel has an effect on what they are willing to learn. Some seem bound to certain concepts regardless of their factual basis. The challenge is to help students shift from sympathy to empathy, while instilling a sense of responsibility for their awareness. Students who consciously enter the helping professions often do so with a belief that they understand a great deal more than they actually do, especially about those they want to help. Prior exposure to the disability experience often creates a false sense of understanding; it is also often emotionally laden.

The revelation that people can choose to be aware and that an emotional response to disability is integral to that awareness can also be a challenging balance for a student with a disability, but for different reasons. The gap may not be between one's sympathy and empathy for a personal connection, but between anger and empathy. In the situation with my TA, once he realized that someone's ignorance, including his own, could be by choice, his tolerance for it greatly decreased. This may lead some disabled students to rage against others, further distancing themselves, or to get more involved in their newly discovered "community" as self-advocates.

The Balance in Practice

Students can easily dissociate from the disability experience and keep it in the realm of "deviance" if only one aspect of the disability experience is highlighted. Simply providing information about the ills of society may merely reinforce the perceived status (inferior) of disabled people through their "struggle to overcome." Yet, having a disability is both a personal experience as well as a societal one. A connection to that personal side is necessary if disability is to be perceived as part of the human condition and not deviant. The continuing challenge is to focus on the personal aspects of disability without further stigmatizing it.

As with other groups, understanding the personal is to "get inside another's skin" and see life from the inside out, both experientially and emotionally. While this goal may be similar in other diversity courses, the objective may not be the same. Others may first aim for a recognition and acceptance of difference; empathy may be secondary. Because their identity as a cohesive group is not commonly recognized, people with disabilities have an individuality that is filtered through a specific disability type. One of my objectives is to break down the artificial constructs that separate individual identities. In order to do that I first focus first on the similarities as human. All disabled people can feel and adapt. It is this emotional level that I target for the class to understand.

As in the case with other groups, understanding that disabled people are more similar than they are different comes by acknowledging that we all are human beings. As such, we all react (feel). We all are capable of adapting given our specific abilities and limitations. Although somewhat controversial, simulation is one method I have used to facilitate the personalization of disability on an affective level.

I have found that it is possible to create an experiential component and, for learning about disability thereby, elicit a more personal response and a more direct connection. The disability community often criticizes the use of simulations because they tend to emphasize the difficulties of the experience rather than the normality of it. I have found, though, that this activity can bring the students a little closer to the experience. By emphasizing how it feels to interact with the environment as a simulated disabled person, what is seen, and the "normalcy" of much in that experience, I can direct students to consider aspects of the disability experience more completely and through a different lens.

The focus of my simulations, then, is not on the disability itself. The aim is to draw out the emotions of (1) having to adapt to new and unexpected situations, and (2) having to deal with a less-than-hospitable environment. Both are important in the disability experience. Discussion and feedback on reaction papers are directed at emphasizing these key points.

This activity often creates anxiety and tension. Not only do the students not know what functional limitation they will have (although they do know there are three possibilities—mobility, visual, or hearing/speech), but they also are paired with someone they do not know. They are required to either assist or be dependent upon this stranger. Over the years of reading their reaction papers, I have found this to be the most "eye-opening" experience for the class. The challenge for me is to maintain a focus on the similarities and adaptability of humans and decrease the deviant status. Some students, for example, want to try the other disabilities. In response, I emphasize that it is not the specific disability per se that creates the experience. Rather, it is the interaction of a person, an event (disability), and the environment (Vash 1981). Understanding this human side of disability helps to reinforce empathy and the universal nature of human adaptability.

Emphasizing different aspects of a simulation does not, unfortunately, eliminate the perception of *struggle*. As a result, some students still express increased admiration for people with disabilities. While on the surface this may be positive, admiration for disabled people who are simply "getting on" with life also can be a paternalistic (and oppressive) response, further distancing the disabled person from the non-disabled "admirer:"

> When confronted with someone who is evidently coping with tragic circumstances, able-bodied people tend to deny the reality of the adjustment. The disabled person is simply making the best of a bad job, putting a good face on it. There may be some truth in this. But when it becomes obvious that there is also a genuine happiness, another defensive attitude is taken up. The "unfortunate" person is assumed to have wonderful and exceptional courage....This devalues other disabled people by implication, and leaves the fit person still with his original view that disablement is really utterly tragic. (Hunt 1998, 25)

Seeing these kinds of sentiments in student reaction papers, in addition to vague statements such as "now I know what it feels like to be" disabled, calls for careful feedback on my part. Responding to such "positive" regard without appearing to be negative (unappreciative) is difficult. My feedback, therefore, is aimed at refocusing students on why they found the experience difficult (i.e., unexpected, no practice) and reemphasizing the affective connection in dealing with the difficulty. Despite my best efforts, however, some students still find this a difficult concept to embrace. To reinforce written feedback, I'll often take the next class session to focus on stereotypes related to people with disabilities (including admiration) and the effects these stereotypes have on those with disabilities.

The discussion of stereotypes, both negative (e.g., drain on society) and positive (e.g., courageous), focuses on the impact stereotypes have on a person who may feel quite normal inside but who is perceived by others in either one of two roles: one step away from the lower dregs of society, or close to sainthood. Again, the impact of these words and images is brought down to the personal level by addressing their connection to self-concept, self-esteem, and sexuality, human aspects with which all students seem to be familiar. This familiarity normalizes the issue; it is not merely a disability concern but one to which each of us has a connection.

Societal influences are highlighted as primary contributors to the development of anyone's self-concept and self-esteem. There is always more to the story than just personality. I try to shift class discussion away from surface descriptions to problems with dichotomies that note only the positives (e.g., amazing and courageous) and the negatives (e.g., poor and pathetic). I comment on the stress for those with disabilities when presented with only those "abnormal" images of their supposed selves. Such terms as "marriageable," "contributing," "participating," and "normal" are rarely used to describe people with disabilities, and yet that is often how they see themselves or want to be seen. Perceiving individuals as "admirable" for simply living their lives can be as damaging as seeing them as poor, unfortunate cripples. For those students who are able to grasp this concept, they may then also come to understand how everyone can be implicated in perpetuating this damage.

Some students are uncomfortable with this implication. One student in particular insisted that the professionals with whom he worked in special education did perceive their students as normal, and their behavior reflected that belief. It was difficult for him to see that these influences permeate society. My challenge was to help him see that stereotypes are intertwined with systemic practices, policies, and other manifestations. The effect is not simply negated by the behavior of a few individuals. What I tried to emphasize was the impact these stereotypes have on people with disabilities and how they view themselves. I could only hope that, in time, he would be able to see the world with a more critical eye.

Self-concept and self-esteem are intimately and naturally linked with sexuality, another central aspect of the human condition that everyone shares, disabled or not. Marriage, parenting, sexual identity, sexual abuse, and other issues related to one's sense of self as a woman or man are always hot issues within any collegiate environment. Discussing how these issues relate to people with disabilities creates another link with non-disabled peers. However, as an emotionally laden topic, it also can elicit resistance and distance.

Rather than having a specific class discussion of sexuality that may cause some to be uncomfortable, I often use a video *Toward Intimacy: Women with Disabilities* (1993), featuring four women with disabilities. While the medium may appear to be more passive than a full class discussion, it helps focus the interrelationship between disability and sexuality in a very direct manner. For example, one woman with an obvious physical disability states that her gynecologist encouraged her to consider birth control before it was too late because "unlike her face, her vagina had developed beautifully." The sensitivity of the topics, the candor, and the types of disabilities presented by these women have proven both engaging and thought provoking. What emerges as stories unfold is society's impact on the expression of the women's sexuality. While a factor, their disabilities are clearly in the background. The stories of the women help normalize not only the issues but also the women's disability experiences. As their personal stories unfold, so too do their societal struggles, broadening what our students learn.

For students with disabilities, the normalization process is in discovering that their reactions, as well as their experiences, are not unique. One example illustrates this process very well. The personal reactions of disability can be examined through the reactions to loss (i.e., denial, bargaining, anger, guilt, depression, etc.). While a grief reaction is somewhat expected for those who acquire a disability, it is not often noticed in those who grow up with a disability. Yet, when presented in the context of the disability experience, one student with a learning disability was able to recognize that he himself had experienced these reactions. Told to simply tell their stories, guest speakers with congenital and acquired disabilities often identify particular emotional responses associated with this process. Such connections illustrate how a theoretical construct is manifested. At the same time, students with disabilities are able to identify with others on this emotional level regardless of the type of disability. Understanding that feelings of loss are part of the human condition and occur regardless of how a disability comes about helps students see the experience as understandable, not unique and deviant.

Another connection I have seen students with disabilities make is illustrated in their reactions to a presentation on learning disabilities. While providing an explanation of learning disabilities to non-disabled students, including what it feels like to have one, the video I use also seems to provide a great deal more for learning-disabled students. By advocating a climate of safety and comfort, the depiction of a student's personal experience seems to help normalize the disability and connect it to others who have a similar disability. It usually is not until this class period at this time in the semester that some students will self-identify themselves as having a learning disability and attest to the support they receive. Students who have struggled on their own end up seeking support, as if they no longer need be ashamed.

The content of presentations and class discussion provides the opportunity to dispel myths and assumptions through facts and figures. The discussions, the simulations, and the topics related to the self are all aimed at touching the students on a personal level, connecting them to the human side of disability and normalizing it. To minimize the distance and resistance to the idea that disability is part of the human condition, I have found that maintaining a balance of heart and head is the art of teaching this class.

Self-Disclosure and Authority

Informing through the perspectives of people with disabilities has been an important strategy for me in teaching this class as a disability studies course. I not only identify as a person with a disability, but my educational and employment background gives me knowledge about issues from a professional orientation, as well. The challenge for me has been to balance my professional and personal perspectives and to bridge the gap my training has not provided, i.e., the skills I need to teach. My vocation is as an administrator; the teaching aspect came about by chance, not as part of my job description. I have had the challenge of both finding my place as an instructor and finding the time to do both vocation and avocation.

Having a physical disability, I am aware that I may be the first visibly disabled instructor my students have had. As with other diverse instructors, this can create an initial discomfort and/or confusion. After introductory information and an overview of historical perspectives, and to ease any discomfort, I present myself as the "first guest speaker." The goal is to establish both my personal and professional expertise. This approach gives the class the opportunity to know me as a person, as a disabled person, and as someone with an authentic knowledge base. It also gives me a chance to set the tone of the class. I am always very open, answering questions and giving details when asked.

However, aware that comfort with self-disclosure varies with individuals, I am mindful that other guest speakers may not be as open as I am, especially if class questions pertain to more personal aspects. Some students may feel "offended" if another guest speaker declines to answer a question or does not offer more personal details. Therefore, I give students the opportunity during the following class session to ask me any question they did not have answered. While I may not be able to answer all questions, I do know my guest speakers personally, and that has given me a level of confidence that most questions will be within my reach.

One difficulty for anyone speaking as a representative of a group seems to occur when information is disconcerting for others. When I first started teaching this course alone, class evaluations indicated that some students felt I was too judgmental, too opinionated, or too biased in presenting information. As a result, I began to differentiate between opinion and fact or research more deliberately. I added qualifying words to statements so that data would not be interpreted as absolute (e.g., "sometimes this happens," "often this is a result," etc.). Separating my experience from researched knowledge has taken a great deal of self-examination so that I can offer useful insight without appearing biased.

While some students have confronted me with different opinions about specific issues, others have argued about specific facts when they seem contrary to their own experiences. Because I strive to have the class be open to different ideas, I've had to learn how to validate certain perceptions while at the same time challenging students to reframe their ideas. Rather than being drawn into a debate, I try to emphasize that the disability experience as a whole is more than simply the sum of individual situations.

I have come to realize, however, that whether or not I am a "good" instructor may not be as important as being enthusiastic about and engaged with what I am teaching. As a disabled person who has been able to relate to my experience from both personal and professional levels, I can bring to the class the best of both, even if I lack traditional academic and pedagogical training. In addition, to keep fresh, I constantly seek new information to incorporate into the class. As a result, my understanding of the disability experience and my own disability is ever expanding.

Over time, I have found what works well and what does not. Although the original flavor of the course has been retained, the disabilities studies approach has proven much more fulfilling for me as the instructor and hopefully for my students as well. My personal and professional goal is to have the students at least "think" about disability in a way that doesn't spark their own resistance, rage, or fear of new ideas. Fortunately, I believe that goal has been reached more often than not, as illustrated by the following comments from a recent semester (Spring 2002):

- Teacher was very knowledgeable, enthusiastic, interesting material.

- This was a wonderful class. The assignments and readings were beneficial to me personally and for the class. Because of them, I am aware of my surroundings and my language usage. I liked seeing the videos.

- An unbelievable teacher with a strong connection to the subject. She is always willing to help and her class is one that everyone should take. It would greatly better our campus and society.

- Great class. Changed my way of thinking.

Yet, one student provided a reminder of how difficult it still may be to reach some students:

I think it would be hard for a person who is herself disabled to teach this class in an unbiased manner. I felt as though I couldn't speak up about different ideas or perspectives because it would hurt her feelings or make her mad.

Establishing a safe, yet challenging class environment obviously is as difficult with disability as it is with any diversity experience.

Conclusions

In teaching about the disability experience to a class of primarily non-disabled students, I was aware of the similar reactions elicited in other diversity courses; resistance, rage, and fear. However, until I volunteered to write this chapter, I had not thought much about those reactions. That is not to say I did not deal with them; I simply did not think about how they may have impacted me, the class, and what I had done in response to experiencing them. As an administrator, my expertise does not lie within the classroom. Therefore, much of what I have developed as an instructor has been by trial and error, not from an academic understanding of the process of teaching. This chapter has given me the opportunity to examine how I've dealt with the various reactions and what has guided my responses. It is likely not as sophisticated a reflection as are the others in this text. It does, however, describe the challenges I've identified in teaching disability as a diversity topic.

Understanding the disability studies perspective is the foundation of my efforts; providing a disability perspective is the cornerstone of the course. How I do that seems to influence how successful students are in learning about disability as part of the human condition.

Students who take this course often are majoring in the helping professions. Part of the goal, and challenge, of the class is to critique those fields without disconnecting the students by attacking their self-esteem. The balance I've developed is to include both the positive and negative aspects associated with the systems that help, while encouraging systemic change so as to minimize ways in which the system hinders. While students are introduced to ideas that may cause them discomfort, I have found that the ways information is presented are as critical as the content is. For non-disabled students, the disability experience often is seen as distant from their own. For those with disabilities, their perspective is up close and personal rather than communal. The challenge has been in making the distant more personal to one group and more global to the other.

Disability engenders emotions that can make the content very personal (e.g., simulations), but care is required to keep it on an empathetic level rather than a sympathetic one. Making the experience more global also can elicit emotional reactions that can be difficult to channel into empathy. This has meant finding a fine balance between the emotional aspects (heart) and an intellectual examination of the experience (head).

As the instructor, presenting a disability perspective to a primarily non-disabled student body, how I establish my authority and credibility is influenced by both content and technique. As an instructor, I have had to be mindful of my own informed opinion, the perception of others, and a great deal of research. Establishing an environment that combines all these sources is not always easy.

One limit to teaching about the disability experience is in gauging whether or not belief systems change and whether behavior actually changes. Although people do make choices to be aware or not, oppressive behavior is not only a result of negative intentions. Since disability is part of the human condition, so, too, is how individuals respond to it, either on a personal level or a systemic one. Explaining why specific societal behavior exists hopefully gives a deeper understanding of the impact on individuals. By examining and questioning the assumptions of society, students often come face to face with their own. For many, it is the first time they realize they have bought into those societal assumptions. The challenge is in responding to the reaction of both non-disabled and disabled students (e.g., resistance or rage) as their consciousness is raised.

Self-disclosure has allowed me to present myself as a person with a disability and as someone with professional expertise. While the personal aspect helps me make the information real, presenting too much of my personal story can make me seem opinionated. A careful selection of guest speakers and videos reinforces the authenticity of the content of the class. Setting the tone for participation, sharing of experiences, and responding to opinions that may be in conflict with other views, including my own, are also part of the complexity of teaching this course.

After fifteen years of teaching disability from a disability studies perspective, I find myself continuing to learn new aspects about this field and how best to teach it. My association with other diversity areas has helped me realize the similarities as well as the differences of teaching through a diversity perspective. Not only have I been able to incorporate ideas from other areas (e.g., sexism, racism, and their relationship with ableism), but a diversity perspective also has helped me normalize the experience by establishing a connection to other groups who also are judged (without merit) as deviant by society. We are more alike than we are different, and that concept, I find, helps normalize the disability experience more than any other.

It has been a privilege to be able to contribute disability to this discussion on teaching diversity. I hope others will be able to do the same in the future.

References

Hirsh, Karen. 2000. *Advancing disability studies.* Presentation at AHEAD (Association of Higher Education and Disability). Kansas City, MO.

Hunt, Paul. 1998. A critical condition. In *The disability reader,* edited by Tom Shakespeare. London: Cassell.

Linton, Simi. 1998. *Claiming disability*. New York and London: New York University Press.

Martin, Judith N., and Thomas K. Nakayama. 1997. *Intercultural communication in contexts*. Mountain View, CA: Mayfield.

Oliver, Michael. 1990. *The politics of disablement*. Basingstoke: MacMillan.

Philipsen, Gary. 1992. *Speaking culturally: Explorations in social communication*. Albany, NY: State University of New York Press.

Shakespeare, Tom, ed. 1998. *The disability reader: Social science perspectives*. London: Cassell.

Thomson, Rosemary G. 1998. Incorporating disability studies into American studies. Kansas City, MO: AHEAD 2000.

Toward intimacy: Women with Disabilities. 1993. Directed by Debbie McGee. 60 min. Filmakers Library, National Film Board of Canada. Videocassette.

Vash, Carolyn L. 1981. *The psychology of disability*. New York: Springer.

Wright, Beatrice. 1983. *Physical disability: A psychological approach*. New York: Harper and Row.

Alien Perspectives in Accented Voices: Classroom Dynamics When International Female Instructors Teach Diversity Content

Silvia Sara Canetto and Evelinn A. Borrayo

Introduction

Teaching about human diversity is exciting. It engages students and instructors with scientifically rich and personally meaningful issues such as gender, sexual orientation, ethnicity, or social class. It involves participating in a journey that can be intellectually and personally transforming. At the same time, teaching about human diversity is challenging. Personal identities are shaped and loyalties are formed around dimensions of diversity such as gender or ethnicity. A scholarly analysis of diversity issues inevitably leads to personal reflections on one's experiences with diversity. Thus, teachers and students of diversity have to contend with the personal meanings and emotions the diversity content stimulates (Garcia and Van Soest 1999).

Teaching about human diversity also engages students with issues of equity and justice, power and powerlessness. In courses about diversity, students are exposed to the social influences in people's lives and to the consequences of these influences in terms of status and opportunities. They learn about people's privileges and oppression and about their places on the social map. For many students, learning about social stratification and inequalities is threatening because it challenges their assumptions about other people and about themselves, as well as the reasons for their places in the world. For example, for some students it may be personally challenging to consider that achievement is not simply a function of merit. Some react to threatening content through denial and resistance. Feelings of shame, guilt, anxiety, and anger also may be triggered. In some instances, students turn their negative feelings against the instructor, who becomes the target of hostility (Condit 1996; Davis 1992; Garcia 1994; Garcia and Van Soest 1999; Jackson 1999; Kirkham 1998/1999; Marks 1995; White 1994).

For all of these reasons, classes on human diversity are difficult to teach. These are classes that tend to generate challenging student dynamics, independent of who teaches them. At the same time, the kind and intensity of challenges one faces when teaching about human diversity vary across teachers and contexts. A teacher's knowledge, experience, and teaching style are certainly important factors in these diversity classes' dynamics. Equally important, however, are the teacher's personal characteristics (such as his or her ethnicity, sex, and age) as well as the meanings of these personal characteristics in terms of perceived credibility, expertise, trust, and power. For example, some students may particularly value ethnic-minority instructors for classes dealing with ethnic-minority content. For these students, the instructor's personal experience with the class content is an asset. In the eyes of other students, having a personal experience with the course's diversity content—especially a personal experience of discrimination and disadvantage—makes the instructor less credible. The latter students may dismiss ethnic-minority teachings about the ethnic minority experience as biased and self-serving.

Another example is that of male professors teaching women's studies. Male professors may have to struggle to establish their credibility as teachers of women's studies, at least in the eyes of some students. At the same time, because most professors at institutions of higher learning are males, male professors (particularly those who are also European American and older) often enjoy automatic respect and power in the classroom. Most college students are used to male professors. They also are used to respecting the authority of male professors and to learning from male professor's about all kinds of topics, including female-related topics. On the other hand, female professors, particularly ethnic-minority female professors, are rare. They often have to establish their authority and credibility with students, *even* in classes about women's and ethnic-minority issues (Davis 1992; Friedman 1985; Garcia and Van Soest 1999; Jackson 1999; Kikham 1988/1989; Smith 1999).

In this chapter, we draw on our experience of teaching diversity content as foreign-born and foreign-raised female psychology professors at a Midwestern, land-grant university in the United Sates.

Our observations as teachers of diversity have developed in undergraduate and graduate general psychology courses (e.g., abnormal psychology, adolescent psychology, lifespan developmental psychology) as well as in psychology courses that are explicitly about diversity content (e.g., diversity issues in counseling, psychology of women, psychology of gender). Our goal as psychology teachers is to broaden students' knowledge of the human experience and prepare students for professional, community, and family roles in an increasingly diverse and global society. We give students access to information about understudied groups in the United States. We also teach students about the lives of persons outside the U.S. so students can appreciate that "the U.S. is not the whole world but only one corner of it" (Kaye/Kantrowitz 1999, 42). Across topics and populations, we encourage students to think about human diversity categories (e.g., ethnicity) as complex and dynamic. Finally, we alert students to issues of language, how language influences thinking, and how language can inadvertently reinforce exclusion and oppression (Walker 1993). Finally, in our assignments, instead of memorized information, we expect from students a critical, scientific analysis of U.S. theories and research. For example, we ask students to examine the samples and questions used in influential U.S. psychological studies, and consider who the findings apply to, and to whom they are irrelevant.

While we have faced some unique issues when teaching diversity, we also have noted many similarities in our classroom experiences. Having reviewed the literature and discussed our experiences with each other and with U.S. teachers of diversity, we have come to the conclusion that what we have seen in our classes is in some important ways different from what our U.S. colleagues describe, including our U.S. female colleagues. We think our common and special experiences are likely due to our being female international teachers.

Throughout this chapter, we address the issues and challenges we have encountered when teaching diversity content as female instructors with foreign accents and mannerisms.[1] What we describe here is neither exhaustive nor necessarily representative of the classroom dynamics that take place when international instructors teach human diversity content in the United States. The dynamics we describe are simply the ones we have found to be most pervasive and most challenging in our classrooms. We hope that by writing about our experiences, we will encourage others to do the same and thus contribute to advancing the knowledge on teaching about diversity.

Teacher and Institutional Characteristics:
Who We Are and the Context of Our Teaching

Research suggests that the personal characteristics of teachers affect how they are responded to and how they are evaluated by students. For example, there is evidence that the gender of the teacher affects students' perceptions of the teacher's competence, with female professors being viewed as less knowledgeable than their male colleagues (Basow 1998). There also has been extensive discussion of the role of the teacher's ethnicity on perceptions of his or her skills (Farnham 1996; Williams, Dunlap, and McCandles 1999). Scarce attention, however, has been given to the impact of a teacher's nationality and language of origin on students' perceptions of the teachers' competency, skills, and credibility, particularly as reflected on course evaluations.

In order for our readers to evaluate the role of our personal characteristics and cultural backgrounds on the classroom dynamics we describe, we believe it is important that they know who we are—that is, who our students see and hear when they take our classes. Here, in summary, are our biographies.

Silvia Sara Canetto was born, raised, and educated in Italy through her first doctorate. She is a first-generation university graduate; neither of her parents completed high school. Her high school education focused on the study of ancient and modern Mediterranean cultures, histories, philosophies, religions, and languages. Her international experience in her first twenty years involved occasional family car trips around Europe. When she started university studies in psychology, she was proficient at translating texts from ancient Greek, Latin, and French, but her knowledge of English was rudimentary. After gaining a doctorate in experimental psychology at the University of Padua, Italy, she won an international research scholarship for a year in Israel. She ended up spending the next four and a half years in Israel, where she completed a graduate degree in general psychology. Being a student in Israel expanded her language skills. She learned to understand and speak Hebrew, follow the lectures, and take exams. She also learned to read and write in English to access class and library texts and prepare research papers. From her French roommate she picked up considerable French, and communicated with her South American friends she taught herself conversational Spanish. While in Israel, she lived for the first time in an internationally diverse community. Eventually, she moved to the United States for a second doctorate in clinical psychology and gerontology. It was in the United States, as an adult, that she finally learned to speak and understand English. In this country, she has worked as a clinical and academic psychologist in urban and rural settings across a variety of locations, from Illinois to Montana, Vermont, and Colorado.

The other author, Evelinn A. Borrayo, is of Latin American descent. She was born and raised in Guatemala City. She was first exposed to the U.S. mainstream culture and education when she immigrated to the U.S. at eight-years old. As an elementary school student in Los Angeles, she learned English without formal training. She had direct exposure to the experience of many immigrants who struggle with being ridiculed or ignored when unable to communicate in the dominant language. She achieved enough fluency in English to complete elementary school but returned to Guatemala to complete the equivalent of a high school education. Her high academic achievement and her bilingual skills allowed her to win a competitive scholarship to pursue an undergraduate degree at the University of the Ozarks in Arkansas. She later continued her graduate education and earned both a master's and doctorate in clinical psychology, with a specialty in health psychology, from the University of North Texas. Her post-doctoral training is in gerontology from the University of South Florida. Her first tenure-track faculty appointment is at Colorado State University. All together, she has had the experience of living in five different states.

There certainly are commonalties in our experiences. These commonalties may account for our similar approaches to teaching in general, and teaching diversity specifically. We both grew up in a foreign country, speaking a language other than English. At some point, we both became intellectual nomads. We both received a doctorate from a U.S. university and eventually settled in this country. Our experiences across communities, cultures, and languages probably also changed us personally in similar ways. We both made human diversity a key professional interest.

There also are similarities in our physical characteristics that may trigger similar responses from students in our classes. To start, we both are females and physically small. These similarities, however, coexist with many visible and invisible differences, including differences in ethnic appearance, age, academic rank, and religion. Based on our experiences, we suspect these differences are less salient to our students than the fact that we both are female professors with a foreign accent.

It is important to recognize that the context of one's teaching makes a difference in terms of whether one is perceived as different and strange. Teaching as a female professor in a women's college is a very different experience than teaching as a female professor in a university where the majority of one's colleagues are men. What may make one unusual and unfamiliar in one place may be the norm in another setting.

In this spirit, we think it is useful for us to describe our institutional context, that is, our students and colleagues. Students at our institution are overwhelmingly U.S.-born, native English speakers, White (of northern European descent), young, and Christian. Many grew up in local, rural communities and have limited experience traveling even out of the state. They tend to be religiously and politically conservative. The most common type of professor these students encounter in their classes is someone in many ways like them—U.S.-born, native English speaker, White (of northern European descent), Christian, and politically conservative. The majority of the faculty at our institution are male.

Familiarity

One obvious factor in our classroom experience is that our students are unfamiliar with the type of professors we are. When they take our classes, they have to adjust to a different image of what a professor looks and sounds like. Since so much teaching depends on visual and aural clues, it is impossible for our students not to be aware of the way we look and sound different from the typical professor at our institution. Our voices, appearances, and mannerisms constantly remind our students of our alien status. We think these aspects of ourselves are not just the instruments of our teaching. They give our lectures a unique rhythm, texture, color, and ambience. In other words, we think that how students react to the diversity content in our classes needs to be understood not just in terms of what we teach, but also in terms of who we are, how we look, speak, and act, and what these different physical clues trigger in our students. We think our physical diversity can be a real challenge for some students.

The issues we face as foreign female professors are in some ways similar to those of U.S. professors who are a numerical and low-status minority in their institutions (e.g., U.S. female professors in predominantly male-faculty institutions). For example, like our native born female colleagues, we tend to be addressed by our first name or to be called with an appellative (such as Miss or Mrs.) that assumes we are not a 'professor.' As noted by Basow (1998), college teaching is overwhelmingly a male occupation. Female professors remain uncommon, especially in the higher ranks; thus, "male professors are [viewed as] professors [while] female professors are female professors" (150).

As foreign professors, we face extra challenges. Our native born female and male colleagues can count on the common denominator of being "Americans."[2] We have to contend with the distrust and anxiety associated with "aliens," as foreigners often are called in this country. Our "alien" status is enhanced by the limited and stereotyped international coverage our students tend to be exposed to via the media. Many of our students are uninformed about the world outside the U.S. As a result, some find it difficult to relate to our experiences and perspectives as foreign professors.

Credibility and Authority

A teacher's credibility and authority are essential to effective teaching. Credibility and authority are related to status and power. High-status teachers tend to enjoy greater credibility, independent of the topic they are covering (Basow 1998; Marks 1995). In his article on teaching about gender, Marks notes that being a male works to his advantage, even when he teaches about the female experience. "The legitimacy of my power and authority will go unquestioned even if I am not appreciated as a person, whereas female instructors may find that they must work extra hard to earn their legitimacy" (Marks 142).

Credibility and authority also are affected by a teacher's personal relationship with the subject matter. Having personal experience with the subject matter affects one's credibility in the eyes of students. The direction of this effect seems to depend on student characteristics. For example, being a Native American instructor may increase one's credibility on Native American topics among Native American students, but it may diminish one's credibility among some European American students, especially those with limited experience beyond the European American canon (Smith 1999). Similarly, we find that our students rarely challenge us, and they may even treat us as reliable informants if we cover international issues in a manner that reinforces their perception of the U.S. as a leader and model country. Our credibility on international matters, however, is questioned if we present information that is critical of U.S. customs and values. Actually, our knowledge and competence have been disputed when we have simply challenged the generalizability of U.S. psychological theories and research to all people in the world.

Our experiences concerning authority and credibility as international female professors are similar in some ways to those of U.S.

professors who are a visible[3] numerical minority in their institutions (such as ethnic-minority professors in predominantly European American institutions). Like other visibly different professors, we sometimes are assumed to be less knowledgeable and less qualified than our colleagues. At the same time, there are unique challenges we face as a result of being international professors. For example, female, U.S.-born teachers of human diversity may have the advantage of being perceived as informed about national issues by virtue of having been born and raised in this country. As international professors with accents, we often are thought to be ignorant about national history and affairs, even though we have advanced degrees from U.S. institutions and we have actually lived longer in the U.S. than most of our students. Another advantage of U.S. professors, even those who are a visible minority in their institutions, is that they may be presumed to be loyal to America (whether that is true or not). For this reason, they may be allowed to be critical of U.S. ways or products (in our case, of U.S. psychological science) in a way that is not tolerated in foreign professors. On the other hand, international instructors who critique the U.S., we may be suspected of being anti-American.

To encourage class discussion about issues of diversity, including our own diversity (and to give permission to students to ask questions about our background), we sometimes have informed students of our international backgrounds at the beginning of a course. We wonder if such self-introduction increases our credibility and improves our rapport with students, or rather gives them an early and explicit rationale to discount us. We also wonder if we contribute to diminishing our credibility by relying on less-authority-oriented teaching methods. For example, in our classes we tend to discourage memorizing of information. Rather, we expect students to critique our courses' content in class discussions as well as in homework assignments. While these teaching methods are a good fit for the diversity content of our classes, they also may reduce our authority in the classroom. We suspect that some students interpret our teaching style to be a sign of our lesser knowledge and competence. In our review of the literature, we found at least two authors who argued that a student-centered classroom may be counterproductive for teachers whose credibility is already suspected (Condit 1996; Marks 1995). One African American female instructor was quoted as saying that it would be dangerous for her to adopt pedagogies that diminish her voice and authority in the classroom: "I am *already* out of the center," she noted in her article. "Many of my students act as if they have more of a right to be here than I do" (quoted in Marks 1995, 142-143).

Resistance, Anger, and Retaliation

Teaching about human diversity is teaching "against the grain" (Cochran-Smith 1991). It involves challenging students' fundamental assumptions about themselves and their place in the world. While some students welcome this opportunity to examine their worldviews, others resist and become angry. Still other students deal with their anxiety about the class by contending with the instructor in various ways (Condit 1996; Jackson 1999). Faculty in this situation have mentioned a variety of difficult student behaviors: chatting, sneering, late attendance or early departure from class, challenging and/or questioning the teacher's expertise or the validity of the theories and content of the class, persistent silence, and passivity (Jackson 1999; Williams et al. 1999). One teacher of human diversity reported "being verbally attacked by students and having students act out by not turning in assignments and giving faculty poor evaluations" (Jackson 1999, 32). According to other educators, these difficult student behaviors represent a "defensive behavioral reaction," a form of resistance in response to being "challenged to modify or to change one's worldview" (Williams et al. 1999, 11). These student behaviors also have been compared to transference reactions in psychotherapy. One author noted that, like most transference reactions, these behaviors often feel "disorienting and misplaced to the faculty member" (Jackson 1999, 30). According to Jackson, the transference resistance "keeps the focus on the faculty person, and the student avoids having to explore the anxiety that he or she may feel about the topic under discussion" (32).

A growing literature has been documenting how students' resistance in diversity classes operates differently depending on the teacher's identity, status, and power within the institution. It also has been repeatedly noted that the consequences, for faculty, of these difficult diversity class dynamics vary a great deal depending on institutional support (Condit 1996; Farnham 1996; Williams et al. 1999). For example, three Black female educators described the challenges of teaching about diversity to students with limited exposure to diversity content and no experience with women of color as professors (Williams et al. 1999). At the same time, they emphasized how their supportive institutional environment allowed them to deal constructively and creatively with their difficult classes. They consistently noted the value of being in a department that was aware of the complexities of teaching about diversity. They wrote that their colleagues did not treat their teaching difficulties as personal failures, but rather were unquestionably affirmative of their authority and competence. Similarly, others (e.g., Garcia and Van Soest

1999) commented on the importance of supportive departmental conditions so faculty who teach about human diversity can take chances, make mistakes, and develop new skills and insights.

Once again, we find that our experiences as international and female professors of human diversity have involved student responses similar to those encountered by some of our U.S. colleagues. Like our U.S. colleagues, we have encountered resistance in our diversity classes. We also have run up against a variety of indirect as well as direct forms of hostility. Some of these behaviors are clearly linked to our being foreign professors while others are not obviously so. To start with, some students explicitly mentioned the fact that we are not "American" as a justification for challenging our competence and authority to define class content, structure, assignments, and grading criteria. For example, we have been told that what they learn in our classes is different from what they learn in other classes, and that therefore our class must include incorrect information. Some students have argued that, as non-native speakers of English, we are not competent to evaluate their written assignments. Others have resisted learning from us by missing weeks of classes without providing justification. Yet others have ignored our class requirements or simply failed to complete the class assignments, but then complained to other students and faculty that we gave them low grades to punish them for having disagreed with our "political agenda."

In addition to resistance, we have seen students respond to our classes with verbal hostility. We have been angrily accused of insensitivity by just about every student constituency. Some politically and religiously conservative students have complained that we offended their values. Some European American students and some male students have accused us of silencing them. Some ethnic-minority students have attacked us for being too conventional in our class content and requirements and complained we were not supportive enough of their perogative. In fact, students of just about every background have charged us with favoritism of whomever they saw as different from themselves. For example, some European American students have accused us of being uniquely lenient in our evaluation of ethnic-minority students. At the same time, some ethnic-minority students have complained that we have been too hard or even biased in our assessment of their work.

Finally, we have seen students engage in a variety of hostile actions against us or against our courses. Some students have given us negative course evaluations, with our being foreign professors and the diversity content itself being cited as the primary reasons for their negative comments. Other students have complained about our courses and our teaching competence to our colleagues. Yet others have taken their complaints through various administrative channels with a persistence that is rare for students dissatisfied with a course. This is perhaps because they had been advised to do so by some of our colleagues, as some students later told us.

We believe that one reason for the resistance and hostility we have encountered in some of our classes is that many of our students and colleagues do not see integrating diversity content in the curriculum as a scientific and educational contribution (see Padilla and Lindholm 1992 for a similar analysis). Also, among those who value diversity content, many define diversity narrowly as local ethnic diversity. For them, studying diversity means studying U.S. Ethnic-minority experiences. In their view, consideration of other diversity categories, such as gender, sexual orientation, social class, and physical ability, is at best secondary; and inclusion of international material is downright inappropriate. For example, one of us was warned against including international content in her classes. Her annual evaluation report noted she should maintain a "distinction between American diversity versus cross-cultural psychology," with only the former being considered "fit to her job description" in terms of diversity teaching.

As we discussed earlier, an obstacle in bringing diversity content to our classes is the ambivalent institutional context in which we operate. On the one hand, according to official university documents, all courses should include information on diverse populations. In reality, in our institution as in many others (Kowalski 2000; Padilla and Lindholm 1992; Simoni et al. 1999), most courses do not comply with official diversity content goals. Rather, the absence of diversity content is ignored while integrating diversity content into one's courses brings constant scrutiny to those courses, with the diversity content needing to be constantly justified. For example, one of us has had to contend with yearly peer reviews of the content of a developmental psychology course that had diversity content. There also have been yearly proposals to drop such a course out of its required status. At the same time, other courses' lack of diversity content did not stimulate a call for a course review or for changes in the course status. One consequence of this institutional climate is that our classes are often the only psychology classes in which students systematically encounter, and have to learn, diversity content. Another consequence of this climate is that students learn that it is permissible and even expected to challenge our classes in a way they would not dare to do in other classes.

Another institutional factor in our class dynamics is that those of us who bring diversity content to classes tend to be the least powerful and/or the most junior members of the department. As noted by other educators, this diminishes the status of the diversity content and increases the likelihood of students' resistance and hostility (Hills and Strozier 1992). One of us observed that in a university where senior White male faculty routinely covered diversity content in their classes, minority faculty of all kinds and faculty in untenured positions did not encounter student or institutional resistance when teaching diversity. There are other problems when the least powerful faculty carry much of the burden of diversity teaching. Untenured faculty are particularly vulnerable to the risks involved in dealing with difficult dynamics of diversity-content classes, since their advancement depends in part on class evaluations (Garcia and Van Soest 1999; Hills and Strozier 1992).

Having pointed out these negative experiences, we would now like to address what have been the exciting and rewarding aspects of teaching diversity. First, we find diversity content academically and personally compelling. Second, many students have eloquently expressed their appreciation for what they have learned in our classes, both in class evaluations and letters to the department chair. Several have selected a diversity topic for their thesis or dissertation based on their positive experiences in our classes. Others have made a diversity topic the focus of their whole career and given us credit for the inspiration.

Our commitment to integrating diversity content into the curriculum also is supported by curriculum trends in colleges and universities around the country (Kowalski 2000). A diversity and global focus is the direction business, political, and education leaders around the world are pointing us to (Ownby and Perreault 1994; Turlington 1998). In fact, according to an article published in *Academe*, "today's arguments for diversity focus not so much on *why* diversity is important but *how* it is important" (Baez 2000, 45).

Discussion

In this chapter, we have discussed our experiences as female international professors teaching about diversity in an institution where we are a minority both as female professors and as international professors. Like many teachers of diversity, we have had experiences of resistance and hostility. Like these other teachers, we have realized that class resistance and hostility are not necessarily problematic responses to diversity content. Rather, they often represent "normal processes students...experience when confronted with course material that is uncomfortable" (Jackson 1999, 33). While the negative student responses are "frustrating" (Williams et al. 1999, 16) and even "exhausting" (Garcia and Van Soest 1999, 162) for instructors, they should not be avoided, as they offer students opportunities for cognitive and emotional learning. The intense dynamics of diversity-content classes also are a stimulus for growth for us as teachers. They keep us engaged with our own feelings and conflicts about identity, role, status, and privilege. They also are an occasion for us to "develop insight and pedagogical skills into how to help students come to terms with their social identity and social status issues" (Garcia and Van Soest 1999, 156).

Negative student reactions, however, become problematic if instructors have to worry that their colleagues will treat these negative reactions simply as a sign of incompetent teaching, without consideration of the unique dynamics of diversity-content classes. This is not to say one should dismiss student complaints in diversity-content classes. Rather, it is to note that teaching about diversity tends to generate negative class dynamics and student complaints. If instructors do not have institutional support in undertaking the sometimes treacherous journey of teaching diversity content, they may give up and drop the diversity content, with the result being that the quality of the class also will drop. Those teachers who maintain high standards of diversity content in their classes, despite an ambivalent or unsupportive institutional environment, may increasingly "experience...alienation" from their peers, and also be individually penalized for their efforts in terms of difficulties in professional advancement, including annual evaluations, tenure, and promotion (Hill and Strozier 1992, 49). Therefore, as cautioned by Garcia and Van Soest (1999, 164), "It is important that deans and directors recognize the issues involved in preparing the student to become...[diversity] competent practitioners and that they try to create conditions in which all faculty can risk, make mistakes, and develop skills without fear of negative consequences for their efforts."

We believe our status as outsiders makes us particularly vulnerable to the negative classroom reactions the diversity content tends to engender. In our experience, the students' awareness of our international, "alien" status creates a climate of suspiciousness about our authority, credibility, and trustworthiness. These suspicions can easily consolidate into resistance when the students, feeling challenged, look for ways to dismiss what we are teaching in order to avoid revising their assumptions about themselves, the U.S., and the world. We believe our classroom experiences are intensified by an institutional climate that is often ambivalent and sometimes hostile to diversity content. For these reasons, teaching about diversity has been, for us, personally and professionally demanding.

It has been argued that support for a human diversity perspective is pervasive in institutions of higher education (Baez 2000). For many colleges and universities, this support involves a global diversity curriculum agenda, not simply a local diversity focus. Most major research universities in the United States already "think of themselves as 'world class' institutions" (Mestenhauser 1998, xvii). In reality, many offer a curriculum that is U.S.-centered and taught by faculty who are overwhelmingly U.S.-born and U.S.-trained (Gielen and Pagan 1993). Judging from the increasing number of conferences, policy statements, and studies of global issues, the internationalization of U.S. higher education seems to be an important common goal (Hauberger, Gerber, and Anderson 1999).

It has been argued that one way to globalize the curriculum is for U.S. students to study international perspectives about the U.S., or, as Sarles (1998, 135) puts it, for U.S. students to explain themselves "through others' cultural visions." If Sarles' position is fulfilled, classes like the ones we teach (in which we examine content about human diversity, within and beyond the U.S., building on our experiences as foreign-born professors) may become valued and perhaps even common at U.S. Colleges and universities.

We hope our reflections about the challenges of teaching about human diversity as international female professors will stimulate a dialogue that can benefit all of those who teach about diversity. We especially hope to reach and inspire a response from those who, like us, teach diversity from alien perspectives and with accented female voices. By comparing across experiences, we can perhaps learn to distinguish the idiosyncratic from the normative and expand our understanding of the general factors influencing the class dynamics of diversity-content classes.

Notes

1. From this point on, the term "we" is used to indicate the experiences and perspectives of either or both authors.

2. The term "American" often is used to refer to U.S. nationals. We, however, think it is inaccurate and exclusionary since it renders invisible all other "Americans," meaning Central, North, and South Americans. To highlight its problematic meaning, we bracketed the term "American" between quotation marks.

3. Some professors come from a minority group but their difference is not visible. This applies, for example to lesbian and gay professors or to professors from a minority religion, such as Jewish professors.

References

Baez, Benjamin. 2000. Diversity and its contradictions. *Academe* 86(5):43-47.

Basow, Susan A. 1998. Student evaluations: The role of gender bias and teaching style. In *Career strategies for women in academe: Arming Athena*, edited by Lynn H. Collins, Joan C. Chrisler, and Kathryn Quina. Thousand Oaks, CA: Sage.

Cochran-Smith, Marilyn. 1991. Learning to teach against the grain. *Harvard Educational Review* 61:279-310.

Condit, Celeste M. 1996. Theory, practice, and the battered (woman) teacher. In *Teaching what you're not: Identity politics in higher education*, edited by Katherine J. Mayberry. New York: New York University Press.

Davis, Nancy J. 1992. Teaching about inequality: Student resistance, paralysis, and rage. *Teaching Sociology* 20:232-238.

Farnham, C. 1996. The discipline of history and the demands of identity politics. In *Teaching what you're not*, edited by Katherine J. Mayberry. New York: New York University Press.

Friedman, Susan S. 1985. Authority in the feminist classroom: A contradiction in terms? In *Gendered subjects: The dynamics of feminist teachings*, edited by Marge Culley and Catherine Portuges. Boston: Routledge and Kegan.

Garcia, Betty, and Dorothy Van Soest. 1999. Teaching about diversity and oppression: Learning from the analysis of critical classroom events. *Journal of Teaching and Social Work* 18:149-167.

Garcia, Joseph E. 1994. Reflections on teaching diversity. *Journal of Management Education* 18(4):428-431.

Gielen, Uwe P., and Monica Pagan. 1993, February. International psychology and American mainstream psychology. *The International Psychologist* 16-19.

Heuberger, Barbara, Diane Gerber, and Reed Anderson. 1999. Strength through cultural diversity: Developing and teaching a diversity course. *College Teaching* 47(3):107-113.

Hills, Hope I., and Anne L. Strozier. 1992. Multicultural training in APA-approved counseling programs: A survey. *Professional Psychology: Research and Practice* 23:43-51.

Jackson, Leslie C. 1999. Ethnocultural resistance to multicultural training: Students and faculty. *Cultural Diversity and Ethnic Minority Psychology* 5:27-36.

Kaye/Kantrowitz, Melanie. 1999. How did "correct" become a dirty word? Theory and practice for a social justice classroom. *Transformations* 10(2):42-51.

Kirkham, Kate. 1999. Teaching about diversity: Navigating the emotional undercurrents. *Organizational Behavior Teaching Review* 13(4):48-67.

Kowalski, Robin M. 2000. Including gender, race, and ethnicity in psychology content courses. *Teaching Psychology* 27(1):18-24.

Marks, Stephen R. 1995. The art of professing and holding back in a course on gender. *Family Relations,* 44:142-148.

Mestenhauser, Joseph A. 1998. Introduction. In *Reforming the higher education curriculum: Internationalizing the campus*, edited by Joseph A. Mestenhauser and B.J. Ellingboe. Phoenix, AZ: American Council on Education/Oryx Press.

Ownby, Arnold C. and Heidi R. Perreault. 1994, February. Teaching students to understand and value diversity. *Business Education Forum* 27-30.

Padilla, Amato M., and Kathryn J. Lindholm. 1992, August. What *do we know about culturally diverse children?* Paper presented at the American Psychological Association Conference, Washington, D.C.

Sarles, Harvey B. 1998. Explaining ourselves through others' cultural visions. In *Reforming the higher education curriculum: Internationalizing the campus*, edited by J.A. Mestenhauser and B.J. Ellingboe. Phoenix, AZ: American Council on Education/Oryx Press.

Simoni, Jane M., Kathy Sexton-Radek, Karen Yescavage, Harriette. Richard, and Arlene Lundquist. 1999. Teaching diversity: Experiences and recommendations of American Psychological Association Division 2 members. *Teaching of Psychology* 26:89-95.

Smith, Theresa S. 1999. Teaching who we are: Testing limits of tolerance in a course on religion and sexual diversity. *College Teaching* 47(2):55-61.

Stricker, George. 1993. Diversity in clinical psychology. *The Clinical Psychologist* 46:(20, 88-89).

Turlington, Barbara. 1998. Foreword. In *Reforming the higher education curriculum: Internationalizing the campus*, edited by Joseph A. Mestenhauser and Brenda J. Ellingboe. Phoenix, AZ: American Council on Education/Oryx Press.

Walker, Alexis J. 1993. Teaching about race, gender, and class diversity in United States families. *Family Relations* 42:342-350.

White, Aaronette M. 1994. A course in the psychology of oppression: A different approach to teaching about diversity. *Teaching of Psychology* 21:17-23.

Williams, Michelle, Michelle Dunlap, and Terry McCandles. 1999. Keepin' it real: Three Black educators discuss how we deal with student resistance to multicultural inclusion in the curriculum. *Transformations* 10(2):11-23.

The Institution's Commitment to Diversity: An Aid or Hindrance to Teachers of Diversity

James H. Banning

Introduction

I think this book is about the struggles, challenges, hardships, and triumphs that instructors representing a variety of disciplines encounter as they attempt to "teach about diversity." For me, two themes appear to emerge from the chronicles of these instructors: (1) The task of teaching about diversity is not an easy one and (2) The context in which the effort is embedded is of critical importance. In a supportive and collegial environment triumphs seem more likely to occur. In environments that are not supportive, the assignment of teaching about diversity is a labor of love, but with little institutional or collegial recognition regarding its importance or its difficulties.

My interest resides in the intersection of the two foregoing themes: How can the context of the institution aid or hinder the teaching of diversity? The basic premise of my thinking is rather simple: Institutions that support diversity provide a context by which instructors and administrators who have major responsibilities in teaching and supporting diversity are aided, rather than hindered, in their work. The opposite is equally straightforward: Institutions that do not support diversity, despite their claims of doing so, make it more difficult and hinder the efforts of instructors and administrators. The institutional context can have a synergistic effect and aid in the teaching or an antagonistic effect and hinder it.

Today, nearly all colleges and universities proclaim that they are supportive of diversity. I know of no institution that has made a proclamation against the efforts of diversifying its student body, its faculty, and its classroom teachings. In fact, diversity is a very socially acceptable and embraceable concept for institutions of higher education. What I want to write about are two observations: (1) Despite institutional proclamations for full support of diversity, there are ways to conceptualize the institutional commitment level; and (2) There are ways to conceptualize the institutional "approach" regarding diversity by examining campus artifacts.

Surface and Deep Diversity

For me, the notions of surface and deep diversity have their origin in the ecological literature. This literature points out that not all is right between humankind and nature (Tobias 1988), and many legitimate doomsday scenarios have emerged. Responses to these scenarios have been conceptualized as occurring at two levels: environmentalism and deep ecology (Bookchin 1980, 1982, 1986; Devall and Sessions 1985; Tobias 1988).

Environmentalism, while often seeming to move in the direction of solving ecological problems, frequently offers solutions that are political, technical, and economical and that fall short of addressing other basic issues. Deep ecology is offered as a concept that goes beyond these shallow approaches to restore the balance between humankind and nature.

Ecological problems from the "deep" perspective are seen as being woven into the complexity of our worldviews, philosophies, spirituality, and the way we see ourselves. They are not problems that technological tinkering can resolve. In addition, the concept of deep ecology calls for personal action:

> Deep ecology is a process of ever-deepening questioning of ourselves, the assumptions of the dominant worldview in our culture, and the meaning and truth of reality. We cannot change consciousness by only listening to others; we must involve ourselves. We must take direct action. (Devall and Sessions 1985, 8-9)

The purpose of my review is not to provide an exhaustive comparison of surface vs. deep ecologies, but to introduce the terms so that they can serve as an analogical base for examining our colleges' and universities' commitment to diversity. I want to provide a way to understand whether institutional policies are reflective of surface or deep commitments, and to present a conceptual approach using campus artifacts to understand institutional approaches to diversity.

To continue the analogical strategy: There is a growing awareness that all is not well on college and university campuses. While hard numbers are available, they are not needed to make the point that campuses continue to struggle with diversity. Consider the following:

- Inability to attract ethnic minorities from the communities that an institution proclaims to serve.

- Graduation rates for ethnic-minority students that lag behind the rates for majority students.

- Ethnic minority faculty and staff not present on campus and, if present, they are found in positions with low or no authority.

- Persistent underrepresentation of both women and minority faculty among the full-time tenured faculty.

- Underrepresentation of women faculty occurs even in departments where the majority of the students are women.

- Lack of female presence in many of the decision-making groups within the institution.

- Buildings, labs, and classrooms that are not accessible to students in wheelchairs.

- Gay, lesbian, and transexual students who are subjected to harassment and assaults.

- Gay, lesbian, and transexual faculty and staff who are unable to obtain partner benefits from the institution.

The list could go on, but Devall and Sessions' (1985, 2) remark concerning world ecological problems is an appropriate summary regarding institutional diversity efforts—"something is drastically wrong, out of balance in contemporary culture."

Do the concepts of surface and deep diversity have applicability as a way to conceptualize institutional responses to diversity? Can some institutional responses be viewed as surface responses without a serious commitment, despite their (apparently good) intentions? An answer in the affirmative seems appropriate when you note the following:

- The development and public distribution of institutional diversity plans and goals that never get translated into action programs. The document serves public relations purposes but never results in reaching the stated goals.

- The hiring of diversity personnel into "token" positions that do not have the level of institutional support to allow success.

- The cosmetic inclusion of "persons of color" on campus recruiting materials and posters, university web sites, etc., without this inclusion really representing conditions on campus.

- The placement of very visible handicapped parking signs in lots that lead to buildings without elevators or mechanisms for access.
- The development and implementation of diversity policies that do not address sexual orientation.
- The development of "assertive" recruitment strategies, but a failure to address retention strategies for students, faculty, and staff.
- The over-inclusion of diversity faculty and staff on institutional committees, but a failure to recognize the importance of institutional service at the time of tenure and promotion.
- The awarding of special research funds to diversity staff, but the refusal of tenure and promotion committees to acknowledge the significance of the research topics or to grant publication venues for diversity faculty.

While institutional efforts may be well intended, the lack of results often points to the factors noted in the environmentalism approach to ecological problems. They often are politically and economically based, and may not face the serious societal and campus issues surrounding racism, sexism, heterosexism, and discrimination against persons with disabilities.

At the other end of the spectrum is deep diversity. It, like deep ecology, focuses on institutional actions that are based on a strong commitment. Actions are taken not simply to gain favor with the public or avoid disfavor with particular legislative or community groups, but because of a deep commitment to social justice, the celebration of diversity, and the belief that differences can make communities stronger. Deep diversity calls for the institution to view itself as the target of change. It involves an internal focus whereby the institution is committed to self-examination and significant change, not to short-term public posturing for external groups.

If the concepts of surface and deep diversity are useful to describe institutional diversity efforts, how can institutional efforts be assessed? Few institutions would confess to intentionally or consciously employing a surface diversity approach, but many such efforts are quite apparent. For example, I was invited to a state university to give a seminar on diversity. The letterhead on the invitation was standard university stationery. It included the university's logo and the following statement at the bottom of the stationery: "Quality; Diversity; Personal Touch; Committed to Affirmative Action and Equal Opportunity." In my scanning of the institution's physical environment, I found on the exterior surface of one of its main campus structures—easily visible to all who use the campus—the following graffiti: "Nigger Nigger go back to Africa." The stationery, then, represented the surface commitment to diversity. On the other hand, the graffiti (which I discovered had been visible for over six weeks) represented the lack of deep commitment. No policy existed for the removal of derogatory or "hate" messages.

This example illustrates not only the concepts of surface diversity and deep diversity, but also the methodology I use in trying to understand an institution's level of commitment and approach to diversity—assessing campus physical artifacts.

The Institutional Commitment to Diversity

A switch in analogies from ecology to psychoanalysis is needed to pursue the concept of "institutional behavior." Sigmund Freud introduced two important concepts to understanding human behavior: the conscious and the unconscious mind (Mayer and Sutton 1996). The conscious mind is aware of surrounding events and interacts with these events. The unconscious mind, on the other hand, is a repository of ideas and impulses that are outside of awareness, but that direct a person's behavior. While Freud used these concepts to understand an individual behavior, they also are concepts that can be applied to an organization. For example, are there organizational behaviors that reflect responses to deep organizational beliefs/cultures and that tend to exist outside the immediate awareness of the institution's decision makers? What seems apparent is that institutions have a history of experiences, leaders, constituents, and issues that have molded an institutional culture. If we assume that such cultures often lie outside of our immediate awareness, then how can we assess them or understand their role in decision making? Again, the surface behaviors toward diversity listed previously are not behaviors that the institution would admit it is implementing in a conscious manner. Is it possible to put the institution on the proverbial "Freudian couch" and explore its commitment to diversity?

One of the ways Freud (1901) thought the unconscious could be understood was to note how repressed thoughts manifest themselves in everyday life. For Freud, nothing happened by accident —so through "Freudian slips" of the tongue, "accidental" behaviors, selective remembering, and everyday humor, the unconscious could be revealed. Are there institutional counterparts to these everyday life manifestations so often associated with the behavior of individuals? One strategy for determining this is to examine an institution's cultural artifacts as everyday-life manifestations of institutional culture (Banning 1997; Banning and Bartels 1997). In other words, the artwork, signs, posters, and architecture of the institutional environment may reveal the institution's "unconscious" with regard to the institutional efforts that either facilitate or hinder campus diversity.

Campus Artifacts as Signifers of Institutional Approaches to Diversity

Campus artifacts (artwork, signs, posters, and architectural features) can signify four different approaches to or levels of institutional commitment (Banning, Deniston, and Middleton 2000) in regard to how to diversity is being promoted. The lowest level of commitment is simply a *negative* approach that does not support diversity. The negative approach includes both overt and subtle instances of artifacts in the setting that discriminate, exclude, and produce a hostile environment for diversity. For example, graffiti on the restroom walls ridiculing the celebration of Cinco de Mayo is negative and creates a hostile environment. Subtler examples are posters in classrooms and hallways that depict only white males in leadership positions. (Another example is an institution that failed to place an external building sign for the Women's Studies program office.) On the conscious level, the institution may promote a positive diversity program. But if little attention is given to the messages of posters (cultural artifacts) or the removal of graffiti or the placement of necessary signs, then institutional culture continues to speak a different message on a different level of consciousness, producing a context that hinders campus diversity efforts.

The next level of institutional commitment or approach is termed the *null* approach. The null strategy is based on the work of Freeman (1979) and Betz (1989). The basic principle behind the null approach is that when institutional environments are absent of both negative and positive artifacts, the resulting environment is not neutral, but null. In other words, campus environments that try to remain neutral regarding diversity messages can be seen as inherently discriminatory by persons who are different from the dominant culture, because the "neutral" environment is too often designed in terms of "white male privilege" (McIntosh 2000). These environments, therefore, discriminate against those not included in or belonging to the dominant culture. This is discrimination in the sense that the environment "simply ignores them" (Betz 1989, 137). For example, if a classroom is void of artifacts (like posters) that give specific messages to encourage those that are different, then the prevailing assumptions of the dominant culture remain intact. Success and advancement remain associated with the dominant culture. Again, the lack of artifacts or the null environment can reflect negative diversity messages—ones about which the institution may not have full awareness.

The third level of commitment or approach is a combination of two strategies suggested by Banks' (1999) work in diversity education. This third strategy is a *contributive/additive* approach. In this effort, cultural artifacts are added to the campus environments that support diversity, but the artifacts reflect only those with which the dominant culture is comfortable. The contributive/additive strategy represents a higher level of institutional commitment, but the artifacts most often are presented with little institutional involvement and the presentation typically lacks a diversity-centric perspective. An example of this would be placing a Dr. Martin Luther King, Jr. poster in a classroom for Black History Month without a discussion of his significance and importance. Again, this type of analysis of cultural artifacts is typically not within the paradigm of the institutional psyche.

Finally, the fourth level of commitment or approach combines another two of Banks' (1999) strategies for diversity education and is termed the *transformational/social action* strategy. This strategy or approach has two key ingredients: (1) The transformational/social action approach focuses on artifacts that send a message from a diversity centric perspective rather than the dominant-culture perspective; and (2) The transformational/social action effort calls for a commitment to personal involvement and change (deep diversity). For example, a poster sponsored by the institution that calls upon students and staff to support and create conditions that celebrate all sexual orientations is both a diversity-centric message and a call for personal involvement in change. In contrast, the posting of the Dr. Martin Luther King, Jr. poster as described above does not call for change; in any case, posters of Dr. King lie well within the comfort zone for most institutions.

The foregoing cultural artifact assessment approach to institutional commitment to diversity allows for an evaluation based upon the four levels of commitment—negative, null, contributive/additive, and transformational/social. By classifying the array of campus artifacts using these four dimensions, a summary or composite picture can be created. The value of the composite picture of an institution's diversity efforts is that it can lead to important campus discussions regarding the artifact portrayal of its commitment to diversity. At what levels of commitment is the institution functioning? Does the composite picture suggest "surface diversity," with an eye only to acceptable public relations, or "deep diversity," through which diversity is celebrated and a call to social action is present? These and other questions will help the institution examine its behavior in regard to the promotion or hindrance of diversity.

Impact of Surface vs. Deep Diversity: The Condition of Mistrust

Trust for an individual or institution involves the belief that the conditions of honesty and benevolence will exist (Larzelere and Huston 1980), and that when these conditions are not present, mistrust can develop. When institutions make assertions of support without follow-through, a condition of mistrust is established. Gibbs (1978) outlines the impact of trust and non-trust relationships:

> Trust makes it unnecessary to examine motives, to look for hidden messages, "to have it in writing," to have someone—priest, minister, lawyer, therapist, or bureaucrat—intervene so that we can understand each other or be sure that neither of us is going to hurt the other. As trust ebbs, we are less open with each other, less interdependent, less interbeing—we look for strategies in dealing with each other; we seek help from others; or we look for protection in rules, norms, contracts, and the law—the ebbing of trust and the growth of fear are the beginning of alienation, loneliness, and hostility. (14)

Blau (1964) notes an important behavioral consequence that occurs in conditions of mistrust—interaction among the participants stops. In addition, when the condition of mistrust is established by lack of commitment and follow-up, the term suggested by Adler and Towne (1987), *pseudoaccommodator,* is useful. In pseudoaccommodation, the party that causes the mistrust fails to face up to the fact that a conflict exists; they assert that nothing's wrong. According to Adler and Towne (1987), the partner in the relationship that definitely feels there is a problem is driven "crazy and causes both guilt and resentment toward the accommodator" (345). These feelings of isolation, lack of interaction, hostility, resentment, and guilt are present in many of the stories in this book of teaching and working for diversity. The posture of surface diversity has serious consequences for institutions, particularly for those attempting to move toward a deeper one.

Conclusion

The instructor who is teaching diversity classes will find aid in the institution's context of diversity, if in fact the commitment is to deep diversity. In deep diversity, the classroom struggle will be recognized, support will be given, context will be included in classroom/teacher evaluations, scholarship surrounding the experience will be valued, and students will find support of diversity not only in their diversity classes but also in other classes, in their residence halls, in institutional policy, and on the bricks and mortar of the campus. The instructors, like those represented in this manuscript, will be aided in their efforts by institutional deep diversity. To fall short of the deepest level of institutional commitment is to hinder those who teach diversity. The institutional contextual difference between surface and deep commitment, in fact, relates directly to Ramsden's (1992) concepts of surface and deep learning. He concludes that surface learning relates to the memorization of facts for the purpose of completing an assigned task. Deep learning, however, involves learning about facts in relation to concepts; it is based upon a desire for understanding. Rote learning about diversity is not enough; there must be a desire for deep learning. In the same way, deep institutional commitment to diversity and deep learning about diversity are synergetic. We must have both.

References

Adler, Ronald B., and Neil. Towne. 1987. *Looking out/looking in: Interpersonal communication*, 5th ed. New York: Holt, Rinehart, and Winston.

Banks, James A. 1999. *An introduction to multicultural education*, 2nd ed. Boston: Allyn and Bacon.

Banning, James H. 1997. Assessing the campus' ethical climate: A multidimensional approach. In *Ethics for today's campus: New perspectives on education, student development, and institutional management*, edited by J. Fried. San Francisco: Jossey-Bass, Publishers.

Banning, James H., and Sharon Bartels. 1997. A taxonomy: Campus physical artifacts as communicators of campus multiculturalism. *NASPA Journal* 35(1):29-37.

Banning, James H., Terry Deniston, and Valerie Middleton. 2000, July. A visual anthropological taxonomy for assessing equity climate. Paper presented at the annual meeting of the National Coalition for Sex Equity. Denver, CO.

Betz, Nancy E. 1989. Implications of the null environment hypothesis for women's career development and for counseling psychology. *The Counseling Psychologist* 17(1):136-144.

Blau, Peter M. 1964. *Exchange and power in social life*. New York: John Wiley and Sons.

Bookchin, Murray. 1980. *Toward an ecological society*. Montreal, PQ: Black Rose Books.

Bookchin, Murray. 1982. *The ecology of freedom*. Palo Alto, CA: Cheshire Books.

Bookchin, Murray. 1986. *The modern crisis*. Philadelphia: New Society.

Devall, Bill, and George Sessions. 1985. *Deep ecology*. Layton, UT: Gibbs M. Smith.

Freeman, Jane. 1979. How to discriminate against women without really trying. In *Women: A feminist perspective*, edited by Jane Freeman, 2nd ed. Palo Alto, CA: Mayfield.

Freud, Sigmund. 1901. The psychopathology of everyday life. Vol. VI, *Standard edition of the complete works of Sigmund Freud*. London: Hogarth Press.

Gibb, Jack R. 1978. *Trust: A new view of personal and organizational development*. Los Angeles: The Guild of Tutors Press.

Larzelere, Robert, and Ted Huston. 1980. The dyadic trust scale: Toward understanding interpersonal trust in close relationships. *Journal of Marriage and the Family* 42:595-604.

Mayer, F. Stephan, and Karen Sutton. 1996. *Personality: An integrative approach*. Upper Saddle River, NJ: Prentice Hall.

McIntosh, Peggy. 2000. White privilege and male privilege: A personal account of coming to see correspondence through work in women's studies. In *Gender basics: Feminist perspectives on women and men*, edited by Ann Minas. Belmont, CA: Wadsworth/Thompson Learning.

Ramsden, Paul. 1992. *Learning to teach in higher education*. New York: Routledge.

Tobias, Michael I. 1988. *Deep ecology*. San Marcos, CA: Avant Books.

Recalling the Canon

Jane Kneller

Introduction

By training, I am a philosopher raised in the Analytic tradition, a tradition rooted in Positivism and the Anglo American philosophy of the twentieth century. The focus of this method is on arguments and texts, and until recently it has been relatively unconcerned with historical and sociological context. In the days of the Vienna Circle, it explicitly opposed the systematic incorporation of such concerns into philosophical method. This anti-historicism was fueled by the Positivists' opposition to unsavory ideological and political ends associated with German academics in the 1920s and 1930s, many of whom embraced a more historicist and systematizing approach to philosophy. In this context, abstraction from one's own political and social interests in the interest of simple truth and logical meaning seemed to promise a higher ground from which to do philosophy, but it also signaled a retreat from historical texts in philosophy in favor of the development of new systems rooted in logical theory.

But after World War II, and especially with the advent of the Civil Rights movement abroad and in the United States, followed by anti-nuclear and then anti-war movements, philosophers (who, as Hegel rightly noted, typically manifest the wisdom of hindsight) began to readjust their methods to include less "meta-theoretical" work, theorizing about theorizing about subjects, to return to "normative" theory, that is, theorizing about the subject itself. John Rawls' contributions to ethics and social theory may be seen as the paradigmatic case of this methodological shift in the Anglo-American philosophical tradition [see Rawls 1971] perhaps his most influential). These new philosophers remained rooted in analysis of arguments and the rule of Reason, but their subject matter was brought down to earth to the sphere of human activity: ethics, politics, science, etc. The arguments of historical figures again seemed relevant. This new philosophical orientation was the theoretical soil in which the famous "second wave" of feminist philosophy took root.[1]

I make these very general historical comments in order to situate my own work in philosophy and gender studies, and to give the reader of this chapter a sense of what my commitments in the classroom are. Having undergone the rigors of an analytic training that included a serious dose of logical theory, I see the advantage of being able to analyze and critique arguments in a formal way, abstracted from the contexts of our individual daily lives and the prejudices that always accompany our ordinary thinking. If part of our task as educators is to help students grow and develop mentally into more mature and responsible human beings, then there is much to be said for teaching them to be able to distance themselves to some extent from their particular contexts and to discuss an issue dispassionately. At the same time, I am well aware that one person's rational stance is another's infuriating, arrogant attitude, especially when, as an instructor, I attempt to get all students involved in philosophical discussions. The lessons of my normative ethics professor in graduate school were as important to me as the proofs I did in set theory.

Classroom Practice

After fifteen years of teaching and research, I continue to believe strongly that the ability to remain unshaken and unintimidated in a "real-life" argument in which the stakes are high requires prior experience, practice at "distancing," and abstract critical thinking. Students need to be able to critically evaluate texts of all kinds for valid or invalid forms of argument. They need to be able to conduct research with an open mind for the truth of claims being made, no matter how "obviously" true or false they may appear to the uncritical reader. Accomplishing this, however, involves far more than the right textbooks and a few techniques for organizing classroom debates.

As has been well documented, students cannot even begin to test their pre-formed biases and convictions if they do not feel that it is safe for them to do so. A public space like the college classroom can be a very intimidating place for students, especially for non-traditional students, first-generation students, or students who, for whatever reason, may feel they do not really fit in with the other students. Moreover, students enter any given course with vastly different backgrounds in terms of their exposure to argumentative situations. Our prerequisites generally do not include significant oral communications or public speaking requirements. But even when we incorporate such requirements into our programs of study, as some new core curricula have done, teachers still face the problem that argumentative abilities and self-confidence in public discussion are closely tied to individual family and even cultural backgrounds. It is in addressing these latter issues that I have found feminist pedagogy to be especially useful (see Maher and Thompson Tetreault 1994; Minnich 1990).

Feminist theorists, along with others concerned with teaching those of diverse backgrounds and identities in our classrooms, have recognized the problems involved in allegedly free and open discussion in which the discussants include individuals who have been socialized to think of others or themselves as culturally or even biologically less well-equipped to think "logically." Women in white American culture have traditionally been deemed if not generally inferior, then at least less "logical," more emotional, less able to maintain psychological distance, more easily reduced to tears, etc. Although this is most definitely changing, the view of women as more emotional and sympathetic and of men as more rational and distant still persists. These stereotypes, of course, don't stand alone. They are layered over and intersect with stereotypes associated with various ethnicities and religious groups so that the dynamics of classroom discussion are complex and bewildering. Cultural expectations shape them in subtle and not-so-subtle ways, from the tendencies of some to interrupt and speak longer and more loudly to subtle shifts in attention and interest when a certain type of person begins to speak.

At issue is not so much the question of whether these stereotypes are ever accurate—for instance, whether or not men are more self-possessed and distanced in speaking than women. Given that we naturally strive to live up to cultural expectations, and we are, in any case, limited by these expectations, the stereotypes may well be true in many instances. The problem is, rather, that rational discourse has been culturally defined as excluding emotion and feeling, just as objectivity or distance in an argument have come to be seen as excluding, or at least taking preeminence over, care and sympathy. This is especially true in the academy. So if, for whatever reasons, a student is unable to argue without getting deeply self-conscious, uncomfortable, or emotional, or she can't really distance herself entirely from a firmly held belief, then she is easily, even automatically, labeled "irrational" or "lacking in objectivity."[2]

Yet, recent work in neurophysiology and cognitive psychology lends support to what some (until recently rather lonely) voices in philosophy have said all along, by suggesting that there is no sound physical basis for making the sharp distinction between rationality and emotionality (see May, Friedman, and Clark 1996). My own classroom methodology has been affected by these traditions and recent research, together with my own research interest in the nature of aesthetic experience. What I try to teach in the classroom is continuous with what I deal with in my research—namely, the development of what has been called "feeling reason" (see May, Friedman, and Clark 1996), that is, a sort of sympathetic disinterest.[3] My end goal for students is that they come to feel self-confident in their own abilities to analyze and discuss claims calmly, and that they learn to present themselves orally and on paper without becoming deeply self-conscious. This does require being able to keep emotions in check and to abstract temporarily to a certain extent from one's own personal history.

At the same time, however, I would emphasize two equally important points: First, the best arguments usually are those whose conclusions truly matter to the individual, and second, lack of compassion and "coolness" toward an opposing position is itself a form of emotional response; indeed, it is an emotional response that often hampers the progress of rational debate. In rational debate, *coolness and dispassion therefore need to be tempered as much as do rage or fear.* As a pedagogical strategy, I have found that this emphasis works well. It allows students to feel less self-conscious when their voices shake or their faces turn hot and flushed, and it serves to remind them that a "cold" attitude in itself may require disciplining. I have found that keeping in mind the ubiquity of emotion in all human discourse is useful to pedagogical practice in several ways.

Modeling

By modeling good listening behaviors for those students who readily perceive an instructor's attitude toward other students when *they* speak, an atmosphere of mutual respect can quickly be created. If a student begins to break down, ramble, or become confused due to nervousness or deep emotional commitment to a topic, I try to listen even harder, visibly focusing my attention on that student, occasionally asking questions that help him or her get back to the issue at hand, or drawing other students in to help the faltering student construct his or her position. It is important to make the discussion process less painful by setting up an environment in which there is no disgrace in occasionally breaking down emotionally, "ramblings" or simply losing the thread of a point a student is making. How the facilitator/teacher responds is crucial in guiding the responses of the rest of the class.

Similarly, students who argue just for the sake of argument, without regard to the impact of their "total coolness" on other students, can be reminded that the issue at hand is important and should not be taken so lightly. Sketching out in some detail a hypothetical situation where it *would* matter to that particular student is an effective way of kindling a moral fire in the excessively detached or apathetic student.

Sharing Relevant Personal Stories

In trying to set up an atmosphere conducive to everyone's involvement, I find it enormously helpful to share anecdotes with students about my own experience as an undergraduate who was very quiet in class and rarely spoke for fear of sounding stupid or saying the wrong thing. Typically they find this astonishing and want to know what happened and how that changed. This gives me a chance to personalize the experience of coming to self-confidence and assure them that I do in fact still get quite nervous before speaking publicly. After this kind of "confession," I find many of my most timid students are willing to open up, or at least come to me during office hours to confess similar fears and ask for advice.

It is useful on occasion to illustrate a point by relating a situation where it mattered personally to me. Students feel less afraid of taking a genuine interest in a subject, even abstract ones like the nature of substance or the conditions of knowledge, when they see their professor getting personally involved. This approach should be used with some discretion, however. Too much personalizing on the part of the instructor can create unnecessary resistance. (For example, talking a lot about one's spouse or children might suggest to some students that the instructor is unsympathetic to the plight of single students without children, or to nontraditional families, etc.) Personalizing issues in discussion is a matter of pedagogical judgment, for which there can be no rule. In the end, individual instructors simply have to proceed in light of their own comfort level and that of the students in any given class. Unfortunately (or perhaps fortunately), there is no formula for the art of teaching!

Offering Advice on an Individual Basis

This holds for overly aggressive and gregarious discussants as much as for the quiet folks. Nearly every year, in at least one of my classes, I have an overly vocal student whom I ask to meet with briefly after class. I give this student heartfelt thanks for his or her many contributions, and explain that if I ever cut him or her off or don't call on him or her it's simply because I want everyone to have the chance to speak, and that I want everyone to have the benefit of hearing all their classmates' views. It also sometimes works nicely to enlist the help of overly vocal or unintentionally intimidating students in an attempt to draw in others while refraining from talking so much themselves.

For the timid or quiet student who wants to speak but has trouble, I find that very concrete suggestions help. My colleagues in speech communications have shared with me all sorts of tricks for overcoming stage fright, and I try to pass these on to students. In some cases I have simply referred them to a good beginning speech class. My favorite case, however, involved a very young, very bright and very shy Iranian student with whom I spent the whole semester working to overcome her nervousness (which she desperately wanted to overcome). At one point, we were reduced to dredging up every bit of my own past experience of stage fright in search of some helpful advice, when I thought of the singing lessons I had taken years ago in college and how they had improved my posture and breath control. It was the perfect solution. She signed up for private voice lessons, she enjoyed very much and which helped her overcome her fear of hearing herself talk in class.

Letting Go

If a student simply cannot speak or discuss no matter what I've tried, then it is acceptable in my classes to simply sit quietly and not say a word. Again, this approach depends upon the class content and work itself. Obviously in a speech class one can't waive the oral presentation aspects. But in other courses in which grades depend on participation, alternatives to oral presentation can be found for the exceptional case. I find this is especially important for students who may have suffered some trauma, as well as for students from cultures that place a high value on restraint, including keeping to oneself in public.

Finally, we need to forgive our own pedagogical blunders. It may seem obvious, but making mistakes in the classroom is no crime and some failures are inevitable. The harder I try, the more aware I become of my mistakes and failures, and therefore the more painful they are. Sometimes we need to relax and trust our developed instincts, letting the occasional train wreck drop from our minds as we move on. (I must confess that I find this nearly impossible to do, and yet I know that it is absolutely essential to avoiding teacher "burnout.")

Course Content

Perhaps the most interesting pedagogical development for me, in the course of several years spent working on a curriculum development project that focuses on gender issues, has been the incorporation of new materials into my courses. For most courses, the "infusion" has been relatively simple and obvious, without need of justification in the eyes of my peers. However, my course on 17th- and 18th-Century European Philosophy has for years presented me with a real dilemma. I have fifteen weeks to teach two centuries of philosophy. The standard approach often limits the course to the "big three" rationalists—Descartes, Spinoza, and Leibniz—followed by the "big three" empiricists—Locke, Berkeley, and Hume—with a few days toward the end of the semester spent gesturing at Kant. (I happen to think that Hobbes and Rousseau also are important to the metaphysical and epistemological thought of this period, but philosophy departments rarely address social theory in such classes, with the hope that it will be covered elsewhere). I also have the students read a bit of Galileo, Copernicus, Bacon, and Montaigne at the beginning of the course to give them a sense of how the leading questions originated in the immediate "pre-history" of the period. This leaves precious little time for me to *breathe* during lectures, much less afford my students the time to discuss at length the fascinating metaphysical and epistemological ideas they are reading. So although I have been advising other professors for several years now on ways to infuse gender and multicultural content into their courses, it has been a major difficulty of my own in this particular course, into which I simply could not imagine crowding in more material.

There is the further problem that even if I had more time to include women's voices, until very recently there has been *lack* of material with which to represent them. We read "great books" and study "great thinkers," but in the history of early modern philosophy that I teach, these have not typically included women. But recent feminist scholarship has rediscovered dozens of women philosophers from that period, and finally the larger philosophical community is beginning to take a closer look at what they were saying.[4] The results are only just beginning to come in but they are very promising—not only for feminists, but for philosophy in general (see O'Neill 1998; Conway 1996; and Cavendish 2001).

What has fascinated me as I find places for them in my course is how my study of these women's theories has transformed my view of the philosophy of the period. Although these women could not be called "feminists" in contemporary terms, their work often is oriented around themes that have in some respects come to be associated with "the feminine." That is, they tend to be focused on spiritual, religious, and educational themes, with a concern for social improvement. These are, of course, not the sole domain of women, and male philosophers also took up these issues. But these women are remarkably consistent in putting social and spiritual themes front and center in their work. Moreover, their more abstract metaphysical and epistemological concerns were often associated with what later became "loser" philosophies of the period (i.e., theories that were downgraded by later historians of the nineteenth and twentieth centuries as "marginal" or "secondary" to the then-dominant metaphysics of rationalism and empiricism). For instance, two of the most well-known and acknowledged women philosophers in seventeenth-century England, Margaret Cavendish and Anne Conway, were deeply influenced by, and themselves contributed to, the neo-Platonic tradition in seventeenth century English philosophy. The importance of this tradition has been played down in twentieth century histories of philosophy and often altogether ignored in favor of the view that Britain's greatest contribution to philosophy begins with Locke, who broke from this tradition and is considered the founder of British empiricism.

What I found as I tentatively added a few sessions to cover these women's materials in the course was that the theoretical contributions of these eclipsed traditions are unique, engaging, and, as my students have themselves suggested, oddly compelling in the twenty-first century. Conway's and Cavendish's philosophies, for instance, embrace vitalism and dynamism—that is, they view matter as itself alive and capable of self-motion. They are concerned with the unity of nature and the human and with the continuity between human beings and other animals. Their accounts of space and time are challenging and very different from many of the more widely studied figures. The students found it fascinating and their interest sent me off to do more research into this entire tradition (which, too, is primarily associated in academic work with the more famous male philosophers who espoused it). I believe the result will permanently change the way I look at and write about the history of the philosophy of this period, its newly discovered women, and their neglected male cohorts, all of whom have now re-entered the canon as far as I'm concerned.

All of this was the result not only of my desire to incorporate women's voices into my course content, but also of the hard work and scholarship of feminist philosophers who have made these works available (and in affordable form for my students). As for the problem of squeezing yet more content into a crowded course, I am still struggling, and no doubt always will, to justify every paragraph I choose to have them read, knowing that it means cutting out some other text from an era that deserves a year-long class to cover. But this has always been a difficulty with teaching survey-type courses. For that matter, if we are doing our jobs properly, it can only get worse. The more we research these historical periods, the more material we will find that needs to be added to the canon or that forces us to rethink what is canonical in the first place. Indeed, something would be wrong if, over time, it did *not* get harder to teach all this material in one semester. In this respect, good scholarship, be it feminist, multicultural, or other, will always make our task as teachers more challenging. But, to paraphrase my grandmother, if this is the worst problem we ever have to solve as teachers, we should count ourselves blessed.

Notes

1. I am intentionally distinguishing feminist philosophy from the actual social movement of Feminism, or the women's liberation movement, which of course has been far more visible. Feminist academic philosophers often have tied their work closely to the women's movement and social activism, but whatever their ties to the "real" world of practice, feminist philosophers attempt in their theoretical work to make gender their central conceptual tool.

2. Here I am using the generic "she." Of course, the stereotypes do not always hold. Quiet or emotional men from all cultures and backgrounds may be the beneficiaries of the sort of expanded accounts of rationality and disinterestedness that I want to give.

3. My own research in the history of aesthetic theory and in feminist aesthetics has involved work on a Kantian notion of aesthetic disinterestedness that is closely tied to moral feelings and feelings of love for nature and humanity. Overview essays are contained in Kelly 1998 and Kneller 1998a; 1998b.

4. A good indication of this is the inclusion of Anne Conway's work in a recent series on the history of philosophy published by Cambridge. See also Waithe 1991 and Atherton 1994.

References

Atherton, Margaret, ed. 1994. *Women philosophers of the early modern period*. Indianapolis/Cambridge: Hackett.

Cavendish, Margaret. 2001. *Observations upon experimental philosophy*. Edited by Eileen O'Neill. Cambridge: Cambridge University Press.

Conway, Anne. 1996. *The principles of the most ancient and modern philosophy*. Translated and edited by Allison Coudert and Taylor Corse. Cambridge: Cambridge University Press.

Kelly, Michael. 1998. *The encyclopedia of aesthetics*. Oxford: Oxford University Press.

Kneller, Jane. 1998a. Feminism and Kantian aesthetics. In *Encyclopedia of aesthetics*, Vol. 3, edited by Michael Kelly. Oxford: Oxford University Press.

Kneller, Jane. 1998b. Disinterestedness. In *Encyclopedia of aesthetics*, Vol. 2, edited by Michael Kelly. Oxford: Oxford University Press.

Maher, Frances A., and Mary Kay Thompson Tetreault. 1994. *The feminist classroom*. New York: Basic Books.

May, Larry, Marilyn Friedman, and Andy Clark, eds. 1996. *Mind and morals: Essays on cognitive science and ethics*. Cambridge, MA: MIT Press.

Minnich, Elizabeth. 1990. *Transforming knowledge*. Philadelphia: Temple University Press.

O'Neill, Eileen. 1998. Disappearing ink: Early modern women philosophers and their fate in history. In *Philosophy in a feminist voice: Critiques and reconstructions*, edited by Janet Kourany. Princeton, NJ: Princeton University Press.

Rawls, John. 1971. *A theory of justice*. Cambridge, MA: Harvard University Press.

Waithe, Mary Ellen. 1991. *A history of women philosophers*. Dordrecht: Kluwer Academic Publishers.

Teaching about Diversity Issues in Natural Resources and Outdoor Recreation Courses: Challenges and Complexities

Nina S. Roberts

Introduction

The field of natural resource management has grown to encompass not only environmental sciences such as forestry, biology, and ecology. It also has broadened to include human dimensions of resource use, including the need to both understand and affect people's knowledge of and behavior toward natural resources and their management. In order to prepare the best-trained professionals, our curriculum typically requires students to take specialized courses in areas relating to natural sciences as well as the social and political sciences. Increasingly, it is being recognized that students trained in natural resource management, including recreation resources, should be exposed to the principles of multiple-use, competing land uses, political science, economics, business management, ecology, biology, environmental law, environmental ethics, social psychology, and communication strategies (Robinson, Pfister, Shultis, and Safford 1997).

Ideally, management of our natural resources, such as parks, protected areas, and open space, involves many voices in creating agendas for policy, planning, and outdoor programming or interpretive activities. People of various racial and ethnic backgrounds are becoming a fast-growing and significant proportion of the population (U.S. Bureau of the Census 2000), yet the voices of ethnic minorities have not been heard enough. It is imperative that this change. Curriculum change, then, should be fundamental; it should also be compelling and, above all, practical.

My primary goal in this chapter is to focus on the importance of race, ethnicity and culture, and, in a less extensive way, gender for teaching natural resource management and outdoor recreation courses. However, I will not address all the forms that human *difference* can take and the issues associated with each. In this chapter, I will share my own experiences and strategies for maintaining the integrity of the curriculum (e.g., principles and best practices of recreation resource management) while moving toward a more comprehensive curriculum that employs more aspects of diversity. Additionally, I provide relevant references for making a connection between diversity and the world of natural resource management.

I am convinced that changes in society require broader approaches, since students will face a changing workplace and more diverse groups of outdoor recreation program participants. Moreover, many possibilities currently exist for addressing diversity issues in natural resource management and outdoor recreation classes. Most students seem to be open to diversity content, yet a small proportion often display some sort of resistance. As the instructor, and as a woman of color in a mostly white environment, I have found that diversity content can affect the emotions of other students and undermine my own safety and comfort. This creates an added challenge for me given my own background and experiences.

Personal Identity and Exposé

To better understand my arguments here, it may be helpful for me to describe who I am and what I bring to this field and the classroom. I am a woman of color who has been involved in the field of parks, recreation, and natural resource management for twenty years. I have developed intense passion for my work and for the young people I have taught in varying capacities. I believe it is important to note that I bring a multi-racial perspective to my teaching from a unique cultural heritage. My father is a white man whose ancestors are from England and Switzerland. My mother, on the other hand, is quite a mix. That is, my maternal great grandmother was from Madras, East India, while my great grandfather was Native American—Cherokee. My maternal grandfather is from the West Indies (St. Lucia). As a prodigy of this uncommon ancestry, my skin color is light chocolate brown; I have dark brown eyes and curly brown hair. When I was growing up, it seemed like everyone but me fit into a neat cultural box where they had a label to call their own.

I have never met an individual yet who can figure out what I am. And, as with my teaching, I always encourage people to ask rather than assume. Some think that I am Black, while others approach me talking in Spanish thinking I must be of some Hispanic descent. Some believe I "must" be a mix of some sort and often ask, "What are you anyway?" It is my awareness of who I am that allows me to assess, question, and, at times, challenge many of the assumptions my students commonly make about other people based only on how they look. Additionally, while I understand the oppression that faces ethnic-minority females, I also recognize the privileges associated with my middle-class position in society. My advanced education adds another degree of privilege in my life, and all that contributes to shaping my personal and professional "filters."

When I received my master's degree from the University of Maryland, I was immediately given the opportunity to join the staff as an "adjunct faculty" member. A couple of years later I was also contracted as adjunct faculty at George Mason University in northern Virginia. I have been active professionally on boards and committees as well. Having high energy, I was told by friends and colleagues that I would make a great contribution to higher education as a professor. Many encouraged me to continue my education for a Ph.D. Now, as a doctoral candidate at a predominantly white, middle-to-upper-class, conservative institution, the opportunity to be an instructor is available to me. As I have gotten to know other professionals and practitioners over the years, I have quickly discovered that I am one of a very few ethnic minorities teaching and doing scholarly work in this field.

My own experiences have not fit the most widely cited biracial identity development model (i.e., Poston 1990). This model does, however, provide the closest framework to help explain my personal growth and changes through life. I began the journey to understand these contradictions between theory and experience many years ago, and this has guided much of my work ever since. As a classroom instructor and social scientist, I want to explore how diversity fits into my teaching and my work as a scholar, and how this can contribute to a positive classroom climate.

"But I've Always Done It This Way"

One very important consideration for me in designing my curriculum and ensuring a positive classroom climate is the disequilibrium that people often experience when they face the reality and pervasiveness of social oppression, regardless of the discipline. For students and professors who are used to doing things a certain way and who have a certain attitude about how things "ought to be," having diversity content in the curriculum can create a state of disequilibrium. For example, according to Adams, Bell, and Griffin (1997), students may be thrown off balance by discussions of what oppression is and how it affects people. Invariably this calls into question deeply held assumptions these students might have. For me, that is when profound change can occur. When a stagnant classroom is shocked out of complacency by discussions that involve diversity (e.g., inequality of social groups), intense learning can result. To illustrate, social groups evolve from common histories, cultures, and traditions, so that our understanding of what it means to be female or male, lesbian or heterosexual, Latino or Black, for example, makes sense to us or has significance to our lives depending on our social context. Therefore, a certain degree of instability can be upsetting or even terrifying if students experience disagreements and begin to realize that previous ways of thinking about natural resource management or principles of outdoor recreation programming no longer seem adequate.

The experiences of particular social groups, such as Latino and gay or Black and female, are extremely important to understanding nontraditional means of managing parks and other natural resources. In other words, without this diversity and within homogeneous groups, people can more easily analyze policies, explore the history of outdoor education, or examine principles of recreation programming that support a particular vantage point of their group (e.g., white male). When this occurs, oppression results and multiple perspectives get lost. In the classroom, it is essential that students recognize the stereotypes and prejudices we learn about various "targeted" groups (e.g., ethnic minorities, gays, lower-class people) that develop as part of our socialization process or upbringing. Too often, program leaders and park managers neglect the need for change or open-mindedness.

What is learned at the individual level then, is reinforced by institutional and societal structures of privilege and disenfranchisement. Stereotyping and prejudice may occur no matter what the setting. Too often, "difference" also means inequality. That is, according to Lustig and Koester (1999), all people do not have equal opportunities; some feel empowered while others are systematically devalued. Receptivity and responsiveness to students' needs, both collectively and individually, become critical.

When natural resource and related courses are taught in a way that omits the history, experience, and cultures of ethnic minorities, women, or people with disabilities, learning is limited. Without "new" knowledge, it is unlikely that students will be able to understand other people's experiences or what their outdoor recreation interests are. Too often, culture- or gender-specific ideas are omitted, e.g., that Latinos differ widely in their recreation patterns.

As affirmed by Banks (2001), this *construction of knowledge* must be implemented by teachers in a way that helps students understand first how knowledge is created and second how it is influenced by the racial/ethnic, cultural and social-class positions of individuals and groups. Many European American instructors in the field of natural resources are unaware of how their personal experiences and positions within society influence the knowledge they produce. Teaching traditional content, or omitting diversity concepts, is often justified with "we've always done it that way." Students, however, must understand, even within natural resource management, how cultural assumptions and stereotypical frames of reference influence the curriculum content developed by their instructors. By moving beyond traditional content, basic assumptions can be challenged and students informed about seeing concepts, issues, themes, and problems from diverse ethnic, gender, and other cultural perspectives. Each group of students, then, brings their own perspectives about the changes in course content that must occur.

Many of the concepts relating to cultural assumptions and prejudices can permeate an entire campus and influence other aspects of social life. For example, Henley, Powell, and Poats (1992) discuss several issues adversely affecting campuses across the country: racial tensions (and in some cases violence); lack of culturally enriching activities and/or cultural awareness; feelings of isolation and perception of insensitivity to the needs of underrepresented groups; lack of faculty involvement as role models and mentors with students of color; and accusations of "political correctness" (4). Unfortunately, these problems never improve when there is the general feeling that "that's just the way it is," with little effort made to change.

Although we, as instructors, like to believe campus life has changed and that we embrace diversity better, many of the difficult issues continue to exist. In many areas, I think diversity is still left out because of this "we've always done it that way" attitude (i.e., maintaining the status quo). Regardless of course content, tensions based on differences can carry over into the classroom and become "problems" (e.g., discomfort, conflict, misunderstanding, and exploitation) if not attended to with care and concern. However, if a diversity of opinions is defined as a *problem*, I do not think it can be "solved." In other words, diversity becomes a problem for some classroom instructors only when it is interpreted as obstructing "the way things should be." In reality, any notion of the way things "ought to be" only reflects some set of preconceived abstractions and not any concrete "truth."

Scientific research has elevated our understanding of ecosystems within park wilderness, and the human dimensions of natural resource management have begun to provide an increased knowledge of land uses and recreational preferences. Yet, with respect to education or recreation in the outdoors, the dominant group (i.e., European American students and instructors) may believe that *all* people share the same interests, and to some extent, a common experience. The truth is that white people cannot really know the experiences of ethnic minorities (Ngan-Ling Chow, Wilkinson, and Baca Zinn 1996; Stanfield and Dennis 1993). In contrast, ethnic minorities are typically very well informed about the white experience because that is considered the "norm" (e.g., wilderness values) (Rodriguez and Roberts 2001). By using a normative reference to *wilderness values*, the context relates to a romantic ideal of preserving nature and admiring the scenic wonders, whereas cultural connotations often relate more to sustenance, for example, the Native American heritage of living off the land.

My own multicultural perspective, personal experiences, and marginalized status (as a female and an ethnic minority) allow me to address diversity issues in a direct way in my classroom. It also may be that I am able to do this with a degree of comfort that some of my white male colleagues in natural resources lack, perhaps finding these issues too complex. Instead, they continue to teach content in ways with which they are more comfortable.

As an example, Timpson and Bendel-Simso (1996) write about teaching as both "a science and an art." Their position is that successful teaching demands two essential ingredients: (1) your commitment as an instructor to gain certain skills, and (2) your ability to integrate these skills with your own personal style. The *science* of teaching includes the underlying theories, facts, and tactics that underlie effective instruction and facilitate learning, while the *art* reflects your own gifts. Clearly, an instructor's capability to achieve this will vary with her or his background and experiences. For me, combining science and art in pedagogy helps me to define who I am, who my students might be, and what we can learn together. It is also important that I take into consideration the differences among my students, that is, their backgrounds, motivations, needs, preparations for class, knowledge level, and individual learning styles. Just because some instructors have "always" taught a certain way with which they are comfortable does not mean it is the only way or the best way. Thinking about the art and science of teaching as well as my students' backgrounds and needs challenges me to explore new possibilities.

Teaching and Learning: Connection with the Outdoors

When structuring learning experiences around natural resources, environmental education, and outdoor recreation opportunities, I find it critical that I sharpen my ability to make certain adjustments that are based on student assumptions and expectations. For instance, my classrooms are usually quite homogeneous, composed primarily of students who are European American. Accordingly, I find that the topic of ethnicity and culture can be sensitive and confusing at times. I often sense discomfort and/or lack of awareness when students respond to discussion or readings with "…but we're all the same so why does it matter?" or "I treat everyone as equals so this doesn't pertain to me." I know I must be sensitive to students' comments and questions. However, I also feel the need to respond in a way that broadens their thinking and puts them on the edge of their comfort zone. When a white student says "people of color can do anything they want to, if they just try hard enough" or "I think men are just biologically more adapted to being outdoor leaders than women," I want to invite students to step onto that edge. One way I respond is to open the classroom doors but insist on respectful dialogue as they talk about their beliefs. I also provide the freedom for other students (e.g., allies or those who "get it") to join in the discussion and provide new information—for example, more depth about the concept of oppression and its effect on participation in the outdoors. I encourage students to view this type of discussion as "food for thought" rather than attempts to change individual students on the spot. As reported by Adams, Bell, and Griffin (1997), few can focus or learn when they feel defensive or criticized.

I know I must provide a safe environment for all students, regardless of their "awareness" or knowledge. I have to help them think critically and be open-minded about the attitudes and experiences of ethnic minorities and other underrepresented groups. Also noted by Blazey and James (1994), we can teach "with" diversity by maintaining a focus on inclusive language, inclusive content and topics, and an inclusive teaching style.

Regardless of where a student falls on the diversity awareness continuum, I want him or her to know that his or her perceptions, curiosities, and feelings all have a place in my classroom. I try to be encouraging, allowing students to express themselves fully. I validate their experiences, whatever their background, while challenging them to think "outside the box." No matter what their contributions, even if their assumptions reflect structures of domination (e.g., racial or gender privilege), I try to honor their comments and questions about course materials, readings, or interactions in class. My students all need to know they have a voice in our classes. Although I never have been in a classroom when a blatantly racist comment was stated, I try to be alert to those comments that surface in more subtle or covert ways, and identify how these contributions can be learning opportunities for everyone and exercises in truthtelling.

Whether stated consciously or implied subconsciously, a racist comment or stereotypical perception based on gender is something I also need to challenge without using personal attack or a condescending reply. Students are encouraged to engage with one another, to challenge each other's remarks and questions in a way that supports learning. Again, I find it critical to balance this inclusive style with my responsibility to have students examine the costs of maintaining their personal perspectives if they are closed to viewpoints of other people or to diverse cultures generally. As a teacher, I must invite comments (verbal or written) while challenging, and halting, any oppression that may surface, then try to offer creative alternatives. I do not discourage honest opinions when physical safety is not threatened. Rather, I provide a forum for students to talk about the psychological threat some people may feel (e.g., diminished or offended) when their sense of justice is being violated. One approach I use is to get students engaged in dyads (i.e., one-on-one conversations for a selected period of time) to share with their partners a situation when they remember being on the edge of their comfort zone because of something negative that another individual had said or done to them. I want them to reflect on how they felt and reacted.

Although personal identity development and concepts of privilege may be rare in a class on outdoor recreation programming or social aspects of natural resource management, they are still important. For me, that is part of the challenge. I want to help students begin to appreciate how situations can be understood from different perspectives. I want to help them appreciate how their own assumptions, observations, and interpretations are influenced by their social identity and ethnic background (see Gross-Davis 1993).

I have found that the most interesting descriptions about ethnic-minority involvement in outdoor recreation as well as perceptions about natural resources generally are those that take into account the viewpoint of each student. In some respects, this student self-awareness becomes more important if some useful understanding of diversity is to emerge at all. My own optimism about students understanding themselves first is key. However, if I let certain viewpoints go unchallenged, stereotypes can be negatively reinforced (e.g., some ethnic minorities do not participate in wilderness activities because "it's a white thing"). Self-awareness in students does not automatically produce growth as potential leaders or even acceptance of other people. One way to facilitate this is for me to step in if students seem to be ignoring the perspectives of others. Gross-Davis (1993) suggests that intervention may be an effective means of making it clear that an instructor values all comments.

During the course of any given semester, many European American students in my class hold onto a "melting pot" ideology through which ethnic differences are shed and opportunities for education, job training, recreation, and public policy are available to all people. I must admit that I become annoyed by the attitudes of these students, even angry at times, because presently opportunities are *not* available to everyone. As an instructor, I know I must channel my frustration, uphold my professionalism and ethics, and maintain my desire for being inclusive. At the same time, I try to respond honestly, expressing my own displeasure when they are unable to grasp someone else's "truth" (i.e., different views). I must also refocus my efforts to increase student knowledge about the persistent gap between the dominant culture and ethnic minority group members for access to resources and opportunities.

Some people believe that racial and ethnic differences are among the most enduring and potentially divisive factions within our society (e.g., Johnson 2001; Salett and Koslow 1994). Certain research in the natural resources field indicates that class differences are of equal concern (see Arnold and Shinew 1998; DeLuca and Demo 2001). Yet, in my experience, ethnicity and culture are the primary variables that make it challenging to build safe and trusting relationships. While we all have the potential to change our socio-economic class position, ethnicity is associated with the physical self and impossible to change. Johnson (2001), for example, notes that "the cultural assumption of white racial dominance can override any class advantage a person of color might have" (27). In my classes, this often leads to discussions about privilege and power. Yet, talking about these aspects of life is not something people do easily. My aim, therefore, is to help these future outdoor leaders and resource managers address these real-world challenges.

I also continue to find it very interesting that my own credibility may be questioned when attempting to teach students about managing forests and parks and what it takes to be an *effective* outdoor leader. For instance, the tradition of the outdoors as a white male domain often raises questions about my role as a female, minority instructor. How can I possibly know what I am talking about? To be both an ethnic minority and a woman generally places me outside the power structure of what students are used to. I sometimes feel compelled to clarify my identity and validate my educational background as well as defend twenty years of experience in this field. My survival in both the outdoor environment and the classroom environment has been a bicultural experience, simultaneously socialized in two separate cultures yet able to draw experience and value from each.

Furthermore, as an educator with a feminist philosophy, I support values that deeply affect my classroom instruction in a way that is attentive to relationships and equity. Buried in some of these students' young minds, however, may be some imagined, idealized or socially ingrained definition of what it means to be a feminist. For me, feminism means drawing on facets of my life and doing the difficult work of being genuine and trustworthy with my students, honoring the complexity of my own life as well as being conscientious about adding their experiences into the dialogue. Part of my intent is to build upon a multicultural viewpoint that challenges the status quo, finds common ground while honoring differences, and develops the self-esteem and confidence of my students so that they can better live their own lives. One technique I use in the classroom to help accomplish these goals has students keeping a journal as part of their semester assignment. This typically includes reactions and reflections from class discussions, occasional responses to assigned readings, and any other experiences or opinions they wish to share. I collect these randomly throughout the academic term and find time to meet with students individually as needed.

As I continue to work with students in natural resources and review the current research, several additional and related questions regarding teaching and learning also have troubled me: How can ethnic minorities enjoy our national parks in ways that are consistent with their cultural views and values? How can educational institutions help develop and nurture ethnic-minority students as future leaders and our white students as allies? How can research more adequately reflect and account for the experiences of ethnic minorities in the outdoors? It seems to me that this is all part of a dynamic system in perpetual motion.

Complex and Intricate Connections with Nature

Too often, the outdoors is considered the domain of European Americans. There is a common misperception that many ethnic minorities simply lack interest in nature and outdoor recreation. I also encounter stereotypes that "minorities can't afford it" or "they don't have the transportation to get there." The issue of access inevitably surfaces as a constraint to broaden public enjoyment of natural environments beyond urban borders. In contrast, many whites typically view parks as places for solitude or as sanctuaries from urban stress. Many ethnic minorities, on the other hand, report less enthusiasm or even negative attitudes about parks and wilderness because these places often are reminders of their historical subjugation and oppression (Ewert, Chavez, and Magill 1993; Johnson, Bowker, English, and Worthen 1997; Meeker, Woods, and Lucas 1973). For example, Native Americans have long battled with Congress to maintain their traditional access to and use of natural resources on reservations or other public lands across the country. It also has been argued that the "collective impressions" of African Americans about slavery, sharecropping, and lynching may contribute to their own lack of interest in and appreciation for natural resource recreation (Johnson 1998). More complete analyses about these issues are often missing from our textbooks and class discussions.

There are many topics within natural resource management, outdoor recreation, and environmental education for which we can discuss relevant aspects of diversity in the classroom. Possibilities include understanding issues of ecosystem management; sustainable use and biological monitoring of flora and fauna; visitor effects connected with crowding; conflict; motivation; satisfaction (e.g., benefits of participation), and risk management. Critics like Field (1996) insist that, since scientists and managers within land management agencies have largely been European American males, the academic community's analysis of trends related to people and resource management has often been limited.

In most instances, I think that my white male colleagues who are teaching students about outdoor programming and natural resource management lack the background and knowledge to adequately address related issues involving diversity. Too often, then, these aspects are left out of our students' education or merely touched upon as a minor detail. Attention to the changing demographics in this country is only one, albeit fundamental, reason for building understanding about the influence of race, ethnicity, and culture, both in outdoor experiences and in public involvement in protection of our parks and protected areas.

More specifically, research is still in the early stages of knowing how an individual's ethnic and cultural background affects her or his recreational experiences in a national park. We have made considerable and noteworthy progress since the 1960s in our understanding, yet this field still has a long way to go (e.g., Allison 1988; Floyd 1999; Johnson et. al. 1997; Rodriguez and Roberts 2001). Researchers, for example, have learned about ethnic patterns of recreation, preferences for participation, and styles or "modes" of participation. Regardless, there is still a lack of understanding about the role ethnic and cultural identity plays in the creation, maintenance, and expression of outdoor recreation experiences. Additionally, we need to know how the study of ethnicity and culture in natural resource contexts can make contributions to what is known about ethnicity and culture more generally. Such gaps and questions continue to constrain managers who are trying to provide a quality recreation experience for all visitors as well as manage the natural resources within their jurisdictions (Carr and Williams 1993; Floyd 1999).

Most natural resource students are studying to become park managers, leaders, and decision makers within various environmental and natural resource careers. This is why the challenge is so great. I try to bring a much-needed multifaceted perspective to the classroom. For example, I find that getting students to understand the *meaning* or significance of participation for an individual or a group is at times an overwhelming challenge. By and large, white people struggle to comprehend what it means to be "stared at," to be uncomfortable or feel unwelcome in a national park or forest. As people of color, on the other hand, we are too often reminded of our minority status, even in wildland areas.

In order to help students better understand this notion of minority status when in the wilderness, I pose two questions: (1) what additional knowledge is needed? and (2) what additional readings or materials are needed? I attempt to address diversity and culture in an *emerging* way. That is, I strive to address broader issues of social change and to challenge students to be intentional with their personal and professional actions regarding equity, economic justice, environmental harmony, and nonviolent conflict. I attempt to raise awareness and increase their knowledge through hands-on community experiences, guest speakers, and structured discussion groups organized around supplemental reading and role modeling.

Since the majority of natural resource instructors are European Americans, as are most students majoring in this field, I began to understand why some students look to me for help in understanding how ethnic minorities might experience the outdoors.

There are some complex questions for which I do not have easy answers because I have no direct personal experience or have not seen any useful research on that particular subject. For instance, I have been asked if minority group members with differing levels of acculturation also differ in their perception of discrimination in outdoor recreation areas. Gordon (1964, cited in Gramann 1996) has theorized that greater cultural assimilation will lead to reduced levels of perceived discrimination. It is clear to me that more work is needed in this area. We need to address more multifaceted questions, such as those relating to the interaction effects of race, class, and gender on outdoor recreation choices (Shinew, Floyd, McGuire and Noe 1995; Rodriguez and Roberts 2001).

As instructors, we also will need to address these missing links of race, class, and gender course readings if students are to understand the context of history. As an ethnic-minority instructor filled with passion for the outdoors, I understand the role of different values and beliefs in shaping students' perceptions. I also try to create linkages. For example, I often assign multiple readings throughout a semester to provide a historical context for understanding the similarities between our nation's treatment of Blacks and Native Americans (e.g., Taylor 1989; McDonald and McAvoy 1997).

Among some tribes of Africa and within some Native American communities, nature itself is thought to be sacred, and humans participate in that sacredness according to their degree of integration with natural processes. In their early work, Meeker et al. (1973) explain the need for Blacks and Native Americans to see themselves in, and not separate from, natural settings where they can seek spiritual relief. Alternatively, many European settlers seized public lands and wilderness areas as places of refuge from the "evils of civilization" in urban areas. Over time, "the red man" and "the black man" began to develop very different views of wilderness than those sentiments common among individuals of European descent. Referring to Blacks and Native Americans, Meeker et al. (1973, 5) point out that "for the past few centuries, both groups have learned in pain that their association with the land is a source of misery and humiliation, not of peace or fulfillment."

Various ethnic minorities also have concentrated on natural areas as a focus in their struggles for social and environmental justice and for political power (e.g., Ewert et al. 1993; Kaplan and Talbot 1988; Taylor 1989). While all people have some connection to the natural environment, how relevant and meaningful that relationship is raises different questions. Native American cultures, for example, often emphasize relationships of mutual respect, reciprocity, and caring for the earth. Yet the national parks often are known as places of humiliation for them because of their suffering and loss of land and traditional lifestyle (McDonald and McAvoy 1997; Meeker et al. 1973). The all too visible absence of meaningful education about Native cultures provided to visitors to the parks has caused mistrust and conflict.

In the classroom, these historical "facts" can be taught whether or not students like what they hear. These kinds of lessons can be difficult for anyone who does not have the knowledge, skill, ability, and/or willingness to process this kind of complex, emotionally charged issue. A first impulse may be to ignore the facts rather than engage in possibly contentious discussions. One of my goals is to bring a bit of order and coherence to students' perceptions about history, to provide some insight into the ethnic minority experience, and provide examples relevant for outdoor recreation and visitation to national parks. Specifically, I try to achieve this by using a variety of approaches—lecture, writing assignments, small and large discussion groups, guest speakers, and student interviews with community leaders from diverse backgrounds.

Breaking the Mold

In the field of natural resource management and outdoor recreation, while the study of race/ethnicity has been going on for the past thirty years, it is still relatively new in its depth and breadth(Rodriguez and Roberts 2001). However, research also continues to highlight theories that are based on traditional racial categories (Ewert 1996; Floyd 1998). As indicated earlier, I myself do not fit into any of the neat little racial or ethnic boxes as stratified on forms pertaining to demographics. That makes for an added challenge to my teaching. Because my ethnic background is not compartmentalized into any such "box," I find it difficult to relate to certain historical contexts (e.g., the relationship of African Americans to slavery) or recreational preferences based on cultural values (e.g., Hispanic kinship and extended families). Nonetheless, I am comfortable in discussing the issue of representation and visibility of ethnic minorities in natural resources from a broad perspective.

Here I can draw on a useful reference by Thorton (1996). He notes how "racial differences are given cultural explanations without obvious measures of experience or attitudes" (104). He proclaims that, although "race" is a valuable organizer of life—a measure of our worth in the eyes of society and where we fit into the hierarchy of societal preferences and opportunities—it does not automatically determine with whom one feels the closest bonds. In fact, the author contends, these "bonds" are not predetermined, no matter what we may believe. From a sample of published literature on this issue (e.g., Banks 2001; Lustig and Koester 1999; Salett and Koslow 1994), I can see that most people from a specific lineage feel a special affinity to that heritage. Without a particular (singular) lineage, I have been able to freely cross a number of racial and ethnic boundaries throughout my life.

Some students, however, either doubt my ability to mix easily with different racial groups or become quite curious about what this must require. Since I was born multi-racial, I have the chance to try viewing different ethnic landscapes (in the U.S.) from the wondrous yet troubling perspective of an *insider/outsider*. From this vantage point, I have come to believe that there are certain aspects of an ethnic minority's experience that are difficult, if not impossible, for a member of the dominant group (European American) to grasp and articulate (Baca Zinn 1979). The unique advantage I have as a "minority" scholar is that I am less apt to experience distrust, hostility, or exclusion when interacting with other ethnic minority groups. Clearly, there are still nuances, cultural norms and in-group behaviors that I may not understand. Still, I am usually able to gain acceptance into several ethnic minority communities by virtue of my mixed-race background, distinct appearance, and what I believe is a high degree of intercultural competence.

I also can relate to a degree of "aloneness" from being in the wilderness as one of few, if any, visibly identified minorities. That experience, however, is somewhat bimodal for me. On one hand, I do not feel *alone*, although I am always aware that there's nobody out here who looks like me. On the other hand, I feel extremely comfortable outdoors, and that allows me to both enjoy the tranquility of nature as well as wear my "educator" hat.

Through my own multicultural lens, I am best able to tell students about the meaning of the outdoors. Principles that derive from a *socio-cultural* approach in the literature (Ewert et. al. 1993; Sasidharan 2002) provide a broad framework for describing the association between ethnicity and culture and the meanings individuals and groups regularly ascribe to natural resources.

Where to from Here?

First, the changing demographics of our population are forcing us to rethink our attitudes about ethnicity and education. According to Ramirez (1996), not only will friction probably increase between ethnic minorities and whites, but conflicts also may arise between minority groups themselves until they learn to balance their conflicting claims. Second, because of the limitations of thinking about racial categories on forms, we need to focus on how we can best empower ethnic minorities through increased representation as well as the development of new paradigms. Racial and ethnic identity matters too much to be ignored through a color-blind approach that negates the fact that race and ethnicity (like gender and class) *do* matter in shaping ideas, attitudes, and opportunities (Banks 2001; Ngan-Ling Chow et al. 1996). Students must learn how and why such limitations could impact their lives.

For me, building in multicultural perspectives on different experiences is an important part of how I structure learning in my classes. I encourage my students to develop their ability to articulate their ideas, take responsibility for their opinions, and acknowledge how different people can see nature from different vantage points. What I want students in my classes to understand is this: When people acknowledge their vested interests and their biases as part of a dialogue, the playing field becomes more level. Rather than taking a European American, dominant viewpoint as universal, we can recognize multiple perspectives as valid. For example, it is primarily whites who are visitors to wilderness areas, creators of outdoor equipment and gear, and owners of outdoor-based retail stores (Cordell, Green, and Stephens 2000; ORCA 2000). I guess it is no wonder why many people from other ethnic backgrounds perceive the outdoors as places for white people. However, we do have to note that the socio-economic status of some minority groups is improving (U.S. Bureau of the Census 2000). Their disposable income will, accordingly, continue to rise, leveling the playing field. Nonetheless, in the absence of effective marketing strategies by the outdoor industry to ethnic-minority populations, differences will continue to exist.

In the section of my class that addresses human dimensions of natural resource management, I like to discuss these issues and invite different perspectives. I want to encourage dialogue and constructive debate. For example, discussions in my classes can get heated between those who support waiving national park entrance fees for Native Americans with a tribal identification card and those who believe the interests of all visitors in protecting the park and providing quality services would be better served by all people paying the entrance fee. Both sides tend to be convinced of the legitimacy of their particular perspectives.

Closing Thoughts

As an instructor, I find that the process of shifting perspectives and making personal values and beliefs explicit requires substantial emotional and intellectual flexibility on my part. An added challenge is for me to remain grounded and balanced, with an internal compass, if you will. Working with issues of diversity will always require personal direction and an act of imagination on my part, followed by a great deal of courage and perseverance. To me, this is exactly what is required of all of us, whether in academia or in the general society. How else can I teach my students to respect each other even when they disagree? How can I convey that certain comments or attitudes are not okay? How else can I bring the richness of my own varied perspective to bear on issues that ultimately concern all of us?

At core, I believe my greatest success in structuring learning experiences for students on issues concerning ethnic minorities in the outdoors has come from face-to-face interactions. I want students in my classes to learn the importance of socio-demographic changes and then to help build inclusive communities. I hope this will be an emergent part of their professional lives and not just an afterthought. Students must learn that the benefits of nature reflect an ongoing venture, not just an outcome, and that they may be experienced differently by people from diverse cultural backgrounds.

Teaching is unquestionably both a science and an art. However, addressing multiple perspectives requires awareness about complex issues and solid skills for interacting across differences. My own multiple identities and roles in higher education continue to evolve. I am an objective social scientist who also brings a multiracial perspective to the classroom. I have transformed feelings that once were rooted in anxiety into creativity and productivity. My visibility and minority status are inseparable, ever present, and always apparent to me and to my colleagues. Negotiating for power among different belief systems is not a new experience for me or other minority instructors and scholars. I will continue to critically evaluate current research and challenge it. I can only hope the discussion of diversity in my field is undertaken prudently and with due respect for the great issues at stake.

References

Adams, M., L.A. Bell, and P. Griffin. 1997. *Teaching for diversity and social justice: A sourcebook*. New York: Routledge.

Allison, M. 1988. Breaking boundaries and barriers: Future directions in cross-cultural research. *Leisure Sciences* 10:247-259.

Arnold, Margaret L., and Kim J. Shinew. 1998. The role of gender, race, and income on park use constraints. *Journal of Park and Recreation Administration* 16(4):39-56.

Baca Zinn, Maxine. 1979. Field research in minority communities: Ethical, methodological, and political observations by an insider. *Social Problems* 27(2):209-219.

Banks, James A. 2001. *Cultural diversity and education: Foundations, curriculum, and teaching.* Boston: Allyn and Bacon.

Blazey, Michael, and Katherine James. 1994. Teaching with diversity. *Schole* 9:55-62.

Carr, Deborah S., and Daniel R. Williams. 1993. Understanding the role of ethnicity in outdoor recreation experiences. *Journal of Leisure Research* 25(1):22-38.

Cordell, Ken, Gary Green, and Becky Stephens. 2000. Outdoor recreation: An American lifestyle trend. Retrieved on the world wide web, April 20, 2001. http://www.srs.fs.fed.us/trends.

DeLuca, Kevin, and Anne Demo. 2001. Imagining nature and erasing class and race. *Environmental History* 6(4):541-560.

Ewert, Alan W., ed. 1996. *Natural resource management: The human dimension.* Boulder, CO: Westview Press.

Ewert, Alan W., Deborah J. Chavez, and Arthur W. Magill, eds. 1993. *Culture, conflict, and communication in the wildland-urban interface.* Boulder, CO: Westview Press.

Field, Donald R. 1996. Social science: A lesson in legitimacy, power, and politics in land management agencies. In *Natural resource management: The human dimension* edited by A. Ewert. Boulder, CO: Westview Press.

Floyd, Myron F. 1999. Race, ethnicity, and use of the National Park System. *Social Science Research Review.* Spring/Summer 1. Department of the Interior: National Park Service.

Floyd, Myron F. 1998. Getting beyond marginality and ethnicity: The challenge for race and ethnic studies in leisure research. *Journal of Leisure Research* 30(1):3-22.

Gramann, James H. 1996. *Ethnicity, race, and outdoor recreation: A review of trends, policy, and research.* Miscellaneous Paper R-96-1. Vicksburg, MS: U.S. Army Engineer Waterways Experiment Station.

Gross-Davis, Barbara. 1993. *Tools for teaching.* San Francisco: Jossey-Bass.

Henley, Barbara, Theresa Powell, and Lillian Poats. 1992. Achieving cultural diversity: Meeting the challenges. In *Diversity, disunity, and campus community,* edited by M.C. Terrell. Washington, DC: NASPA, Inc.

Johnson, Cassandra Y. 1998. A consideration of collective memory in African American attachment to wildland recreation places. *Human Ecology Review* 5(1):5-15.

Johnson, Cassandra Y., J.M. Bowker, Donald B.K. English, and Dreamal Worthen. 1997. *Theoretical perspectives of ethnicity and outdoor recreation: A review and synthesis of African-American and European-American participation.* General Technical Report SRS-11. Atlanta: USDA Forest Service, Southern Research Station.

Johnson, Allan G. 2001. Privilege, power, and difference. Boston, MA: McGraw Hill.

Kaplan, Rachel, and Janet F. Talbot. 1988. Ethnicity and preference for natural settings: A review and recent findings. *Landscape and Urban Planning* 15:107-117.

Lustig, Myron W., and Jolene Koester. 1999. *Intercultural competence: Interpersonal communication across cultures,* 3rd ed. Reading, MA: Addison Wesley Longman.

McDonald, Daniel, and Leo McAvoy. 1997. Native Americans and leisure: State of research and future directions. *Journal of Leisure Research* 29(2):145-166.

Meeker, Joseph W., William K. Woods, and Wilson Lucas. 1973. Red, white, and black in the national parks. *North American Review* Fall:3-7.

Ngan-Ling Chow, Esther, Doris Wilkinson, and Maxine Baca Zinn. 1996. *Race, class, and gender.* Thousand Oaks, CA: Sage.

ORCA 2000. *Human powered outdoor recreation: State of the industry report.* Boulder, CO: Outdoor Recreation Coalition of America.

Poston, W.S. Carlos. 1990. The biracial identity development model: A needed addition. *Journal of Counseling and Development* November/December:152-155.

Ramirez, Deborah A. 1996. Multiracial identity in a color-conscious world. In *The multiracial experience: Racial borders as the new frontier* edited by M. P. Root. Thousand Oaks, CA: Sage.

Robinson, David, Robert Pfister, John Shultis, and Ed Stafford. 1997. New directions in resource recreation management: A response to the educational challenge. *Schole* 12:1-11.

Rodriguez, Donald A., and Nina S. Roberts. 2001, Winter. *State of the knowledge report: The association of race/ethnicity, gender, and social class in outdoor recreation experiences.* National Park Service Social Science Review. Fort Collins, CO: Colorado State University.

Salett, Elizabeth P., and Diane R. Koslow, eds. 1994. *Race, ethnicity, and self: Identity in multicultural perspective.* Washington, DC: National Multicultural Institute.

Sasidharan, Vinrod. 2002. Special issue introduction: Understanding recreation and the environment within the context of culture. *Leisure Sciences* 24:1-11.

Shinew, Kim J., Myron F. Floyd, Francis A. McGuire, and Francis P. Noe. 1995. Gender, race, and subjective social class and their association with leisure preferences. *Leisure Sciences* 17:75-89.

Stanfield, John H., and M. Dennis Rutledge, eds. 1993. *Race and ethnicity in research methods.* Thousand Oaks, CA: SAGE.

Taylor, D.E. 1989. Blacks and the environment: Toward an explanation of the concern and action gap between blacks and whites. *Environment and Behavior* 21(2):175-205.

Timpson, William M., and Paul Bendel-Simso. 1996. *Concepts and choices for teaching: Meeting the challenges in higher education.* Madison, WI: Atwood Publishing.

Thornton, Michael C. 1996. Hidden agendas, identity theories, and multiracial people. In The multicultural experience: Racial borders as the new frontier, edited by M.P. Root. Thousand Oaks, CA: Sage.

U.S. Bureau of the Census. 2000. Overview of race and Hispanic origin. Retrieved on the World Wide Web, August 21, 2001. http://www.census.gov.

Student Voices

William M. Timpson

As an instructor for various courses that address diversity content, I strive to be sensitive to feedback from students—how they are dealing with the often difficult, complex, and emotion-laden issues that can and still do divide people according to ethnicity, gender, sexual orientation, social class, disability, religion, region, etc.—the categories by which we organize our thinking. As societies everywhere struggle with their historic and evolving differences, as they mediate their internal conflicts and tensions (or not), as they organize and govern themselves, as they work together and trade with others, issues routinely surface and challenge the status quo. Tension and conflict are inevitable. It is no surprise, then, that learning about diversity is fraught with both intellectual and emotional challenges. Accordingly, I design varied student assignments and routinely solicit feedback, that includes a more formal mid-semester student feedback session. I want to know as much as I can about student progress through this kind of curricular terrain and how I can best guide learning.

For many years, ED 430, "Diversity and Communication," was a required course for the teacher licensing program at Colorado State University. As I noted at the outset, and as you've seen through the various chapters, teaching courses with diversity content has its own set of special challenges and joys. Issues of ethnicity and gender, class, and religion are frequently in the news, at the center of some storm, somewhere. Because so many colleges and universities have taken a leadership role in confronting intolerance, promoting greater inclusiveness, and challenging society to address past wrongs, current inequities, and the demands of increasing global interdependence, students in these courses usually find diversity issues compelling, meaningful, real, and, often, emotionally difficult.

These kinds of issues also can feel dangerous, threatening to long-held values and beliefs. Some of my students come from small, rural communities and often reflect a conservatism that is deeply rooted in ranching and farming. While their own ancestral roots are primarily from Europe, many have relied historically on the cheap labor of migrant families from predominantly Hispanic backgrounds. Other students come from homogeneous suburbs and reflect fairly moderate views on most issues, relatively secure in their privileges and largely sheltered from much diversity, except for what they see on television, in other media, or through their music. Those from the cities, in turn, tend to be more liberal, a few even radicalized by exposure to poverty, racism, and alternative viewpoints. Most students come to class with sincere beliefs in fairness and justice but with some fear that diversity content is fraught with its own land-mines. Most of my students live in Colorado, itself a relatively conservative state. As one young man from a ranching background put it,

> [I thought] we would be learning how everything is the white man's fault and that in order for us...to get to a more accepting country, we must break the white male and disregard all that he has done in making this one of the most respected countries in the world.

Many white students feel guilty about past wrongs but are reluctant to make comments for fear of being misunderstood. They worry about being insensitive or labeled "racist." When discussing low academic performance by some students, for instance, some wonder how they can raise the issue of personal responsibility without "blaming the victim." It often seems easier to "blame the system"—that the problem lies with lousy teachers, inadequate resources, poverty, etc. It can seem insensitive to raise the issue of individual effort. As a participant in a classroom discussion, how can anyone ever know in advance if someone else will feel offended by a particular question, no matter how seemingly innocent? How can anyone ever know in advance what someone else wants to be called? Do you use "Hispanic," "Latino," or "Chicano"? "African American" or "Black"? "White" or "Anglo" or "European American" for that matter? As an instructor, what terms do *you* use? How do you guide everyone through treacherous classroom emotions?

For their part, ethnic-minority students often come into class with their own apprehensiveness, often worrying that they may become the focus of classroom attention when issues of ethnicity arise, that they will be singled out and expected to be a "spokesperson" for their group. These students of color can feel very isolated. Succeeding in college can be tough enough without these kinds of additional emotional burdens.

The challenge for me as an instructor, then, is this: A certain kind of anxiety and vulnerability that seems to lurk just below the surface of classroom discourse, at times suppressing student involvement and choking off open discussions and honest questions. Classroom climate can erode as students shrink from participation. In this chapter, I want to highlight the reactions of students as they worked through complex and highly charged diversity content. You will get to read some of their more thoughtful and heartfelt testimonials about the factors that were problematic as well as those that helped build a sense of trust and, thus, permitted a deeper exploration.

Admittedly, you will read mostly positive references, describing how problems were confronted and new insights emerged. Because these quotes were plucked from required assignments, they may also reflect what students felt I wanted to hear, and there is probably some truth to that. I did want to see some new understanding. As instructors addressing diversity, we all want to see some evidence of learning—not mimicry or mindless obeisance, but rather a thoughtful, heartfelt respect for, even appreciation, differences. Be that as it may, I believe there are insights here into student thinking that you will find useful to others.

In particular, I am indebted to those students who enrolled in ED 430, "Diversity and Communication" during the summer of 2000. As you might expect in a course of this nature, their reactions were quite varied—certain content and activities worked better for some and less well for others. To assess impact, I collected and analyzed student reactions to a variety of assignments. I asked students to post their reflections on readings, class presentations, and discussions, guest speakers, film clips, etc. to our course website. I also conducted mid-semester and end-of-semester course evaluations, which included individual responses, as well as a public debriefing. Evaluating all this data, I noticed that particular themes emerged, although, again, there was a great deal of variation.

Because this book focuses on teaching and the college classroom, the bulk of the writings reflect instructor "voices." However, I felt it important to include the reactions of students as well—their testimonials to what works and what is problematic in a class on diversity as well as their ideas for improvement. I continue to be impressed with the insights students have about their own learning, their metacognitive capabilities if you will. It is obvious to me that we need to keep our communication with students open and honest if we are to address the complex and challenging aspects of diversity with any degree of effectiveness.

Untold and Troubling Stories

First, most of the students appreciated exposure to the real *history* of various populations and not the superficial overview that too often passes for social studies in schools. As a result, many became angry when they learned what omissions and misconstructions existed in their school texts. For example, Ron Takaki's (1994) biting rewriting of immigrant history of the U.S. alerts students to the power of profits that drove the exploitation of various groups, from the early waves of "savage" Irish, to European Jews in New York sweat shops, to ugly stories about slavery. One student, for example, said the chapter on African Americans in the urban North proved clarifying in deep and important ways:

> [It was] enlightening because it was a part of history that I had never studied in depth before. We read many works of the Harlem Renaissance in my high school English classes but I didn't have a clear understanding of the environment generating this writing. Knowing where these writers were coming from makes me want to go back and reread Hurston's *Their Eyes Were Watching God* and Hughes' poems. I think it is critical that teachers take time to explain the history and factors affecting ideas...I could have learned a lot more than just to appreciate good writing.

Another student admitted to some very strong reactions, how she had to unpack old perceptions as she worked through Takaki. Implicit here is an indictment of past instruction that focused mostly on rote memorization of historical facts and mainstream interpretations without much reflection about deeper implications or alternative perspectives:

> Some of his book devastated me when I realized how cruel people can be. I have always known this...but to see it in a different light...really made me think. Growing up, we never read many of the things that Takaki wrote about. Of course, I knew about large topics like slavery and the Civil War, but he talked about so much more...I really had to change my way of thinking and realize that history is not all facts and dates. It is determined by who is telling the story, and what they want us to remember. No wonder history repeats itself; it is never told (from more than one) perspective.

In class that summer, we had an extensive discussion about the impact of material illustrating just how cruel people can be toward each other. While everyone placed a high value on historical accuracy—getting everyone's story told accurately and not just what mainstream historians or textbook writers deemed important—some were still uncomfortable. "My only real dislike about Takaki is that he tells it like it is and sometimes gets a little too graphic in his description." As instructor, then, I have to ask: How do we best handle the worst of human brutality—enslavements, genocide, atrocities, slaughter? Do we gloss over them because to focus means so much emotional wear and tear? Or do we take time because we believe that lessons learned must be relearned or risk being repeated? And if the latter, how do we best prepare students and subsequently conduct our classes?

Applied and Service Learning

Most students valued the service learning component of the course as a way to get more direct experience with different populations. One student saw that her learning really deepened by personal involvement: "This class has been very educational for me, as the material we learned was put into practice." Invariably, however, there are mixed results when students go into the field. For example, three students took on the challenge of volunteering at a local mission serving the homeless. Seeing an entire family there as well as men in suits shook their stereotypes about what the homeless were like. These students were disappointed, however, when local mission rules kept them separate from these homeless people after they had helped serve dinner.

One of my intents in this class was to utilize approaches that required students to actually apply the ideas and skills under study. Notice the self-awareness of this student as she identifies areas for her own further growth:

The debate model was absolutely fantastic in encouraging listening skills and creating an environment in which a successful debate, rather than a heated or emotional debate, can take place. I find that I am very likely to get too involved emotionally in my cause to be effective, and I think that this is probably very likely among students who...have strong feelings.

In this next comment, I find it hard to imagine how anyone could get to this level of self-awareness solely through lecture or direct instruction: "My favorite lesson was learning classroom debate techniques because it made people realize how they may have misunderstood a person's point of view, and that it was necessary to understand each other before arguing with them."

Self-Awareness

The emphasis on self-awareness in this course also seemed important to many. Personal reactions to readings, class activities, and course assignments proved illuminating and clarifying as students explored their own thoughts and feelings. As one student noted, "It was a very empowering experience to have our experiences and beliefs drive the direction and climate of the classroom."

A cultural and communication autobiography asked students to reflect on their lives and make some sense of their experiences. As another student reported:

I did not realize how many experiences I had had with diverse groups in my life until I sat down to write that paper. I was afraid that I wouldn't have enough, but once I began writing, the memories came flooding back...Recalling my experiences with people different from me allowed me to reflect on how my attitudes have changed over the years, and what role family, friends, and society have played in altering my perceptions.

Finally, two case study projects asked students to interview people different from themselves. This assignment provided some useful impetus for initiating contact that otherwise would not have happened. As one student wrote, "I learned a lot from my interviews; they made me realize that people I see all the time have had much different life experiences. This was a valuable discovery because it highlights the diversity to be found all around me as well as proves that people's similarities tend to outweigh their differences."

For those instructors who see their responsibilities ending at the pedagogical border between content delivery and learner acceptance, a focus on student self-awareness can seem irrelevant (even indulgent) outside the parameters of content coverage, beyond the scope of their expertise to grade objectively, and certainly time consuming. Indeed, some students struggle when course focus strays from a strictly content-coverage-and-examination format. There are obvious benefits here for lifelong learning. Although we all face limitations on our time, focus, and energy, I believe that a part of our core mission as educators is to help students address some of the big life issues we all face. For example, at a very foundational level, I was encouraged by this student's comments:

When I started [this course] I decided that this...had no point in my life and was full of common sense that we already had....but the more I think about it the more I understand how important the concepts and issues we have discussed [are]. I have learned a great deal in this class, but most importantly I have learned about myself.

Communication Skills

The importance of good communication skills—listening, empathy, consensus building—became evident quickly when discussion issues became sensitive when feelings were hurt or anger aroused. Taking time to teach and practice different models of communication helped. One student put it this way: "The ability to truly listen and process what we hear honestly and humbly are our best tools for becoming great communicators...The opportunity to be challenged by a different experience or another perspective has been valuable for my learning."

Another student offered this:

The class discussions were helpful to me because we really learned how to get along with each other...There were agreements and disagreements and there were days when people left feeling uncomfortable...[However], I was able to learn a great deal about how to deal with things. I appreciated the emphasis on getting to know one another from the beginning because that set us up to be able to do the activities that we did.

One other student noted the connection among listening skills, self-assessment, and learning:

Many times it was hard opening myself up to others' opinions and beliefs when they were different from mine, especially when it was a topic I felt so strongly about. But I know that listening skills are more important than [speaking skills] stating an opinion. [Listening] helps open the lines of communication and understanding. It also allows more dialogue to take place in a safe environment. I found that many times if [people restate what the others say], they usually can...come to a resolution or understanding much faster and easier.

In this next comment, notice the sophisticated interaction of factors as a heightened self-awareness, an appreciation for diversity, and the challenge to apply new skills co-mingle with ideas about effective communication to produce deeper and more complex insights: "A stranger walking into our class would have thought it was very homogeneous...However, after hearing everyone's stories, I know that we represented a variety of life experiences. Knowing about people's different backgrounds helped me relate to them better; I like feeling I knew them more as individuals, and I tried to communicate with them in the most effective way for them."

Classroom Climate

A climate of trust and personal safety is important for self-exploration and openness to other ideas and experiences. Nearly everyone in this ED430 class pointed positively toward the "culture boxes"—a requirement for students to share something of their own background: beliefs and values, favorite photos, books, etc.—which gave others some insights into what defined them. Most students noted how rarely they ever got the opportunity to know much about their classmates within a traditional class structure. Getting to know each other on a more personal level helped them focus on acceptance. As one student said:

> [The culture boxes] helped create such a strong community and bond...With such a large class and short period of time, I really think that they...facilitated an unbelievably warm atmosphere. It brought the course content alive with the practice of acceptance of diversity and communication.

It may take some time and guidance to get students to shift from a strictly content focus to acknowledging, accepting, and valuing each other's ideas and experiences. In our class on diversity, I thought it was imperative that we make this shift. Note this student's reaction:

> There is no better way to get [a positive classroom climate] than [for students] to get to know one another and respect each other's differences. Although I wasn't too thrilled with the Culture Boxes at the beginning, I learned a lot about others and myself through the experience. Building trust is important.

Notice the focus on self-reflection in this next student's comments, as well as her suggestion that even more was possible:

> I think the culture boxes were one of the most therapeutic and helpful aspects of this course. It was hard for me to stand up in front of the class and talk about myself. But I was moved out of my comfort zone to a different place

where I could grow. That experience was enhanced by the close and open culture of the class. However, I think our class could have been pushed farther along those lines. We could have gelled much better and gone much deeper.

One other student noted how much this sharing of personal stories revealed about her classmates:

I learned their personal triumphs, heartaches, and reasons for living. It was amazing how much some of them were willing to share about their lives...[There] was so much diversity within that classroom, even though only a few of the students could be classified as "minorities." Without these culture boxes, we would never have really understood where each of us was coming from or connected with each other like we did.

An older student, returning to college to get a teaching license after many years in business, noted the interrelationships among openness, vulnerability, appreciation for others, and self-esteem:

I was amazed at how much thought each of us put into the culture box presentations. Personally, I had this on my mind for days...I was surprised at how personal they became. Some students were nearly in tears. When all was said and done, I felt better about myself and the class. I felt as though we knew each other... [Each] of us had become vulnerable.

In another paper, this student would extend the analysis further, unsure of the exact nature of all the factors involved but clear about the benefit:. "Perhaps it was because we all felt vulnerable that we were willing to listen. Perhaps it was because we cared about each other after having learned more about each other...I don't know the answer. It may not make a difference; we were willing to listen."

Yet, climate often is impacted directly by enrollment. While more active student participation is possible with smaller classes, more students can make for a greater diversity of opinion. Notice this student's ability to see the benefits and limitations of bigger classes: "On the one hand, having so many [thirty] students in class provided a large spectrum of opinions and points of view. On the other hand, many people were not given the opportunity in class because of [time] constraints."

All in all, the attention given to building a positive climate seemed to pay off in this class. I have to admit that I'm never exactly sure how this will play out. I don't think there is a formula that prescribes the exact balance needed between process and product, between morale building and learning, climate and content. I am convinced, however, that both are necessary. As one student remarked: "The sharing of personal information helped to humanize the classroom and make us more of a family as opposed to classmates."

Multimedia and Technology

The use of film clips added a shared reference to course concepts and theories. Watching the depiction of mathematics teacher Jaime Escalante, in the film *Stand and Deliver,* gave everyone some useful insights, for example, into the oppressive anti-intellectual nature of gang culture in East Los Angeles or the dangers of low expectations of teachers and parents: "Through (these depictions), we were able to really break down the steps of the (communication model under study) in 'real life' teaching situations." Another student put it this way: "The use of videos as well helped personalize our theories to experiences we could visualize."

The use of a course website for posting reflections and reacting to what others wrote allowed for an extension of classroom discussions and permitted additional and varied participation. Interestingly, at different times and over different issues, things were written and feelings were hurt in this cyberspace environment. It then took some time and direct communication in class, among those students, to repair. One student noted that "WebCT® was a positive experience because through this I could communicate my ideas and get responses back from other students about my ideas. It helped me correct my misconceptions and helped me understand others' points of view."

Another saw real growth in classmates: "Some of my peers truly surprised me when they expressed their beliefs and opinions. [I'm so proud of those who] have opened up since the beginning of class."

Reflecting back over the course, another student noted the value in these web discussions despite the complaints from some about time demands:

> [Contributing] to the ownership and sense of belonging [in this class] were the posted reflections and their responses. Although to many this seemed like a time-consuming, repetitive process, I felt [that it] was extremely valuable in that it allowed us to reflect on and clarify the ideas pre-

sented to us in class and from our readings. The reflection process also provided an opportunity for us to articulate our own interpretations in a thoughtful manner. As a result, we were both encouraged and challenged, as others responded to our reflections. Reading others' responses ...helped me hold my ideas and perceptions with more confidence and dignity.

Cooperative Learning and Initiative

A group project allowed students to experience the benefits of a supportive team in addressing a challenging task. Students met within their subject-area groups to develop, present, and assess a twenty-minute lesson that incorporated some aspect of diversity. With some background preparation on the requisite presocial skills (listening, empathy, consensus) as well as some understanding about the strengths and limitations of cooperative learning, several students noted how positive their experiences were. Without this kind of preparation, their experiences with teamwork in other classes had been mixed at best, often rife with frustration as some students felt exploited and unsupported when others got the benefit of a good group grade without contributing much of value.

Guest Speakers

Various resource people also added an important measure of diversity to the class, often undermining student preconceptions and stereotypes, in part by connecting on a very personal and human level. For example, two African American speakers talked about their sense of isolation on a campus that was predominantly white. Our students could relate to times in their own lives when they had felt isolated and alone. These speakers also shared their appreciation for a world that was indeed diverse, requiring that they themselves stretch and grow as well.

Developmental Shifts and Democratic Ideals

The time taken in class to explore various topics and issues and allow for open discussion seemed long for some but pivotal for others. Developmentalists like Piaget (1952), Kohlberg (1981), Perry (1999), and Gilligan (1982) all have written about the shift humans make from self-reference to understanding others. Kohlberg, in particular, worried about the impact on our democratic traditions of what he saw as a decline in moral thinking—for example, that on average, Americans have become less tolerant of dissent. In this light, the significance of these next two students' comment is striking: "I learned that everyone has their own background that makes them who they are. This was the first time I consciously realized that there are opinions out there other than my own." Another student wrote: "This class has taught me to face my challenges head on and try to learn from all different types of people and experiences."

Returning to our first theme about the untold, darker stories of our history as described by Ron Takaki (1993), note the weaving of personal growth amid democratic processes in this next student's comment:

> Takaki's account on history is also very democratic in documenting reality through the lives of ordinary people...His multicultural perspective also allowed me to question my own prejudices that contribute to keeping ourselves down and continue to see the world in racist, dualistic terms...I realized that stereotypes and thinking in categories allows racism, sexism, and materialism to breed to a point where these ideas are simply accepted and used in supposedly scientific ways to keep the laboring class from uniting and taking a stand for their own lives.

Conclusion

At one final session, several students offered insights and ideas about future directions for teaching about diversity. In one case, a young woman recommended more classroom challenge on a personal level. Note the connection she makes between micro- and macro-insights, between the time taken to explore individual differences in the class itself—to unpack stereotypical and premature assumptions—and the implications this would have for generalized feelings and beliefs about peoples in the larger society:

> I think what worked extraordinarily well, and where I learned the most about diversity, came from our culture boxes. Everyone surprised me, in a great way. Some of my prejudgements from the first day about people I did not know came true, but only along with a list of greater things that I would have never expected...If we were really to push the envelope and be open and honest, then I think we could have shared some of these preconceived judgements of our fellow classmates and how we learned that we were wrong or did not judge the whole picture.

As with any difficult and conflicted issue, teaching diversity carries the twin challenges of telling the truth about past prejudices while holding out the potential for progress. Hearing the personal stories of her classmates allowed one young woman to unpack her own assumptions about life's traumas, feelings that evolved from her own family struggles, and find new hope. She posted the following "confession" on the course web site for everyone to see:

> I have changed my entire belief about dysfunctional families. I seriously thought that everyone came from a dysfunctional family because I had, my friends had, and many of the women [with whom I worked had]...Both of my parents are alcoholics. My mom has been addicted to R_x medication off and on. She has stolen hundreds of dollars from my bank account and forged my signature to get a credit card in my name and then max it out and refuse to pay for it. All of my friends have similar situations and often worse. For me to see so many people [in this class] speak so highly of their families—I thought everyone was lying at first, but now I see that you all are just lucky to have a wonderful family. I now have some restored faith in the family unit.

In addition to the power of hope for addressing issues of diversity comes idealism, something especially important to young people. Here is where a student-centered approach can pay dividends as a buttress to the all-too-often cynicism of adults:

> One of the most beneficial aspects of the class for me was to be involved with so many idealistic young people. One of the things that many of us battle as we get older is succumbing to the realities of life rather than to the dream of what life could be like...I felt revived in embracing my ideologies by the infectious sharing of each person in our class.

There are benefits which can be large and life-changing, and in this course I may have had unique opportunities to address some of this content. Because of the uniquely sensitive nature of diversity as subject matter, those of us who teach these classes may have a license, even the obligation, to use more nontraditional means and range further in our approaches because the sources of student resistance may be, in part, shielded from direct instruction. Problems associated with the legacies of racism and sexism, discrimination on class lines, homophobia, and insensitivities toward disabled people are still with us. I know I find the encouragement I need to continue exploring new possibilities in these student voices about honesty, acceptance, hope, learning, growth, and possibility.

Finally, as I consider these student reflections and assessments, I am struck by the importance of the community—the whole—to support a more direct focus on diversity. In *The Courage to Teach*, Parker Palmer (1998) writes about the need for paradoxical "both/and" thinking to fully embrace the complex challenges we face as instructors. Understanding more about our differences allows us to make needed adjustments in any group. Practicing acceptance helps develop the trust needed for individuals to risk some vulnerability and open up to others and to possible change. Through their inherent diversity of membership—think broadly here and include background, personality, and disability—groups also provide an important challenge and opportunity for individuals to grow out of limiting assumptions and beliefs. The commitment of the group to inclusiveness provides the motivation to support individuals in their development. Unity around this kind of climate, along with a study of group dynamics and communication, provide the foundation needed by students to address diversity, fully explore their own differences and prejudices, and begin changing.

References

Belenky, Mary F., Blythe M. Clinchy, Nancy R. Goldberger, and Jill R. Tarule, eds. 1986. *Women's ways of knowing.* New York: Basic Books.

Campbell, Duane, and Delores Delgado Campbell. 1999. *Choosing democracy: A practical guide to multicultural education.* Upper Saddle River, NJ: Prentice Hall.

Davis, Nancy. 1992. Teaching about inequality: Student resistance, paralysis, and rage. *Teaching Sociology* 20:232-238.

Gardner, Howard. 1983. *Frames of mind.* New York: Basic Books.

Gardner, Howard. 1999. *Intelligence reframed: Multiple intelligences for the 21st century.* New York: Basic Books.

Gilligan, Carol. 1982. *In a different voice: Psychological theory and women's development.* Cambridge, MA: Harvard University Press.

Goleman, Daniel. 1994. *Emotional intelligence.* New York: Bantam.

Johnson, David, and Roger Johnson. 1994. *Learning together and alone.* Needham Heights, MA: Allyn and Bacon.

Kohlberg, Lawrence. 1981. *The philosophy of moral development.* New York: Harper and Row.

Limerick, Patricia. 1996. Believing in the American West. In *The west*, edited by S. Ives and K. Burns. Boston: Little, Brown.

Marks, Stephen. 1995. The art of professing and holding back in a course on gender. *Family Relations*, April, 142-148.

Marsh, Herbert. and Lawrence Roche. 1997. Making students' evaluations of teaching effectiveness effective: The critical issues of validity, bias, and utility. *American Psychologist* 52(11):1187-1197.

Mayberry, Katherine, ed. 1996. *Teaching what you're not: Identity politics in higher education.* New York: New York University Press.

Nabhan, Gary. 1997. *Cultures of habitat: On nature, culture, and story.* Washington, DC: Counterpoint.

Palmer, Parker. 1998. *The courage to teach.* San Francisco: Jossey-Bass, Publishers.

Perry, William. 1999. *Forms of intellectual and ethical development in the college years.* San Francisco: Jossey-Bass, Publishers.

Piaget, Jean. 1952. *The origins of intelligence in children.* New York: International Universities Press.

Simon, Sidney, Leland Howe, and Howard Kirshenbaum. 1972. *Values clarification: A handbook of practical strategies for teachers and students.* New York: Hart.

Takaki, Ronald. 1994. *A different mirror.* Boston: Little, Brown.

Tannen, Deborah. 1996. *Gender and discourse,* New York: Oxford University Press.

Timpson, William M., and Paul Bendel-Simso. 1996. *Concepts and choices for teaching.* Madison, WI: Atwood Publishing.

Timpson, William M. 1999. *Stepping up: College learning and community for a sustainable future.* Madison, WI: Atwood Publishing.

Wolfgang, Charles. 1999. *Solving discipline problems.* Boston: Allyn and Bacon.

Analysis: Safety Is the Leitmotif[1]

Raymond Yang

One topic, in one aspect or another, appears as a part of every chapter in this book: Safety. Some chapters refer to the liberating effects of safety—how it encourages openness, sharing, and camaraderie. Other chapters refer to an absence of safety—a palpable sense of intimidation or threat, a rebuke delivered by a powerful person, or a fear of physical harm from a potential assailant. In other chapters, this sense of threat is the chill of potential retribution accompanying a perceived impertinence, or the trepidation felt prior to expressing an opinion that previous discussion suggests will be in the minority (the classic studies of Solomon Asch [1958]).

When the authors of these chapters did not feel safe, they were reactive. They struggled to deliver what they had intended; they felt constrained in meeting their extant responsibilities. Their perceptions of safety seemed to facilitate or constrain their presentations and interactions with students. Essentially, when they felt safe, they could be open to showing and accepting greater diversity. They covered material and raised issues they might not otherwise have broached. They permitted themselves, and thereby their students, to grow. The authors were proactive when they felt safe. They expanded and further developed their roles. Feeling safe, they stretched the limits for themselves and their students. Their teaching became an adventure with their students. Thus, safety appears to be a prerequisite for creating a classroom ambiance that is intellectually broadening and challenging for both teachers and students.

The dictionary defines "safety" as freedom from harm, injury, loss, or risk (Mish et al. 1993). The risk in classrooms can be as subtle as the exclusion felt by persons with physical disabilities. Or, if not a sense of risk, it can be a perception of condescension. Sometimes that perception of condescension is exacerbated when it is accompanied by a disparity between the ostensible invitation (meaning official documents, such as a university catalog depicting an ethnically diverse university community) and the actual situation (meaning the actual percentage of ethnic minorities on campus). Sometimes the risk is a feeling of vulnerability—a reaction to remarks made by persons who were unaware of being overheard. These reactions all relate to a sense of safety, and all are described in the preceding chapters.

These reactions are not confined to any specific group on campus. Students, faculty, and staff all have these experiences within as well as between their respective groups. Certainly students can feel threatened by faculty. But students may be surprised to learn that some instructors—who are putatively more powerful than students—also report feelings of vulnerability and ineptitude to their students (Vacarr 2001). Indeed, some faculty might be surprised to realize that their administrators can feel threatened by them. Apparent or real, the influence of a constructed perception of safety or threat, whether it be embedded in unrecognized privilege or assigned status, must be taken into consideration.[2]

Perhaps safety is related more to "human nature" than to group status or relational aspects of university life; that is, it is a basic need for everyone (Maslow 1968). If so, when they feel safe (or not), people react differently. For the student in the lecture hall, the disdainful gaze of the instructor could discourage asking a reasonable question; for the instructor at the lectern, conversation among back-row students could be presumed to be disrespectful social chatter (when it could be an exchange relevant to the lecture). Both student and instructor could feel their safety threatened. Yet, the student might not speak while the instructor might speak more loudly. Both are equally uncomfortable. Teaching and learning could suffer.

Organizing Safety's Facets under a Larger Rubric

In this volume, Mona Schatz described her fear after being stalked and not receiving any support from her colleagues. Chance Lewis described the chill he felt when entering a classroom in which the students, for the first time, see that he is Black. Eric Aoki described how he is able to self-disclose to his students when he knows he is supported by his department chair and colleagues.

If a sense of safety can vary from the absence of threat to the warmth of genuine welcome, how can we begin to analyze it in a way that has practical implications? Our range is considerable—from a "chilling effect" to forewarnings of physical violence. Broad as that range may seem, if we consider safety to be more than the absence of threat—that safety includes things positive, such as a warm welcome (e.g., Buscaglia 1982)—our purview is even more substantial.

Two Developmental Models:
Carl Rogers and Abraham Maslow

Carl Rogers (1961) is well known for his emphasis on *unconditional positive regard* and its importance in the therapeutic context. Rogers believed that this posture of nonjudgmental acceptance (not only of others but also of self) is an essential element in the process of self-actualization. Rogers called it "the actualizing tendency." An ambiance of unconditional positive regard is the setting in which self-actualization proceeds best. Rogers believed that in educational settings, positive regard is exemplified by a teacher who trusts students' desire to learn, who allows them to select their own paths and grapple with their own mistakes. This successful teacher will nurture confident, caring students who think independently.

In the classroom, the successful teacher builds personal relationships with students. These relationships support students' natural tendencies toward exploration, discovery, and competence building (Rogers 1960). The teacher is a resource. When the teacher cannot be non-judgmental and must exert control, students (and others) use denial and perceptual distortion to cope. According to Rogers, neither of these defenses promotes actualization, and the more experiences students have in which they react with denial and perceptual distortion, the more stunted their development will be.

Abraham Maslow is best known for his model of the *hierarchy of human needs* (1968). These needs begin with the physiological (food, shelter, clothing), then move to safety, then to valued relationships that nurture a sense of self, and then to respect and prestige, which are associated with *self-actualization*. In Maslow's model, movement through these stages of need is inherently motivating. Thus, once the need for safety is met, a person next seeks close relationships. Satiation of lower needs is the motivating force for seeking satisfaction of higher needs. At the highest level, people can have peak experiences. These are times of intensely gratifying engagement and can be momentary or sustained.

The self-actualization process is lifelong, and peak experiences can and do reoccur for individuals. Yet, this developmental process can be blocked and peak experiences can be precluded: Control, deliberateness, caution, self-criticism, and fear all act to prevent this developmental process from moving forward (Maslow 1968). In contrast, the courage to relinquish control and take risks facilitates development. Indeed, true self-actualization requires acts of courage.

Rogers'(1961) and Maslow's (1968) models exemplify how safety is embedded in the broader context of development. They speak to the lifelong relevance of safety, from childhood through old age.[3] Yet, the university campus is populated primarily by those with adult status; and safety for these adults is probably an issue of contextual rather than developmental relevance. But even though the campus is primarily a contextual setting, it unarguably has long-ranging effects on the adults in it, and it surely affects them broadly, not only in their professional preparation but also in their *Weltanschauungen*.

A Community-Contextual Model

As a cultural institution, the university serves as discoverer, repository, and transmitter of knowledge. But in recent decades, American universities struggled to reformulate their values in the changing *Zeitgeist*. Barzun (1968) and Bloom (1987) worried about how universities could serve their original mission when they were driven by dissent (associated with the Vietnam War[4]) and their organizational hierarchies were fractured by competing values (e.g., marketshare profitability versus pedagogy). But universities have been resilient, modifying their goals accordingly. One new trend became the pursuit of "excellence,"[5] although Reading (1996) noted that on closer inspection, the actual pursuit was as much of popularity and celebratory recognition. Nonetheless, college and university campuses have retained a set of values (albeit transformed), hierarchical statuses, norms, prescriptions, and proscriptions for behavior (Gettman 1992; Levine 1996). They have retained their identities as communities of shared norms, values, and mores.

As communities, campuses have sustained their obligation to protect their members. Yet, the changes in goals and policies, such as supporting greater diversity, have inevitably left them with values that in practice, seem incompletely implemented, inconsistent, or sometimes contrary (Banning, this volume). It is these incomplete implementations and apparent contradictions that can create a context for feelings of threat or lack of safety. This is especially visible for recently espoused values—for example, special multidisciplinary programs (e.g., ethnic and women's studies), affirmative action, multiculturalism, and diversity. On-campus support for these activities remains, even today, mixed. Thus, in the context of these new values, issues of safety are especially relevant to that long-standing mission of the university to further knowledge. The institution's sense of community can make it feel both welcoming and threatening to those within and beyond its boundaries.

Proffering Welcome

For the past two decades, universities have substantially increased their marketing and recruitment activities in all areas, including attracting ethnic minorities (Astin, Keup, and Lindholm 2002). And despite some opposition, the numbers of ethnically diverse faculty and students on university campuses have increased (Haynes 2001).

As the authors of the chapters in this volume indicate, their sense of safety is predicated on their perceptions of welcome by students in their classes and from their colleagues. "Welcome" includes a presumption of collegiality and support from other faculty. When the authors felt welcomed, they felt a sense of communal support. They taught with courage, challenging their students (Timpson's "Students' Voices," this volume) and themselves (Aoki this volume) to think beyond their own boundaries.

The welcome that is of most impact for faculty came from those nearby: from students in their classes and from departmental colleagues. It is this proximal welcome that creates a sense of safety (e.g., Aoki's department chair and colleagues). A distant welcome—a letter from the dean, provost, or president—might not have as much of an impact in proffering welcome.

A Sense of Threat

But as the authors of our chapters note, they sometimes feel not so much variations in welcome but an actual presence of threat (Canetto and Borrayo this volume, Shatz this volume). Arriving on campus, some minorities sense not only an ambivalent reception (Feagin and Sikes 1995) but sometimes a palpable opposition to their presence (Takagi 1992; Tochterman this volume). The campus community, when seen up close, seems as ambivalent as the larger community (Cose 1993).

Threat—perceived or real—invariably induces vigilance among those who feel they are potential victims. Once vigilant, these persons, more so than others, may look for additional signs of potential danger. Thus, vigilance can become a self-reinforcing process or at least one that is difficult to extinguish since in many settings, one can find what one seeks. Faculty who feel threatened are placed in a precarious position: They watch their students and colleagues closely, while still devoting their energies to their normal responsibilities. It can only be fatiguing.

Citizen, Steward, Sojourner, Interloper

Threat and welcome are not necessarily dichotomous. Each can vary independently of the other. The proffer of welcome can be received first, and only later might a person become aware of an ambiance of threat.

Conceptually, their relation can be represented by a two-by-two table combining high and low amounts of welcome and threat (Figure 1).

When welcome is high and threat is low, the invitation is unambiguously positive: Come and stay. Guest status, over time, converts readily to citizenship. Faculty, staff, and students become members of the campus community. They will feel, each in their own areas, the responsibilities of contributing to the commonwealth. Morale is high.

When welcome is high and threat is high, the invitation is to come, but only under clear and pre-specified conditions. An individual is useful to the community, but only in ways that community clearly delineates. One is given responsibilities of stewardship, but without any proffer of citizenship. Only with prolonged and faithful stewardship can citizenship be requested; and then it may come with explicit conditions. Not meeting the conditions of service specified by the community may render the person useless. When that person no longer serves a useful function to the community, the welcome is retracted, the person can feel manipulated and conclude that promises made were not kept.

When persons are neither welcomed nor threatened (both welcome and threat are low), the community is indifferent to their pres-

	Threat High	Threat Low
Welcome High	Steward	Citizen
Welcome Low	Interloper	Sojourner

Figure 1. Typology of personal reception.

ence. These persons' stays are temporary—presumably to meet some personal need—and they sustain no status. They are sojourn-ers. Yet, if new needs emerge during their stay, they can prolong their visit without untoward results. These persons view universi-ties as utilitarian routes to self-betterment (e.g., careers).

When welcome is low and threat is high, no invitation is ex-tended and the person becomes an interloper. Self-interest must supercede threat in order for the person to enter the community. The stay is only long enough to meet their self-interest. They leave immediately thereafter.[6]

This typology of personal receptions—citizen, steward, so-journer, interloper—represents a holistic assessment of persons entering the campus community. On campus, faculty can be placed in the typology in several ways. Rank is probably the most apparent: Faculty "stars" recruited from other campuses are granted immedi-ate citizenship (i.e., full professorship); untenured junior faculty can be stewards; temporary instructors—"gypsy" faculty —who truly enjoy teaching and who are usually poorly paid are sojourners. Interloper seems to be the only characterization not readily visible among faculty. However, minority faculty, including women (Kite et al. 2001), sometimes wonder, especially when they perceive their colleagues to be inhospitable or unsupportive (see Borrayo and Canetto, this volume)[7], if they are not interlopers. On our campus, the ratio of female to male full-time faculty is one to four (based on the 2001-2002 academic year)[8]. Although the ratio on our own cam-pus is slowly changing toward more equitable female representa-tion, it is now where most universities were in 1984 (Hamermesh 2002, 28).

Safety Sets the Foundation

We envision that meaningful educational experiences bring stu-dents to a point where they can step beyond their self-established boundaries. This kind of stretching inevitably involves some dis-comfort. Thus, challenge and a degree of tension (Yang, this volume) are essential elements of true learning, especially at the university level (Gettman 1992). Timpson ("Student Voices," this volume) de-scribes students' reactions to this process. But, as Aoki (this vol-ume) indicates, asking students to stretch beyond their comfortable boundaries also can require the same of the instructor. In the best circumstances, an alliance is formed between teacher and students that allows both to grow intellectually. They both tolerate a degree of discomfort so they can extend their respective horizons.

The student side of this alliance has been described by Barr and Tagg (1995) as the new instructional model in higher education—a "Learning Paradigm." In this new paradigm, *success* rather than *access* is offered to students. Success requires that the university take co-responsibility for students' learning. The old lecture model, which offered access to knowledge, is inadequate for this new model. In the new model, the university, at formal and informal levels, becomes a co-producer, with the student, of learning. Student and teacher must meet each other halfway, and the university must formally restructure its programs in order to provide the appropriate context for this partnered learning (e.g., by establishing multidisciplinary programs). According to Barr and Tagg (1995), at multiple levels ranging from direct interaction between teacher and students to the organizational divisions among academic programs (and ancillary support services) to state funding mechanisms, universities are attempting to transform themselves. True education requires a partnership between the teacher (representing the university and supported by it) and the student. Although Barr and Tagg emphasize the impact of this partnership on the student, we believe it can have an impact on the teacher as well.

The foundation for this partnership assumes safety for both teacher and student. In this volume, we have dealt primarily with safety for faculty. But surely when faculties do not feel safe, when the uncertain teacher is standing before students, those students can sense it. Whether it is the discomfort of a first-time teacher, or the equivocality felt by students whose stereotypes are violated (Lewis, Middleton, Tochterman, this volume), the ambiance in the classroom changes, at least momentarily, for everyone. Typically, these first-day jitters subside, and the class moves on. But those jitters can become a source of growing tension that, if not given attention, can detract from the teacher's objectives and ultimately students' learning (Davies, this volume). Thus, the classroom is where the effects of safety—welcome and/or threat—are most apparent. In this setting and those nearby—proximal to interactants—occur the greatest influences. As Banning (this volume) has so well described, distal influences also have an impact. But the distinction between proximal and distal influences is the distinction between immediate effects and those that emerge later. Together, they generate that holistic reaction that characterizes the citizen, steward, sojourner, or interloper.

Not all members of the campus community can or should be citizens. Students ostensibly are on campus to achieve an education and to then depart to other challenges; typically, they are sojourners. But most would agree that no one on campus should feel he or she is an interloper. The processes by which faculty on campus come to these various identities have been described by the authors in this volume. Hopefully, their efforts will contribute to the improvement of safety on campus for all its members.

Notes

1. The editors appreciate the contributions of LeAnn Duran and Michelle Mirr in the preparation of this epilogue.

2. Thus, the wag's observation that "the playing field always looks level to those standing at the top of the hill." For example, in a department faculty meeting, a discussion of promotion/tenure criteria is on the agenda. Senior faculty comment that their discussion, unlike those occurring in other departments, has an ambiance of supportive camaraderie. Other faculty nod in agreement until an assistant professor blurts out, "Well, then, why am I sitting here sweating bullets!"

3. Erik Erikson (1950) emphasizes the longitudinal relevance of safety, too (i.e., his initial stage of "Basic Trust versus Basic Mistrust").

4. Earlier examples are the Social Gospel movement on campuses in the 1920s and '30s (Fogel 2000) and the shift to a research emphasis during the 1960s.

5. Best exemplified by stunningly popular books like *In Search of Excellence* (Peters and Waterman 1982).

6. After the attacks on the World Trade Center in New York on Sept. 11, 2001, any Muslim of Arab descent could feel this way.

7. This perception has been shared with the authors by ethnic-minority faculty who have since left this campus for other institutions.

8. Like it is at many universities, the ratio is more equal at lower ranks (approaching parity for assistant professors), and decreases substantially for full professors (11percent are female) (Annual Report on the Economic Status of the Profession 2002).

References

Annual report on the economic status of the profession, 2001-02. 2002. *Academe* 88(2):47.

Asch, Solomon E. 1958. Effects of group pressure upon the modification and distortion of judgments. In *Readings in social psychology*, 3rd ed. Edited by E.E. Maccoby, T.M. Newcomb, and E.L. Hartley. New York: Henry Holt.

Astin, A.W., J.R. Keup, and J.A. Lindholm. 2002. A decade of changes in undergraduate education: A national study of system "transformation." *The Review of Higher Education* 25:141-162.

Barr, R.B., and J. Tagg. 1995. From teaching to learning: A new paradigm for undergraduate education. *Change* 27(6):13-25.

Barzun, Jacque. 1968. *The American university: How it runs, where it is going.* New York: Harper and Row.

Bloom, Alan. 1987. *The closing of the American mind.* New York: Simon and Schuster.

Buscaglia, Leo F. 1982. *Living, loving, and learning.* Thorofare, NJ: C.B. Slack.

Cose, Erick. 1993. *The rage of a privileged class.* New York: HarperCollins.

Erikson, Erik H. 1950. *Childhood and society.* New York: Norton.

Feagin, J.R., and M.P. Sikes. 1995, Summer. How black students cope with racism on white campuses. *Journal of Blacks in Higher Education* 8:91-97.

Fogel, Robert W. 2000. *The fourth great awakening and the future of egalitarianism.* Chicago: University of Chicago Press.

Gettman, J.G. 1992. *In the company of scholars: The struggle for the soul of higher education.* Austin, TX: University of Texas Press.

Hamermesh, D.S. 2002. Quite good news—for now: The annual report on the economic status of the profession, 2001-2002. *Academe* March-April:20-29.

Haynes, V.D. 2001, April 6. Enrollments of minorities back up in California. *Chicago Tribune.* Retrieved June 28, 2001, from Chicago Tribune Archive on the world wide web: http://www.chicagotribune.com.

Kite, M.E., N.F. Russo, S.S. Brehm, N.A. Fouad, C.C.I Hall, J.S. Hyde, and G.P. Keita. 2001. Women psychologists in academe: Mixed progress, unwarranted complacency. *American Psychologist* 56(12):1080-1098.

Levine, L.W. 1996. *The opening of the American mind: Canon, culture, and history.* Boston: Beacon Press.

Maslow, Abraham H. 1968. *Toward a psychology of being.* New York: Van Nostrand Reinhold.

Mish, F.C., et al., eds. 1993. *Merriam-Webster's collegiate dictionary*, 10th ed. Springfield, MA: Merriam-Webster.

Peters, T.J., and R. H. Waterman, Jr. 1982. *In search of excellence: Lessons from America's best-run companies.* New York: Harper and Row.

Reading, Michael. 1996. *The university in ruins.* Cambridge, MA: Harvard University Press.

Rogers, Carl R. 1961. *On becoming a person: A therapist's view of psychotherapy.* Boston: Houghton Mifflin.

Rogers, Carl R. 1960. *Freedom to learn: A view of what education might become.* Columbus, OH: C. E. Merrill.

Takagi, Dana Y. 1992. *The retreat from race.* New Brunswick, NJ: Rutgers University Press.

Vacarr, B. 2001. Moving beyond political correctness: Practicing mindfulness in the diverse classroom. *Harvard Educational Review* 71(2):285-295.

Teaching about Human Diversity: Lessons Learned and Recommendations

Silvia Sara Canetto, William M. Timpson,
Evelinn A. Borrayo, and Raymond K. Yang

As we all worked on this project, from our very first glimpse of its possibility, arising Phoenix-like out of the ashes of turmoil, literally and figuratively, we eventually saw hints of its conclusion as a manuscript along with its potential for pedagogical transformation of professional development and other new initiatives. Knowing that our efforts represented something new and different on the landscape of the scholarship about human diversity, we wanted to move from our individual reflections, analyses, and studies to shared conclusions and practical recommendations. Admittedly, we still have some differences, although these tend to be over emphases and subtleties. In a book on diversity we accept this inherent complexity.

Defining Human Diversity

Awareness of language meanings and connotations is critical in the field of human diversity, as it is in any area of scientific and human interest. One issue is precision. Scientific communication requires language that is accurate, concise, and clear. The other issue is bias. Scholarly communication about human affairs must pay attention to bias and value judgments implied in certain words or expressions. In this spirit, the 1994 *Publication Manual of the American Psychological Association* issued a recommendation to "avoid constructions that might imply bias against persons on the basis of gender, sexual orientation, racial or ethnic group, disability, or age" (1994, 46). In its 2001 version, the same manual explains that:

> Bias may be promoted when the writer uses one group (usually the writer's own group) as the standard against which others are judged. In some context, the term "culturally deprived" may imply that one culture is the universally accepted standard. The unparallel nouns in the phrase *man and wife* may inappropriately prompt the reader to

> evaluate the roles of the individuals (i.e., the woman is de-
> fined only in terms of her relationship to the man) and the
> motives of the author...[Similarly], contrasting lesbians
> with "the general public" or with "normal women" portrays
> lesbians as marginal to society. (APA 2001,164-65).

As we noted in our introductory chapter, there is a Babel of language and meanings in the study of human diversity. Different terms
(e.g., *human diversity, multiculturalism*) sometimes are used to refer to different domains (e.g., a range of categories of social classification versus ethnicity as a single category of social classifications).
At other times, they refer to similar domains (e.g., *human diversity*
and *multiculturalism* as both meaning a range of human experiences or "cultures"). There is also the issue of the meaning of "culture" in contrast to "human diversity" with regard to what each term
includes and implies.

Having considered these issues in light of our experiences and
what is described in the literature, we decided that the best phrase
to use for what we wanted to encompass in this book is *human diversity*. For us, human diversity refers to the *broad* range of variations in human experience. From this perspective, teaching about
human diversity involves *not only* addressing the experiences of any
group (e.g., women, lesbians and gays, people of color) who have
been absent, under-represented, or misrepresented in the canon. It
also means including a critical examination of the experiences of all
those who have been implicitly presented as the standard or ideal in
the academic canon, including men, the upper class, and people
from industrialized countries. This definition of diversity is firmly
grounded in considerations of power and status, consistent with
new developments in human diversity theory (Rosenfelt 1998;
Sampson 1993). It is also a definition that acknowledges how categories of "difference" (e.g., ethnic classifications) are historically
and culturally produced constructs, yet still affirms that these categories of differences have enormous real and practical consequences for the lives of individuals at a particular time and place
(Rothenberg 1998).

There are important pedagogical consequences for our choices
about terminology, definitions, and a conceptual framework. First,
a pedagogy of human diversity based on our definition is both inclusive of multiple categories of social classification as well as attentive
to the complexities of human experience when different categories
intersect (e.g., gender and ethnicity). It is a pedagogy that discour-
ages students from essentializing from a single dimension (e.g.,
maleness). For example, students are expected to examine how the

experience of being a male differs depending on ethnic background and socio-economic status. Second, a pedagogy of human diversity based on our definition is "transformative" rather than merely "additive." It does not simply "add" women (or people of color) to the traditional curriculum. It changes the basic terms of the discourse; it can reset foreground and background and it recalculates norms. It requires that *all* students re-assess their places on the social map, not only those whose traditions and experiences have been ignored or misrepresented. Third, it is a pedagogy in which ambiguities, multiplicities, and contradictions are expected and even welcomed rather than considered unusual and problematic (Felman 2001; Sampson 1993). Students are discouraged from seeking simple or absolute answers.

To conclude, devoting some effort to analyzing terms and concepts may seem tedious and excessively academic when compared to the host of compelling issues that surround human diversity. Yet, as noted by Wicker (1985, 1101), "the potential payoffs" of critically examining language and theory are "substantial" and can lead to more precise, more sophisticated, and more socially sensitive thinking. It can also generate new insights about what teaching about human diversity means and what is required of teachers and students along the way.

Openness, Safety, and Risk

If we are to ask our students to take on the complexities, ambiguities, and difficulties of a diverse world, to think more deeply about diversity itself, and to accept the challenges of overcoming longstanding biases, then we need to strive to establish a climate of openness and safety for students. Openness means allowing exploration of all ideas, including views that may be unrefined, blunt, or idiosyncratic. As noted in chapters by Kees and Schatz, however, safety requires setting limits, such as establishing rules of language (e.g., no disrespectful terms), style (e.g., use of "I" statements), and/or content (e.g., that one cannot dismiss or accept research evidence).

In practice, then, creating an open and safe classroom involves a complicated and sometimes contradictory set of actions (Bell, Morrow, and Tastsoglou 1999). Openness demands that we listen to all students, but safety may require interrupting a comment that we perceive as offensive—an action that may be seen by some as disrespectful or censoring. Openness could mean allowing a spontaneous flow of contributions; safety, however, may involve managing the traffic of contributions so that there is a diversity of speakers who won't fear retaliation. Students from groups with a history of being silenced may need to be given additional encouragement to talk in order for their perspectives to be heard, while students from groups with a history of dominance and privilege may need to listen more.

For example, according to Fisher (2001), teachers "need to draw certain lines" to ensure that women have a "space" to develop an independent discourse rather than putting others' ideas and needs ahead of their own (147). According to Lewis (1990), this is related to the self-silencing and caretaking imperative that women are socialized into. Thus, the issues of classroom safety must involve different dynamics and tasks for women and men, and by extension, dominant and subordinate groups in general:

> Women need . . . safety so they are free to speak in order to better understand and act against the violations they have experienced in a social/cultural setting that subordinates them in hurtful and violent ways....(484)

Men, on the other hand, need safety in order to do the hard work involved in acknowledging "the pain of their complicity in benefitting from the rewards of this same culture. (Lewis 1990, 484)

Though each of these positions has its challenges, we agree with Kuntz and Kaplan that "it is easier to see oneself as a victim than as an oppressor; it is easier to think about righting wrongs when you yourself do not have to contemplate surrendering power" (1999, 241). Instructors are well aware of the difficulties male students tend to have in engaging in the self-reflection required in gender-content classes (e.g., Lewis 1990). Some have argued that an analysis of gender issues is perhaps the most difficult one to tackle because for *everybody,* gender touches upon personal relationships. "Sexism is the oldest, most established, and least questioned form of social domination," writes Bleich (1998, 151). Similarly, bell hooks comments:

> Sexism is unique. It is unlike other forms of domination—racism or classism—where the exploited and oppressed do not live in large numbers intimately with their oppressors or develop their primary love relationships (familial and/or romantic) with the individuals who oppress and dominate or share in the privileges attained by domination...[For women and men], the context of these intimate relationships is also the site of domination and oppression. (1989, 130)

To come back to the issues of openness and safety, Bell and colleagues (1999, 36) note that the instructor's "position is fraught with tension, as she uses her authority in order to deconstruct authority." Not surprisingly, students' responses to the instructor's interventions to promote openness and safety are not predictable and consistent either. Says Lewis (1990, 148):

> For instance, in one class, I might receive a nod of recognition from students of color when I stop a white student from trying to make an African American student into a "race expert"—that is, stop the white student from assuming that a black student can and should speak with authority about all African Americans. In another class, an African American student who welcomes the chance to tell the truth of her life might see my intervention as white maternalism.

According to Lewis (1990), there are no simple answers even in terms of the format of the diversity-content class: "The lecture format may suppress student participation or encourage it, depending on how the lecturer handles her subject and relates to the students. Discussion in a circle may invite student participation or create an atmosphere of surveillance, so that students feel that their every word and gesture is being judged," notes Fisher (2001, 148). Also, an instructor who encourages self-disclosure may find that "once students begin to connect with and share their own experiences," they may get stuck at the individual level of analysis. In other words, students may become unable or unwilling to put their own experiences in context and examine them critically in light of theory and research data (30). According to Bell and colleagues (1999), this classroom climate may feel like a cozy "space of self-disclosure and support" (36) but it is also a climate that risks reinforcing the very individualistic, "psychologistic" conceptualizations that the human-diversity-content class aims at dispelling (38).

The complexities surrounding openness and safety for students of human diversity are compounded when we recognize the parallel issues for us as instructors. Problems of safety also may arise as students turn their negative reactions about a difficult and painful learning process against their teachers. As the chapter by Canetto and Borrayo points out, the instructor of the diversity-content class may become the target of a range of hostile behaviors, from reading the newspaper in class to noncompliance with class assignments; from constantly questioning the validity of the content presented in class or in the readings to constantly challenging the instructor's judgment about the student's performance; from verbal attacks to poor class evaluations; from accusations of "unscholarliness" (Kuntz and Kaplan 1999) to accusations of incompetent teaching.

Accordingly, being in a "safe" department can be especially important for anyone teaching diversity content. In this case, a safe department means a department that is aware of the complexities of teaching about diversity and does not automatically assume that one's teaching difficulties are a sign of insufficient effort, incompetence, lack of openness to students' feedback, or human diversity biases. It is a department that basically allows those who teach about human diversity to take chances and make mistakes. In his chapter, Eric Aoki writes about the pedagogical possibilities afforded to him by the support of his colleagues and department head as he explored the use of self-disclosure as a gay male in his teaching about identity and human diversity. For Aoki, as for Allen (1995), disclosing being of a minority sexual orientation was a way to "invite and model ways for students to understand their own experiences with social locations such as gender, race, class, and sexual orientation" (136).

At the same time, as authors in this book as well as others have pointed out, the most reliable "protection" when conflicts in teaching about diversity arise may be one's own identity on the "social map." Basically, there may be fewer challenges and dangers in teaching about social differences if one does not embody these "differences." Conversely, teaching about human diversity without (or with limited) individual social privilege (that is, teaching without the privilege of maleness, white skin, or heterosexuality) can be dangerous (Shankar 1996). For example, Henry (1993-1994) tells us:

> Teaching and learning about race/ethnicity, culture, religion, language background, gender, sexuality, and able-bodiedness [sic] are difficult...For me, as a Black woman...there are no safe places...Racism and misogyny organize the minutest details of my classroom practice...For instance, as a Black woman professor, students contest my credentials more than those of my colleagues. Thus, I discuss them "up front" with the class. I try to devise clear, unambiguous grading systems because students question all that is questionable about my modus operandi. (2)

Henry (1993-1994) also contrasts her classroom experiences with those of her White male colleagues: Her "students struggle against...[her] Black female authority [but not] with the authority of...[her] colleagues who do not share...[her] race and gender" (1). Her conclusion is that for people like her:

> There is nothing "safe" about engaging students in rigorous and critical ways. It seems to me that to be able to speak of safety in the "belly of the beast" reveals class and race privilege. Only a certain elite has the privilege of cultivating a safe space in mainstream institutions that perpetuate the very inequities that we fight against as feminist educators. Sometimes a discourse of safety and nurturance can blanket ambiguous politics, double-mindedness, or the fear of jeopardizing one's academic status...I recognize that each of us, as feminist educators, does what we deem necessary to our survival— even if it means choosing not to speak—especially as members of subordinate groups. However, we must be mindful that to "blend in" and "cultivate normalcy" (Cliff 1984, 58) perpetuates the status quo." (2)

These are among the most painful comments we read. And they resonate with experiences and feelings that some of us have had. Our conclusion is that there are no easy solutions and no easy formulas for how instructors can create a climate of openness and safety for students and themselves. One thing is sure: No class is an island. What happens in a diversity-content class in terms of openness and safety is influenced by department and university values, attitudes, policies, and evaluation and reward practices. Thus, one recommendation is that departments and institutions develop forms of teaching support and evaluation that address the specific skills, tasks, and demands created by diversity-content teaching.

A Positive Classroom Climate

This discussion also can be framed around those characteristics or "determinants" that comprise a positive classroom climate and promote the risktaking needed for deep learning about prejudice and privilege. As Timpson and Bendel-Simso (1996, 18) suggest:

> Another challenge for every instructor is to create a classroom environment which provides a foundation for risk-taking. If the students expect to extend themselves in your class, and know that they won't be punished for doing so (either by you or their peers), they will be much more willing to engage with the material and contribute actively.

According to Timpson and Bendel-Simso, there is much useful research to guide instructors in assessing the climate for learning in classes. A colleague can be recruited to lead this kind of "audit" through interviews, focus groups, a survey, or a formal mid-semester student feedback session. Fears and concerns, appreciations and recommendations can surface early enough to allow for course corrections. Perhaps as important, everyone is challenged to see teaching and learning as a shared, co-created process. The following questions have emerged from the research on positive organizational and classroom climate:

- Are students encouraged to ask questions and/or express their personal viewpoints in class?
- Are there expectations for individual student performance?
- Is there flexibility in what is required of students?
- Do students have a voice in what happens in class?
- In what ways do you help students develop problem-solving abilities?
- Is the teacher open to exploring a variety of learning approaches?
- Is instructional and programmatic support available for students who need it?
- Is the instructor interested in students as individuals?
- Have classroom rules and procedures been developed cooperatively?
- Does the instructor consult with students to identify their goals?
- By what means do teachers and students identify and solve conflicts?
- Is effective communication evident?
- Is everyone who is affected involved in decision making?
- Do students have a sense of autonomy as well as a willingness to accept the accountability that goes with it?
- Are effective teaching-learning strategies evident?
- Is there an ability to plan for the future?

In addition, instructional approaches that tap into the rich possibilities of theater and psychodrama can be especially helpful when addressing diversity content and handling the range of reactions that can result. Role playing, for example, can help students explore their reactions in simulated situations and practice alternative responses. As Timpson and Burgoyne (2002, 197-198) note:

An underlying developmental journey moves students from a preoccupation with their peer group toward greater independence—intellectually and emotionally. A similar journey takes young people from fear of the unknown and outright prejudice toward understanding, tolerance of differences, and appreciation for the strengths contained in human diversity...As an instructor, your understanding of the potential role which drama can play in attending to differences and building bridges becomes important...As in the theatre, you have a tightrope to walk when certain views tap into deep feelings or destructive prejudices, when, for example, going to war often means demonizing the enemy and can make any concern for them seem unpatriotic. You must be aware of individual sensibilities and public mores whenever you entertain the controversial. However, knowing the place for tension and conflict in promoting the development of critical and creative thinking will help you to decide what approach to use and when.

The Canon and the Counter-Canon

One dilemma in teaching about human diversity is what to do with the canon, meaning the dominant curriculum that was in place before the new diversity voices and perspectives burst through. This is an issue one of our authors, Jane Kneller, addresses in terms of the teaching of philosophy. "I have to teach two centuries of European philosophy in one semester," she writes. "Once I cover the 'big three' rationalists, Descartes, Spinoza, and Leibniz, and the 'big three' empiricists, Locke, Berkeley, and Hume, with a few days spent on Kant, Hobbes, and Rousseau and a bit of Galileo, Copernicus, Bacon, and Montaigne, how can I possibly find the time to also cover, say, Margaret Cavendish or Anne Conway?" The issue, as Kneller concludes, is not one of female philosophers versus male philosophers. It is a general issue instructors deal with every time they teach the same course: What should I include of the "old" content when other important new scholarship needs to be recognized? Within this perspective, the dilemma of course content is one of riches (due to an increasing wealth of knowledge) rather than oppositions (e.g., female versus male philosophers). "Something would be wrong if, over time, it did *not* get harder to teach all this material in one semester," Kneller notes.

Another canon dilemma in human-diversity-content classes is the one encountered by philosopher Minnich (1990,79) in her classrooms. She found that:

[S]tudents taking a course in philosophy that includes two or three works by women, and/or some works that include consideration of women, come to feel that the course is "ideological." They do not see the men represented and discussed in the course *as men* but rather as philosophers, writers, painters, significant historical figures, important composers. However, they do see women *as women* because they have learned from the use of prefixes in course titles and what's left out of their course requirements that women are oddities in the dominant tradition, that women are always a kind of human, a kind of writer or whatever. They do not notice when a course concerns only men, yet some may feel at first that a course that mentions women more than a couple of times "overemphasizes" women (and sometimes complain that their instructor is "obsessed with women").

Minnich asks: "What...does it mean for us that students find it odd, uncomfortable, uninteresting, even threatening to begin seriously to study the majority of humankind—to learn about women, to learn about men other than privileged European Americans? What does it mean for democracy that only some few kinds of humans can be imagined as our representatives?(1990, 79)."

Similarly Higginbotham (1990), a professor of sociology and social work, writes: "Students can tolerate a certain amount of cultural enrichment, but if this material exceeds more than one or two lectures, they lose their patience because they think the instructor is deviating from the core...Students carry old lessons into the classroom. They have already learned that what happens to people of color (or to women) does not count" (4-5). Minnich (1990) has an inspiring conclusion and recommendation about this dilemma: "If we never startle our students or any of those with whom we share our work, our life, and our world, if they never feel any anxiety, are never aroused to anger or to sudden, intense, personal engagement by what we say, we ought to be concerned. Such comfort can indicate that the learning in which we are engaged is not touching the old errors built deep into the culture" (81).

Professional Development and Personal Growth

While we have general agreement about what constitutes quality scholarship—peer-reviewed presentations, publications, and grants; well-cited articles, chapters, and books—we are much less certain about quality instruction. Course design is one component of quality instruction as is effective course delivery. Accordingly, we want to argue for more substantive investment in professional development (Timpson and Broadbent 1995). A campus-wide commitment to change can help overcome the inherent isolation of teachers and support their sharing, learning, growth, and creative synergy.

To do so, we must be realistic about the longstanding, even systemic, barriers to collective responsibility for quality instruction, especially at our flagship research universities. Timpson and Bendel-Simso (1996, 141) describe it this way:

> Teachers in higher education also tend to work in relative isolation. Rarely are they in each other's classes, except for the occasional guest lecture. Moreover, academic freedom has often been broadly interpreted as meaning that no one is encouraged to visit or say much about anyone else's teaching, except through interpretation of student evaluations. At universities, the demands of research then only compound this problem, skewing the reward system away from systematic or serious attention to instructional effectiveness and faculty development. Consequently, poor or ineffective teaching practices are allowed to persist on many campuses, with little opportunity to nurture innovation and sustain improvement.

A focus on student learning, however, introduces a degree of complexity that defies simple assessment, especially when we take a long-term perspective—that is, how our graduates will perform in the "real world." As Timpson and Bendel-Simso (1996, 15) insist:

> Traditionally, it has been the case that "good professors" were those who were undisputed masters of their fields, who could be counted on to have a good answer for any question put to them, and who poured a ton of information into their receptive students semester after semester. Now, while expertise is certainly essential to teaching, it is only part of the answer: Today teachers must deliver an evolving subject matter to a student body which is itself evolving. The changing shape of institutions of higher education adds more complexity. Creativity becomes a vital element of academic success in this context. And while having answers will continue to be the hallmark of experts, the ability to shape student thinking will always be the hallmark of the best teachers.

A form of professional development that may particularly benefit teachers of diversity-content classes is one that systematically ex-
poses them to the literature on teaching about diversity and
teaching in general. There is a rich knowledge base on teaching
about human diversity, on teaching and learning generally, and on
the nature of change itself (e.g., Sarason 1984; Sarason and
Morentz 1998; Fullan 2001). While we often repeat the faculty man-
tra of "busyness" in our efforts to stay current in our own disciplinary work, we also need to recognize the importance of systematic
exposure to the education literature.

Good teaching, particularly good teaching of diversity-content
classes, requires studied practice and feedback. It requires that we
find good readings. If at all trained in teaching, most faculty have no
formal preparation for the specific skills that teaching about diversity requires. "We define as our calling a critical, feminist, and
antiracist pedagogy...[yet] we have little formal preparation for [it].
In our classroom we grope toward an 'unknown,'" write Bell and her
colleagues (1999), and "with little support from our institutions"
(35). We also agree that teaching about diversity content and for critical analysis may require unlearning traditional teaching practices.
Finally, we agree that becoming a good diversity-content instructor
is a lifelong learning process that "must be nurtured, supported,
and continually appraised and negotiated" (35). Action learning,
peer coaching, mentoring, videotape analysis, and the like all offer
promising avenues for instructional development for diversity-
content faculty (Timpson and Broadbent 1995; Timpson and
Bendel-Simso 1996; Timpson 1999).

One form of practical professional development that may particularly benefit teachers of diversity-content classes is training in
communication skills. Addressing the varied aspects of diversity—
both the challenges in the content itself as well as the complexities
inherent in dynamic interactions and deeper learning—instructors
need to be able to listen deeply themselves, respond empathetically,
identify and address conflicts that arise, and more. Unfortunately,
within traditional paradigms of academic training, precious little
time is ever available for attention to the communication skills of
faculty. Too often, these kinds of skills are thought to be beyond the
responsibility or capacity of instructors. Lowman (1995), for example, argues for the centrality of instructor-student rapport for increasing learning in college. We agree. We believe that a new
instructional paradigm is needed, one which that recognizes the importance of the process skills that make for better interactions and
discussions.

One delicate issue in the engaged, diversity-content classroom has to do with the authority of the teacher. In many ways, these kinds of courses invite a de-centering of authority. On the other hand, the usefulness, feasibility, and process of de-centering oneself as an instructor may have to vary depending on one's personal characteristics, on institutional and systemic factors as well as on specific class dynamics. As many of our authors have reminded us (see, for example, the chapter by Chance Lewis in this book), for instructors whose credibility is automatically questioned due to their physical "difference" (women, persons of color, persons with a disability) from the stereotype of the "competent" professor, protecting one's authority may be important or even necessary (Condit 1996; Marks 1995). "I am *already* out of the center," said an African American female instructor. "Many of my students act as if they have more of a right to be here than I do," she added (quoted in Marks 1995, 142-143). "What does it mean for a '*colored*,' foreign female, triply an 'outsider'...to assume the position of power and authority in a 'First World' English classroom?" asks Shankar (1996, 197). "It is already assumed I am unqualified or incompetent as an Asian American female professor," writes Hase (2002).

Finally, as instructors and contributors to this project, we also have become convinced of the need to commit to our own personal growth as we simultaneously challenge our students to reflect, explore, rethink, and grow personally. For example, reflecting on her evolution as an instructor and as a person, Allen (1995) offers the following insight: "As my experience reveals, teachers who are lesbian, bisexual, or gay must continually confront their own internalized homophobia and weigh the risks of concealment or disclosure" (138). She then goes on to comment on the use of journaling for self-awareness: "Making use of a teaching diary...allows an instructor to debrief from intense classroom experiences and provides a written record of what happens in class. Over time, a teaching diary can become the basis for reflection about effective teaching strategies as well as documentation of the teacher's growth and empowerment" (140).

As instructors, we must assume responsibility for our own personal development—for confronting our own biases as human beings while we simultaneously play the role of disciplinary experts. An important working assumption is the acknowledgment that we all live in systems that promote biases (sexism, racism, classism, heterosexism, ableism, and ageism) and "thus cannot be blamed for learning what we have been taught." On the other hand, we are all responsible "to identify, name, and interrupt the cycle of oppression"

(Bell et al. 1999, 36). This is admittedly complex terrain to navigate and requires understanding, skill, clarity, and courage on everyone's part.

Support for Ongoing Research and Development

Institutionalized changes in higher education will not come quickly or easily. The historic protections for academic freedom and support for discovery put an emphasis on individual initiative and autonomy. Accordingly, we are convinced that special funds ought to be provided to encourage new conversations, sharing of ideas, and new course designs and deliveries. Despite the ubiquitous rhetoric about bringing more human-diversity content into higher education, we still see too much that seems to be just that—rhetorical. Resources are important for real changes. For example, Timpson and Broadbent's (1995) work with the Action Learning Project at the University of Queensland documents the benefits when substantial resources are attached to a systematic university effort at instructional innovation and improvement.

We also want to argue for institutional support for new and original research on topics related to the teaching of diversity. We have benefited much, individually and collectively, from participation in this book project. Because of our work on this topic here, we believe we have a reasonable claim on further investment in this effort by our own university. The pursuit of new knowledge is central to the mission of every research university. In a report for the Carnegie Commission on Higher Education, Kenney (1998), for example, argues that much could be done to reinvigorate undergraduate education if universities did more to connect their research priorities with instruction. We are confident that our work on teaching diversity can contribute something new and useful to the scholarship of teaching and help bridge the deep and historic division between research and teaching.

Accordingly, visionary and vigorous campus leadership is also essential. While individual faculty members can contribute important insights and examples, leaders must emerge to extend this learning across the institution. If the challenges of diversity are to be addressed with new and creative thinking, we need administrators to provide resources for desired institutional research and professional development. One way to move forward is to tie this work into ongoing strategic planning. Our own university has developed a process that reviews progress made and facilitates decision making about future directions. While any centralized planning effort has its shadow side, it also can be an important opportunity for focusing discussion and resources on important areas for change efforts.

Final Thoughts

The teaching cases we have featured and explored in this book involve issues that defy easy answers. Teaching about human diversity means dealing with social hierarchies, privilege, and oppression. Privilege and oppression, whether unspoken or recognized, impact course content and interactions in important and often volatile ways. In Davis' (1992, 232) words: "What makes courses in social stratification most exciting to teach also makes them most difficult. The issues of power and powerlessness, advantage and disadvantage addressed in these courses are charged concepts."

Our own thinking and responses, then, must be correspondingly sophisticated and creative, sensitive to nuances and competing values. One example from Marks (1995, 144) is telling:

If given the opportunity, [students] always have their own stories to tell about playground banter and the kinds of feelings that surround it.

At some strategic point, I ask the women in the class how many of them were "tomboys" or would have been so regarded by many of those around them (more than half raise their hands). I then ask the men, as deadpan as I can, "Now, how many of you were 'sissies'?" Following the snickers and laughter, we have a discussion about the lack of parallelism between these two terms: It's fine for a girl to be boy-like, but a curse of ignominy for a boy to be girl-like (or even for a girl to be too girl-like). Then I offer the empirical generalization: There must be deep-rooted and widespread misogynous convictions that undergird our construction of female and male differences.

Rothenberg (1998) also notes how gender ideology is problematic—"schizophrenogenic." Women, she writes, are considered "both different from men in the sense of being inferior and in the sense of being special. We...do things such as give birth to men's children...[we] care for other people...[something] men tell us they are unable to do. Thus, we are special. Yet, those very capacities render us inferior, since no man in his right mind would want to do those things anyway" (146). In his own classes, Marks (1995, 144) attempts to maintain a focus on honesty and safety:

Unfortunately...there is an ever-present potential in [my] course to polarize into two hostile camps–feminists against anti-feminists, men (and male-oriented women) against women. This is a most counterproductive outcome and it is difficult to undo when it emerges. I think the best way to avoid it is to ground students in an honest and safe exploration of their own gendered identities—what they are, and what is gratifying, and what is painful about them.

Similar arguments can be made about students facing their other identities (e.g., ethnic, physical, religious, sexual orientation).

As we have noted throughout our analyses, diversity-content courses do best when they promote an engaged climate and allow for self-reflection among students and instructors. At the same time, a good diversity-content course also is one that encourages deeper learning. For all students, "The challenge must be offered continually to move beyond individual experience and undertake a critical analysis," write Bell and colleagues (1999, 37). This is because, as bell hooks (1994, 202) puts it, "Without the capacity to think *critically* [emphasis added] about ourselves and our lives, none of us would be able to move forward, to change, to grow."

The importance of these skills is especially evident when facing social problems that reflect an inherent complexity of interacting factors and forces. For example, our colleague, Steve Shulman, teaches an economics course on welfare. Because demographic data clearly disclose disproportionately higher percentages of ethnic minorities among the lower classes, tensions often surface in class when arguments from different places on the political spectrum collide, when talk of governmental action meets questions about personal responsibility. When Shulman provides credible defenses for those various political positions, students must think for themselves when articulating their own positions. As one student said, "I love this class. I'm really challenged. I never know what Shulman himself thinks."

For some students, especially those who are just starting to identify and affirm their own life meanings, this move from personal experience to critical analysis may be slow and difficult. Instructors also may find it useful to establish individual goals based on each student's development. For example, as suggested by Bell and others (1999), teachers can outline "expectations for evidence of 'progress' in each student's understanding of the issues by the end of the course." Students also may be "asked to document and consciously observe their own process of change, by way of writing self-profiles at the beginning and end of the course" (37).

We also believe that case-based and problem-based materials hold much promise for human diversity classes. For example, in his first-year, diversity-content class, Bleich (1998) asks students to write in detail about conversations they have had about homosexuality. This assignment is meant to elicit raw stereotypes of sex and sexual orientation to be used in the course's analysis of sexism and homophobia in the United States. In his course, Bleich does not grade any piece of work because he does not want to encourage self-censoring. Similarly, in her "Global Gender Issues" class, Hase (2002) has her students check in which country their clothes were made. The goal of this in-class exercise is not only for students to become more aware of the differential impact of the global economy on different populations of the world, but also she wants for them "to see in a very tangible way the connections they have to the world beyond the borders of the United States" (99). Finally, Hase also wants to educate students about United States responsibility "in global economy and politics" (102). Using case studies and problem-based learning, human diversity content can come alive with immediate relevance.

A problem- or case-based approach builds on a student-centered foundation and moves toward discovery, or "constructivist learning." As such, it can be a powerful way to pull students into a more focused, reflective, and interactive examination of their own understanding of diversity issues. As Timpson (1999, 87) describes it:

> *Problem-based learning* (or *case-based learning*) is an approach to instruction that is gaining increasing popularity in some parts of higher education, especially in fields like medicine, where students will eventually move into roles calling for a greater deal of critical and creative thinking about real and inevitably complex problems. Because these roles defy overly reductionistic reasoning (e.g., Barrows and Tamblyn 1980), teachers help students learn how to access a range of sources and think through various issues. When compared with a more traditional, linear transmission of knowledge via lecture, a problem-based format addresses course content through a more guided, holistic immersion, with much less predictable outcomes...In the problem-based approach, teachers pose problems, students do the needed research, and together teachers and students explore possibilities. As the teacher, you become a facilitator of understanding, setting the stage, raising questions, probing responses, guiding dis-

cussions, and challenging assumptions, all in an attempt to sharpen and deepen student thinking.

Complex and sensitive content requires sophisticated pedagogical approaches. Building on the experience and wisdom of the many teachers and scholars who have contributed to this field, we have offered some interpretations on the pitfalls and possibilities, the threats and opportunities, the dangers and excitement of teaching about human diversity. We also have suggested new directions for a pedagogy on human diversity. We are eager to hear your responses to our ideas.

However, we also know that there is much more productive work required in this area, and we invite teachers and scholars everywhere to join in. As Nelson Mandela reminds us in his 1994 autobiography, any journey to overcome a legacy of prejudice and oppression requires vision, courage, commitment, reflection, perseverance, and more:

> When I walked out of prison, that was my mission, to liberate the oppressed and the oppressor both. Some say that has now been achieved. But we know that that is not the case…I have walked that long road to freedom. I have tried not to falter; I have made many missteps along the way. But I have discovered that there are many more hills to climb. I have taken a moment here to rest, to steal a view of the glorious vista that surrounds me, to look back on the distance I have come. But I can rest only for a moment, for with freedom come responsibilities, and I dare not linger, for my long walk is not yet ended. (624-625)

References

Allen, Katherine. 1995. Opening the classroom closet: Sexual orientation and self-disclosure. *Family Relations* 44:136-141.

American Psychological Association. 1994. *Publication manual of the American Psychological Association,* 4th ed. Washington, DC: Author.

American Psychological Association. 2001. *Publication manual of the American Psychological Association,* 5th ed. Washington, DC: Author.

Barrows, Howard, and Robyn Tamblyn. 1980. *Problem-based learning: An approach to medical education.* New York: Springer.

Bell, Sandra, M. Morrow, and Evangelis Tastsoglou. 1999. Teaching in environments of resistance: Toward a critical, feminist, and antiracist pedagogy. In *Meeting the challenge: Innovative feminist pedagogies in action,* edited by M. Mayberry and E. C. Rose. New York: Routledge.

Bleich, David. 1998. Homophobia and sexism as popular values. In *The feminist teacher anthology*, edited by Gail E. Cohee, Elisabeth Däumer, Theresa D. Kemp, Paula M. Krebs, Sue Lafky, and Sandra Runzo. New York: Teachers College Press.

Condit, Celeste M. 1996. Theory, practice, and the battered (woman) teacher. In *Teaching what you're not*, edited by Katherine J. Mayberry. New York: New York University Press.

Davis, Nancy. 1992. Teaching about inequality: Student resistance, paralysis, and rage. *Teaching Sociology* 20:232-238.

Felman, Jyl Lynn. 2001. *Never a dull moment: Teaching and the art of performance*. New York: Routledge.

Fisher, Bernice M. 2001. *No angel in the classroom: Teaching through feminist discourse*. Lanham, MD: Rowman and Littlefield.

Fullan, M. 2001. *The new meaning of educational change*. New York: Teacher's College Press.

Hase, Michiko. 2002. Student resistance and nationalism in the classroom: Reflections on globalizing the curriculum. In *Twenty-first-century feminist classrooms: Pedagogies of identity and difference*, edited by Amie A. MacDonald and Susan Sanchéz-Casal. New York: Palgrave MacMillan.

Henry, Annette. 1993-1994. There are no safe places: Pedagogy as powerful and dangerous terrain. *Action in Teacher Education* Winter:1-4.

Higginbotham, Elizabeth. 1990. Designing an inclusive curriculum: Bringing all women into the core. *Women's Studies Quarterly* 1/2:7-23.

hooks, bell. 1989. *Talking back: Thinking feminist, thinking black*. Boston: South End Press.

hooks, bell. 1994. *Teaching to transgress: Education as the practice of freedom*. New York: Routledge

Kenney, S. 1998. *Reinvigorating undergraduate education: The Boyer Commission on Educating Undergraduates in the Research University*. Princeton, NJ: Carnegie Commission.

Kuntz, Susan, and Carey Kaplan. 1999. Gender studies in God's country: Feminist pedagogy in a Catholic college. In *Meeting the challenge: Innovative feminist pedagogies in action*, edited by Maralee Mayberry and Ellen C. Rose. New York: Routledge.

Lewis, Madge. 1990. Interrupting patriarchy: Politics, resistance, and transformation in the feminist classroom. *Harvard Educational Review* 60(4):467-488.

Lowman, Joseph. 1995. *Mastering the techniques of teaching*. San Francisco: Jossey-Bass, Publishers.

Mandela, Nelson. 1994. *Long walk to freedom*. Boston: Little, Brown.

Marks, Stephen. 1995. The art of professing and holding back in a course on gender. *Family Relations* 44:142-148.

Minnich, Elizabeth Kamarck. 1990. *Transforming knowledge*. Philadelphia: Temple University Press.

Rosenfelt, Deborah S. 1998. Crossing boundaries: Thinking globally and teaching locally about women's lives. *Women's Studies Quarterly* 3/4:4-16.

Rothenberg, P. 1998. Integrating the study of race, gender, and class: Some preliminary observations. In *The feminist teacher anthology,* edited by Gail E. Cohee, Elisabeth Däumer, Theresa D. Kemp, Paula M. Krebs, Sue Lafky, and Sandra Runzo. New York: Teachers College Press.

Sarason, Seymour. 1984. *The nature of schools and the problem of change*. Boston: Allyn and Bacon.

Sarason, Seymour, and Elizabeth Morentz. 1998. *Crossing boundaries: Collaboration, coordination and the redefinition of resources*. San Francisco: Jossey-Bass, Publishers.

Sampson, Edward E. 1993. Identity politics: Challenge to psychology's understanding. *American Psychologist* 48:1219-1230.

Shankar, Lavina D. 1996. Pro/(con)fessing otherness: Trans(cending) national identities in the English classroom. In *Teaching what you're not,* edited by Katherine J. Mayberry. New York: New York University Press.

Timpson, William M., and F. Broadbent, eds. 1995. *Action learning: Experiences and promise*. Brisbane, Australia: Tertiary Education Institute, University of Queensland.

Timpson, William M., and Paul Bendel-Simso. 1996. *Concepts and choices for teaching*. Madison, WI: Atwood Publishing.

Timpson, William M. 1999. *Metateaching and the instructional map*. Madison, WI: Atwood Publishing.

Timpson, William M., and Suzanne Burgoyne. 2002. *Teaching and performing*. Madison, WI: Atwood Publishing.

Wicker, Allan W. 1985. Getting out of our conceptual ruts: Strategies for expanding conceptual frameworks. *American Psychologist* 40: 1094 -1103.

Index

AUTHOR BIOGRAPHIES

William M. Timpson
Professor, School of Education;
Director, The Center for Teaching and Learning

After finishing my bachelors degree in American History at Harvard University in 1968, I spent four years teaching junior and senior high school students in inner-city Cleveland. I moved on to complete a doctorate in Education Psychology at the University of Wisconsin-Madison. Since 1976 I have taught at Colorado State University (CSU), although a four year leave of absence allowed me two years as Director of the Center for Teaching at University of California, Santa Cruz, and two more years at the Tertiary Education Institute at the University of Queensland in Brisbane, Australia. At CSU, I have routinely taught courses on diversity and have infused diversity content into my other courses. I also direct the Center for Teaching and Learning on this campus, where I attempt to support needed instructional improvements and innovations.

Silvia Sara Canetto
Associate Professor, Department of Psychology

I was born and raised in Italy, and after gaining a doctorate in Experimental Psychology at the University of Padova, I spent four years in Jerusalem, where I received a second graduate degree in General Psychology. In 1981, I came to the U.S. to pursue a third degree, in Clinical Psychology, at Northwestern University Medical School. Since 1991, I have been on the faculty at CSU, where I have taught "Psychology of Gender," "Psychology of Women," "Life-Span Developmental Psychology," and "Diversity Issues in Counseling." In 1997, my work on gender and culture in suicidal behavior was honored with the Shneidman Research Award of the American Association of Suicidolgy. In 1998, I was elected member of the International Academy for Suicide Research. More recently, I was elected Fellow of the Society for the Psychology of Women, as well as Fellow of the Division of International Psychology of the American Psychological Association. I have published over eighty articles and chapters and edited three books. This is my first contribution to a book on teaching.

Evelinn A. Borrayo
Assistant Professor, Department of Psychology

I was born in Guatemala City and moved with my family to the U.S. when I was eight years old. I learned English as an elementary school student in Los Angeles. After returning to Guatemala for high school, I won a scholarship to the University of the Ozarks in Arkansas, where I earned my undergraduate degree. I received masters and doctoral degrees in Clinical Psychology from the University of North Texas and have post-doctoral training in gerontology from the Florida Policy Exchange Center on Aging (FPECA). I continue to be an Associate Researcher and collaborate with FPECA in conducting policy research. I hold a tenure-track faculty appointment at CSU, where I teach graduate courses in health psychology, ethnic minority psychology, and cultural diversity psychology.

Ray Yang
Professor, Department of Psychology

I grew up in Hawaii, where my grandparents had once emigrated to work on the sugar plantations. I received an education in developmental psychology and have since studied infants, elementary-age children, and at-risk youths. My research has dealt with abusive families, juveniles in adult prisons, and college-age minority students' adaptation to the challenges of university life. I have taught on six campuses, including Cornell University, the University of Georgia, Northern Illinois University, the University of Wisconsin-Madison, and the University of Hawaii. I am currently professor of Human Development and Psychology at CSU. I would like to thank Jill Kreutzer for her helpful comments after reading drafts of my chapter.

Eric Aoki
Assistant Professor, Department of Speech Communication, Interpersonal and Cultural Communication

After completing my bachelors and masters degrees in Speech Communication at California State University-Fresno in 1990 and 1992, I moved to the Northwest and completed a doctorate at the University of Washington-Seattle in 1997. Prior to the defense of my dissertation, I was offered a position at CSU's Department of Speech Communication to begin in August of 1997. At the outset, I found that being part of an ethnic and sexual minority, and teaching Interpersonal and Cultural Communication in a smaller city like Fort Collins, would present both challenges and opportunities. Five years later I still find this to be true.

James H. Banning
Professor, School of Education

I was born and raised in rural Kansas. I received a doctorate in Clinical Psychology from the University of Colorado-Boulder in the midst of the anti-war and civil rights movements. Participation in these efforts helped me realize the important role that systems play in human affairs. In the early seventies, I redirected my career from a being psychotherapist to one in university administration, and I spent nearly ten years as Vice-President for Student Affairs at Colorado State. Currently, as an environmental psychologist, I am a professor in the School of Education, teaching qualitative research, environmental psychology, and campus ecology courses.

James W. Boyd

University Distinguished Teaching Scholar;
Professor, Department of Philosophy

Upon completion of my BA in English Literature and Music at Lawrence University, I taught social studies and music to junior high school students for four years. During that time I also began working on my masters degree in History and Literature of Religions at Northwestern University. In 1962 I received a Fulbright fellowship to study at Banaras Hindu University in India. Subsequently I studied at Vidyodaya University in Sri Lanka and the University of Bombay, and after receiving my doctorate I continued to travel, study, and teach at a number of universities: the University of Shiraz, Iran; Kansai Gaidai University in Osaka, Japan; and within the U.S., at Harvard, Pittsburgh, and Tennessee.

Roe Bubar

Assistant Professor, Social Work

I attended college and worked in Upward Bound at the University of New Hampshire at Durham, where I received a BA in Psychology. After graduation I spent several years in an Indian Education program and became very focused on social justice issues and government policy. After receiving a JD from the University of Colorado in Boulder, I became a lobbyist for a small, Indian-owned corporation. A former director of a Children's Advocacy Center, I worked to develop such facilities in Indian Country and Native Alaskan communities, and I continue to support tribal initiatives in the Colorado area. I am currently an Assistant Professor at CSU, where I have joint appointments in the School of Social Work and the Center for Applied Studies in American Ethnicity.

Timothy Gray Davies

Associate Professor, School of Education

I grew up in Cleveland's inner-city, and were it not for a high school coach who believed in me academically as well as athletically, I never would have accepted the football scholarship that began my academic journey. Having completed a bachelors and masters in English, I began teaching at Macomb County Community College outside Detroit, and over the next thirty years I taught at seven different community colleges, most of them in major urban centers. I see the community college as the most egalitarian higher education institution in the United States, and it was specifically to develop the doctoral program in community college leadership that I joined CSU in 1995.

Nathalie Kees

Associate Professor, Counseling and Career Development,
School of Education

I have been training counselors for the past fifteen years. I am a licensed professional counselor and I've had a private counseling practice for ten years. Before that, I was a school counselor and music teacher. I received my EdD from West Virginia University and an MA in Counseling from the University of Wyoming. I have served as a multicultural trainer at CSU for the past fifteen years. I am also Director of CSU's President's Commission on Women and Gender Equity, and I founded the Women's Interest Network for the American Counseling Association. My writing is mainly about women and diversity issues in counseling with a focus on working with groups.

Jane Kneller
Associate Professor, Department of Philosophy

After receiving my PhD in philosophy in 1984 from the University of Rochester, I taught for a year and then returned to graduate studies in the Department of Germanic Languages and Literature at the University of Cincinnati. I have taught philosophy courses that encourage students' exploration of voice and plurality in ethics, aesthetics, epistemology, and the philosophy of religion. I have become increasingly aware of a wealth of material that remains largely unexplored in my own areas of research, and I bring some of that to my students in the form of newly discovered or republished documents representing historically marginalized or unusual voices.

Rosemary Kreston
Director, Resources for Disabled Students;
Instructor, The "Handicapped" Individual in Society

I received a BA in psychology in 1973 from Wayne State University in Detroit and a Masters in rehabilitation counseling from the University of Northern Colorado in 1976. I was hired by the State of Colorado as a rehabilitation counselor in 1978. In 1980, I was hired to direct the Resources for Disabled Students department at CSU. More than two-thirds of these students have learning disabilities, and the emphasis of the office embraces attitudinal access and advocacy as well as physical access and accommodation. My course focuses on the interdependency between individuals with disabilities and those who provide support.

Chance W. Lewis
Assistant Professor, School of Education

After completion of my BA in Business Education from Southern University I taught for four years in the inner-city schools of Baton Rouge, Louisiana, during which time I completed a masters program in Education Administration. In 2001, I completed a PhD in Education Leadership at CSU while working as Department Chair and faculty member of the Computer Information Systems department at Front Range Community College. Currently, I am an Assistant Professor in the School of Education where I teach in the areas of Education Technology and Multiculturalism.

Valerie A. Middleton
Assistant Professor, School of Education

After graduating from Illinois State University with a BA in Special Education, I spent nine years in public school settings on the southern outskirts of Chicago as a special education inclusion consultant and teacher. In 1992, I became a full-time graduate student and teaching assistant at CSU. During this time I taught courses in teacher licensure to preservice teachers-in-training. Within three years I earned a Masters Degree in Special Needs, and over the next two years I earned a PhD in Teacher Education and Staff Development, both from CSU. I am currently a tenure-track Assistant Professor at CSU, teaching and researching courses on diversity, special needs, and educational methodology.

Angela Paccione
Professor, School of Education

I grew up in the South Bronx, New York. As a child, my love of learning competed for a while with my love of basketball, until both found their fulfillment at Stanford University. I was among the first to receive a full athletic scholarship to Stanford, where I graduated with departmental honors in Political Science. I played professional basketball for a couple years before returning to school to earn my teaching certificate. While pursuing a masters degree in Educational Administration, I was recruited to CSU to enter the PhD program and to work with a teacher preparation program. In 1998 I earned my PhD and was hired by CSU. I have been working as an Assistant Professor with teacher preparation for the past five years.

Nina S. Roberts
Doctoral Candidate, Natural Resource Recreation and Tourism;
Education and Outreach Specialist, National Park Service

I completed my BA at Bridgewater State College in Massachusetts and my Masters Degree at the University of Maryland-College Park. For eight years afterwards I was a park manager and adjunct faculty member at the University of Maryland-College Park and George Mason University. I have been a research associate for the Student Conservation Association (SCA), I have served as Assistant Director of SCA's national urban and diversity programs, and I have participated in leadership training through the National Outdoor Leadership School, Woodswomen, Project Adventure, Pro-Image, Washington Women Outdoors, and the SCA. Currently, I am completing my PhD in Recreation Resource Management at CSU and working for the National Park Service as an Education and Outreach Specialist.

Mona C.S. Schatz
Professor, School of Social Work;
Director, Education and Research Institute for Fostering Families

I completed the bachelors program in Sociology and Political Science at Metropolitan State College in Denver in 1976. In 1979, I completed a masters program in Social Work at the University of Denver, and shortly thereafter moved to the Mid-Atlantic region, where I consulted on projects related to rural health care delivery for young Latino women. After beginning my academic career at Southwest Missouri State University, I completed a doctorate in Social Work in 1986 at the University of Pennsylvania. I have taught in the School of Social Work at CSU since 1985 and have long been a part of the Education and Research Institute for Fostering Families (ERIFF). I currently mentor and teach undergraduates, preparing them for work with Latino and Native American families.

Suzanne Tochterman
Assistant Professor, School of Education

After completing an undergraduate degree at Vanderbilt and a masters degree in Education at The George Washington University, I taught students with special needs in the Washington, DC area. Currently I am helping to prepare secondary teachers across content areas. My courses address methods, standards and assessment, diversity and communication, classroom management, foundations, special education, and literacy. When asked to teach "Diversity and Communication" I was concerned, because faculty of color had traditionally taught the course. I wondered what I might have to offer my students. My chapter in this book is a reflection on my experience.

Irene S. Vernon
Director, Center for Applied Studies in American Ethnicity (CASAE);
Professor, English Department and CASAE

I received a BA in Native American Studies from the University of California at Berkeley. After receiving an MA in History at the University of New Mexico, I returned to UCB, where I received my PhD in Ethnic Studies. My area of specialization is Native American, Ethnic, and Multicultural Studies, and I have taught courses on various aspects of Native life including religion, law, history, literature, and economic development. As the Director of the Center for Applied Study in American Ethnicity (CASAE), I work toward deepening appreciation of our various ethnic traditions, the patterns of interaction among groups, and the nature of problems that arise from the abuses and misunderstandings about ethnic identities.